W9-CHS-315

Swans and Pistols

By the same author

*Do or Die: For the First Time, Members of L.A.'s
Most Notorious Teenage Gangs—the Crips
and Bloods—Speak for Themselves*

Smoked: A True Story About the Kids Next Door

*A Wrongful Death: One Child's Fatal Encounter
with Public Health and Private Greed*

Swans and Pistols

Modeling, Motherhood, and Making It in the Me Generation

Léon Bing

B L O O M S B U R Y

New York   Berlin   London

Copyright © 2009 by Léon Bing

All rights reserved. No part of this book may be used or reproduced in any manner
whatsoever without written permission from the publisher except in the case of brief
quotations embodied in critical articles or reviews. For information address
Bloomsbury USA, 175 Fifth Avenue, New York, NY 10010.

Published by Bloomsbury USA, New York

All papers used by Bloomsbury USA are natural, recyclable products made from
wood grown in well-managed forests. The manufacturing processes conform to
the environmental regulations of the country of origin.

LIBRARY OF CONGRESS CATALOGING-IN-PUBLICATION DATA

Bing, Léon, 1950–
Swans and pistols: modeling, motherhood, and making it in the
me generation / Léon Bing.—1st ed.
p. cm.
ISBN-13: 978-1-59691-481-0 (hardcover)
ISBN-10: 1-59691-481-5 (hardcover)
1. Bing, Léon, 1950– 2. Women journalists—California—Los Angeles—Biography.
3. Models (Persons)—California—Los Angeles—Biography. 4. Mothers and
daughters—California—Los Angeles—Biography. 5. Los Angeles
(Calif.)—Biography. I. Title.

CT275.B57365A3 2009
979.4'94052092—dc22
[B]
2009008904

First U.S. edition 2009

1 3 5 7 9 10 8 6 4 2

Typeset by Westchester Book Group
Printed in the United States of America by Quebecor World Fairfield

For
Gareth Seigel

Contents

Prologue

One summer, when I was about four years old, my mother went to Chicago with her second husband for a meeting with some of his business associates. The meeting didn't include wives, so my mother decided to take a walk and explore the city. She set out with no particular plan; the hotel where she and Barney were staying was one of the great Chicago landmarks, and because it was located just off Lakeshore Drive, my mother figured there had to be interesting sights in almost any direction. She passed famous restaurants with German names and apartment buildings designed in the style of medieval cathedrals. Then she came to a major construction site: steel girders and high-iron workers in hard hats. Those guys spotted my mother in her white linen suit and high heels the instant she rounded the corner, and they let her know it with shrill two-digit whistles and thundering approval of her ass and legs. My mother played it the way she'd been taught at Miss Ransom's School for Girls: she jerked up her chin and pretended not to hear. And, because that tilt of head sacrificed her view of the pavement, she stepped—and slid—in dog shit.

She hopped to the curb and went to work on her alligator pump, and the construction guys rewarded her with a chorus of braying laughter and graphic comments.

"All I had to do in the first place was smile and give a little wave," she said years later when she told me the story. "But I learned a good lesson that day: if you act like you're above it all, you don't see the shit until you're in it."

CHAPTER 1

The Belle of Oakland

I don't remember the exact date I moved from Los Angeles to New York with the idea of making it as a model there; what I recall is the push of relief in my mother's voice when she wished me luck, as if both of us living in the same city placed too much pressure on her. Maybe it was being the lone parental figure that got to her. Maybe I was just a pain in the ass. We'd never been particularly close; she wasn't the kind of mother who offered a lap to sit on, she was never the first to hold out her arms for a hug, and if you moved in for a kiss, you got her cheek. But she was smart and funny and she had a dark, dangerous beauty. She could be silly, my mother, but you had to watch it: she'd pull you along into helpless laughter and then leave you cold when she tired of the game. Still, rooms seemed warmer when she was in them. She danced with a supple, natural grace and she was generous with her gift, refining my first awkward moves to her favorite Billie Holiday and Nat King Cole recordings as she steered me around the living room floor.

"I bought you a fur coat for Christmas . . ."

"Stop looking down at your feet. And don't stick out your behind that way. Lean in when you dance, let the music flow through you." She pulled me closer, her hand a warm presence at the small of my back, and led me through a few more steps. She was right. When I relaxed, my moves seemed less clumsy.

"Better. The boys will fall all over themselves when you go to your first dance."

". . . Gee, baby, ain't I good to you?"

Embarrassment must have flooded my face, because my mother's smile dropped away.

"Don't be such a stick, Mary Léon. Loosen up and enjoy yourself, for Christ's sake." She hummed along with the music for a few seconds. "Know how I learned to dance? I was a sophomore at Miss Ransom's, and Elaine Spaulding and I would ditch class, take the streetcar downtown, and sneak in backstage at the old burlesque theater. The girls thought we were cute, so they let us try on their costumes and then they showed us some moves. That's how I learned to dance."

"Did you ever . . ." I hesitated. I didn't want to say "strip" to my mother. "You know, on the stage?"

She didn't answer. Instead, she sauntered a few steps away, turned, held both arms over her head, and bumped her hips forward. Then she looked at me, arched her left eyebrow, and shrugged. I was twelve years old and able only to wonder at the effortless way my mother spun mystery around herself. It was a reason to love her. It was a reason not to.

Her name was Estelle Dorothy Lang and she kept her surname through five marriages, an outrageous decision in the decades prior to the sixties. She dressed in custom-tailored suits that she wore with the highest heels she could find, liking the contrast between understated severity and on-the-line sensuality. Her only makeup was bright red lipstick. She knew how to make men fall in love with her and she was always the one who walked away. She divorced my father when I was three years old, took him out of our lives as cleanly as she sliced the tips from the stems of gladiolas she bought in crimson masses, and remarried almost at once. That marriage failed as well, not because Barney was a bad guy—although in the strictest sense he may have been: he came up on the streets of Brooklyn's Brownsville section and was in with the Jewish mafia. I knew him only as a kind, soft-spoken man who allowed my mother her way in everything. But, like my father, Barney found himself married to a woman who couldn't connect fully with anyone outside her blood relations. That imposed distance was the reason nearly all her marriages went under. There was no one to blame; it was my mother's nature: she was an only child and her mother, Fanny, was her greatest love. Her father, Léon, was the only man she ever tried to please, the only man for whom she felt true affection. All the rest, the five husbands and countless admirers (Clark Gable among them), were as disposable as the cigarettes she crushed out after two or three puffs. The only times I saw my mother entirely happy was when she was with her parents in their rambling bungalow in the Piedmont section of Oakland, where she'd grown up and where I spent my childhood.

My grandmother's sister and brother, the two who never married, lived with my grandparents in the big house on Jerome Avenue, and before I was a month old, it was decided I should be moved there, too. Years later, when I was old enough to ask questions, my mother's explanation was that my grandmother didn't think my parents were capable of caring for an infant. When I wanted to know the reasoning behind my mother's surrender of her only child, she shrugged, and for an instant I thought there was a spark of remorse behind the practiced coolness of her gaze. That's what I was looking for, but there wasn't any way to mistake the message in that familiar expression: the conversation was at an end. My mother never believed in analyzing past actions. My grandmother didn't either. When I was four or five I asked her about the decision to take me away from my parents. She kept on washing dishes and said nothing, but I knew she heard me because she began setting down each clean plate with an angry little thump. I looked up at my great-aunt Ethel, nicknamed Hotten, who stood drying the dishes at the other side of the sink. She turned her head just enough to avoid my gaze. It was a rare instant of being ignored in a house where I always seemed to be the center of attention.

It was the first time I recognized and obeyed the instinct to let something go.

It would not be true if I said I suffered from the move to my grandparents' home. My childhood was wonderful: I lived in a home with people who loved one another. They said things like "Let me get that for you, I'm going upstairs anyway" and "Nobody in the world can make me laugh like you." I was passed from lap to lap and exclaimed over and made to feel like a precious object. Hotten taught me to read before I went to kindergarten because I'd memorized all the stories she read to me and corrected her when she tried to skip paragraphs. I was an eager pupil; from the moment the letters T-I-G-E-R coalesced into an image of the great striped cats I'd seen at the zoo and B-I-R-D became our parrot, Loretta, as well as the seagulls that swooped in arcs above our house to signal an oncoming rain, I felt as if the world had been handed to me. I didn't want to do anything but read. I sounded out each word in *A Child's Garden of Verses* and joyously moved on to the adventures of Babar, the elephant king.

My grandmother must have worried because I was such a solitary child, so she arranged a playdate with the kids next door. Their parents and my mother had been friends since high school and the youngest daughter was named after my mom and referred to as "Little Estelle." Additionally, both families were members of the congregation at the same synagogue in Oakland. In spite of that history, the two sisters wouldn't play with me (possibly because I was younger, probably because I was an impossible brat), so my grandmother hung candy bars from the lowest branches of the lemon trees in our back yard and told them it was magic.

I had an hour's worth of company, but when all the candy was collected, Little Estelle and her sister went home. I heard the tantalizing sounds of their voices over the stone wall that separated our back yards whenever I went outside, but when my grandmother suggested I go with her the next time she went next door for a visit, I refused. I'd never told her (or anyone else) that when those kids came over that day they slipped me a sandwich. There was mayonnaise and lettuce and Swiss cheese that turned out to be a slice of yellow soap. I took a bite and spat it out as the bitter taste of the soap spread through my mouth like an oil slick. Surprise and hurt changed to anger, and I yelled at them to go back home. Then I stamped off into the house. I made up some story for my grandmother, but the fear of being labeled a tattletale kept me from telling the truth. When I was older I guessed the sisters' motivation had to have been resentment at being coerced into playing with the spoiled little kid next door, coupled with a strong need for revenge. Whatever it was, they never came to play again.

I accepted my solitude with something like relief and went back to the books I loved. I read stories about forest animals like *Bambi* and books about heroic and faithful dogs. When I was seven or eight, my great-uncle Henry, who owned a pawnshop, brought home a beautiful old book. The title, stamped in gilt on the cover and spine, was *A Little Princess*, and the story was about a girl named Sarah Crewe who, three or four years after her mother's death, traveled from her home in India to become the prized pupil at an English boarding school while her father, Captain Crewe, went off to fight the Boer War. That book became my favorite, not only because it was illustrated with the kind of detail that brought each chapter to life, but because Sarah, who was my age and a voracious reader, too, behaved valiantly when she was taken from her luxurious rooms and made to sleep in an attic and work as the school scullion after her beloved father was declared lost in battle. I pretended I was Sarah and that my own father would return to me someday. My copy of *A Little Princess* had belonged to some other child long before it came to me and I found that to be thrillingly mysterious. I wondered who she'd been, what she had dreamed about as she read, if she was now a very old lady, and why her book had been pawned and left with Uncle Henry. I lost myself in my books, savoring the fragrances of paper and ink and time, reading some of them over and over, always held captive to their stories. My family, none of them particularly avid readers, teased me about being a bookworm but their words held an edge of pride, and often, a plate of sugared orange slices or a cup of hot chocolate would appear on the table next to the big chair on the sunporch, my favorite reading spot.

My mother was a glamorous visitor who descended every few days in a swirl of Chanel No. 5. Sometimes she'd stay only long enough to take me out on a short trip around the neighborhood. On one of these visits, we walked hand in hand up the hill to a home where the residents kept a family of monkeys in a tree-sheltered enclosure that faced the street. My mom told me she'd begun calling on these monkeys when she was in her teens, that they were like pets to her. She positioned herself directly in front of the enclosure but I stood behind her, a little frightened, as three or four monkeys raced up to the bars and stared back at us. That's when it happened: My mother turned to say something, and a sinewy arm covered with glossy black fur shot out and a spidery hand grabbed her hair and held on tight. Then another arm reached through the bars and began an enthusiastic grooming procedure, searching for nits and any other dainties it could find. My mom batted at the paws that pulled at her, and all I could do was stare and giggle nervously while she yelled at me to run and get my grandmother. I didn't move; there was no way I was about to leave the spectacle of my fastidious mother in the grip of a monkey rooting around in her hair. She finally broke loose and marched me down the street, looking like a furious early model for the guy in *Eraserhead*. I kept still, figuring I was in for a scolding, but halfway to the house my mom stopped walking and began to laugh. By the time we got home we were both howling. That was my mother: it was impossible to second-guess her because she'd fool you every time.

She brought with her a kind of naughty fun for the longer visits, taking me out in her car and allowing me to sit close to her with my hands on the wheel as we pretended I was driving past the Queen Anne houses and Craftsman bungalows that lined the quiet residential streets of Piedmont. When I sat next to my mother and her attention was on the road, I was able to study her, to examine all the small details of her person: the pale olive skin stretched taut across her cheekbones; the aquiline, finely drawn line of her nose; the cleft in her chin. I was particularly fascinated by her hands: they were long and narrow with tapering fingers and lush red polish on the perfectly manicured nails. But the pads of her thumbs were scored with wounds that looked like tiny, open mouths. That broken skin fascinated me and, because it was my mother's, seemed mysterious and glamorous. I never imagined that she picked at herself because she might have been unhappy or insecure or frightened. And her cool remoteness made it impossible for me to ask why she did it and when it had begun. I was her rapt audience when we were together; when I was alone, all I could do was admire and imitate by savaging my cuticles.

It was during one of those drives when I asked about the words I was forbidden to say at my grandparents' house. What I wanted to know was why it wasn't okay for me to use them since I heard them at home all the time. My mother didn't say anything; she looked out the window and smiled and tapped one long red fingernail against the steering wheel. Then she introduced me to the swearing game. The swearing game became a vital part of our ritual, to be played only when we were alone in my mother's car. I was to call out words like "hell" and "damn" and "mumser" (something my grandmother hissed under her breath when she talked about the old man next door) and my mother would repeat them in a dramatic voice. Then we'd make up sentences for each word and I learned that "mumser" had different meanings, all of them bad. I was crazy about that one. We'd play for ten minutes or so and always, before heading back to the house, we would renew a vow of secrecy that included my promise never to say the forbidden words to another person. The swearing game was for us only; we were the founding members of a club that nobody else could join. I loved my mother with a throat-swelling intensity during those afternoon drives, but sometimes a feeling like sheet lightning inside my head made me want to scream at her and force her to tell me why it was all right for her to leave my father and marry some other man but not all right for my father, whose image had begun to fade from my mind, to come and take me driving in *his* car. I never raised the courage to confront her. I was too grateful for our private afternoons, even when I had to hide a sudden wash of tears. My mother never cried and I was afraid she might stop liking me if I did.

After the drive, my mother would come in the house and sit at the dining room table with my grandmother and Hotten. Cups of strong, fresh coffee and homemade rolls fragrant with melted butter and cinnamon-sugar were set out, and the real talking would begin. I'd pick up a book, fold myself into the armchair on the sun-porch, and pretend to read. That's how I overheard this story the first time my mom told it:

She had just begun to go out with Barney, who, aside from several other business ventures, owned a nightclub in east Oak-land that featured third-rate bands. The patrons who flooded the dance floor were young guys who worked at the shipyards and flashily dressed girls given to gum-snapping and squeals. One eve-ning my mother hectored Barney into taking her to the club; she loved to dance, and the way she saw it, the club was as good a place as any to have fun. And because she had the knack for fitting in anywhere, even Barney (who knew the place was a dive) had to ad-mit the evening was turning out well. When she said she needed to use the restroom, Barney told her she was not to go anywhere near the public facilities in this joint because God only knew what she might catch from a toilet seat or sink top. He stood up, held out his hand, and led my mother around the teeming dance floor and past a maze of tables to his office at the back of the club. It was a small, airless room with a battered desk, a few chairs, and stacks of ten- and twenty-dollar bills piled on every available surface. Barney opened the door of a tiny bathroom and turned to leave. Then he stopped, glanced around at the landscape of cash, and looked back at my mother with narrowed eyes.

"Listen, I'm gonna be waiting in the hall right outside that door there and what I want to hear is your hands clapping. Like this . . . see?" He clapped his hands together in a steady cadence. "The whole time you're in here. Understand what I'm sayin'?"

"Oh, I think so." If he'd known her better, he would have recognized that soft, even voice as a sign of trouble barreling straight at him. "Now, go stand in the hall and listen."

Barney got out fast and closed the door behind him.

My mother began to clap her hands. She went on clapping while she straddled the toilet to pee (she never sat in strange bathrooms), stopped long enough to run water over her fingers, and took up the beat again as soon as she was done. Then she walked out of the bathroom and looked around the grim little office. She had never seen so much money in one place before, not even when her uncle Henry counted up the register at his store.

She stood like that for a long moment, clapping her hands, thinking. Then she yanked up her skirt and exposed the length of one slender thigh. And, without missing a beat, she began to slap the bare skin there with her left hand while, with the right, she scooped stacks of twenties into her oversized handbag.

When she was done, she let her skirt fall back, snapped the bag shut, and began to clap both hands again. After a few seconds, she strolled out of the office and aimed her dazzling smile at Barney.

They went back to their table and Barney ordered up two more beers. They danced again. My mother laughed and flirted and never mentioned the hand-clapping.

Later, when Barney's car pulled up in front of her apartment, he reached out to kiss her. She nudged him back.

"I have something for you."

"You shouldn't be buyin' me presents, honey."

"Don't worry. I didn't buy it."

She opened her bag and turned it over in a single fluid gesture. Twenty-dollar bills showered out. They pooled on the leather car seats and drifted down to settle on the floor on both sides of the console. Barney repeated his earlier ritual: he looked at my mother, looked at the money, looked back at my mother. Only this time, his eyes were wide with shock.

"What the hell . . . ?"

My mother leaned in close to whisper.

"I'm Estelle Lang. I don't steal. If you need to hear applause, get tickets to the opera."

I wasn't afraid to cry when my mother wasn't around. I used tears as a cudgel to get what I wanted, and when sobs weren't enough, I hurled myself into tantrums. I was sprawled on the floor of the guest room one afternoon, kicking my heels in a relentless tattoo and banging the back of my head at a slower (and less strenuous) beat, when my mother strode into the room.

I amped up the performance by a few decibels. My mother's long, unblinking eyes watched for a moment, then she turned and walked out. I squeezed my eyelids shut and bellowed louder and suddenly I felt a pour of cold water across my face and down my throat. I gagged and coughed and opened my eyes. My mother was standing over me with an empty pitcher in her hand. Then, as if she were offering another helping of dessert to a dinner guest, she asked if I'd like some more. I pulled in air for another scream but it died in my throat. My mother said nothing; she only looked down at me and shook her head. Then she walked out of the guest room and closed the door quietly. I never had another tantrum.

Not long after that incident, there was a flurry of telephone calls and whispered conversations between my grandparents, and my mother went to Reno for another divorce. Barney was gone and in a few weeks she'd be married to a new husband who would take her away to live in Los Angeles. When I was introduced to Lawrence, he smiled thinly, shook my hand as if it were a small nocturnal animal, and peered down at me through rimless eye-glasses. I knew he was assessing me, trying to gauge if I was going to be trouble. I looked back at him and realized this new man didn't like kids, really didn't like them. It was the first time in my pampered existence I'd come up against anything like this and it was like a small, poisonous dart piercing my skin. I felt the beginning of a tremble under my lower lip.

I'm not going to cry. I'm not going to let this new man see how much he just hurt me with that look. He's one of those grown-ups who think kids don't see or hear anything more than cartoons on TV and I see more than anyone knows. And sometimes I see more than I want to, like the way Hotten leans over the railing and tries to hear what my grandparents are talking about when they're downstairs and she's upstairs with me, or the way Nonnie pats her chest after dinner and says, "This food lays on my chest like a rock," and even if I think that's a funny thing to say, I know from the look on my grandmother's face it's not funny at all. I see so many things I can't talk about and now here's another. My family thinks Lawrence is perfect because he wants to take care of my mother. I think my mother should have stayed married to Barney. No, I think she should still be married to my real father. I could sit close and read A Little Princess *to him. I'll still read to my mother, sometimes, and Hotten and Uncle Henry, but I will never read anything to this Lawrence.*

Lawrence didn't ask me to call him "uncle" but he did tell my mother that a good boarding school with a rigid curriculum was just the thing for an intelligent, badly spoiled child. He was right: I was spoiled.

I was enrolled as a boarder at a conservative girls' school in Berkeley, fitted for uniforms, and kissed good-bye by my tearful family. I didn't feel like crying; I thought the whole thing was an exciting adventure. I'd be coming home every weekend, and as a kind of bonus, summers were to be spent in Los Angeles with my mother and her new husband. I didn't think I could ever like Lawrence—he was too cold—but if having him for a stepfather meant I could spend more time with my mother, I'd try to get along with him. And, in the meantime, I could be Sarah Crewe, alone at a boarding school for the first time with her father far away and lost to her.

I got along better at boarding school than I had in the public school system, where being skipped from first to second grade made me feel like a pariah. I liked sharing a room with a girl named

Sissy who came from Chicago and had her own horse. I enjoyed wearing the gray and white uniform that made it easy for me to blend in with the other students. I loved the days when classes were over and we scrambled into jodhpurs and boots for riding classes at Mills College.

My grandfather was an executive with the music firm of Sherman Clay and he was inflexible in his belief that I possessed enough talent to play the piano. To that end, he arranged for me to take lessons during my first term. That meant practice, so in the late afternoons, before the brass gong at the foot of the main staircase summoned us to the dining hall, I had to put in an hour on an old upright in one of the housekeeping rooms. I don't remember what pieces I hammered out; my only memory is of Emily, whose room it was I invaded. Her door had to be left unlocked so I could let myself in and now, years too late, I wonder at the intrusion into that quiet little woman's privacy. Emily was a maid; she took her orders from the housekeeper and she was a constant but barely visible presence around the school as she cleaned empty classrooms, mopped hallways, and scrubbed bathrooms. She performed scullery tasks in the kitchen and gathered up bundles of towels and bed linens for the laundry. She was small and timid and everything about her seemed to be mouse gray. She seldom spoke, but when she did, it was with a cockney accent and turn of phrase. She had a hesitant smile that nearly hid a lineup of overlapping teeth, and her eyes were always tired. She looked old to me; she was probably in her early forties.

That hour before dinner was probably the only time Emily had to herself. She would slip in about ten minutes after I began practicing and I'd hear the give of bedsprings as she lay down on the narrow bed behind me. She didn't speak or interrupt in any way and I kept on with whatever piece I was trying to learn, but it seemed queer for me to be so noisily present in her room while she tried to rest, each of us ignoring the other.

Emily had arranged a collection of small porcelain figures on top of the piano and sometimes I gazed up at them while I played.

I knew each figure well: there was a boy in knee britches bowing deeply to a girl holding a bonnet, a sad-eyed dog with a bandaged jaw, a bright blue duck, and a gold-colored horse with three legs. When I grew bored with the music, which was often, I'd swivel around and Emily would open her eyes and smile at me and we'd talk. She said how lucky I was to be here at this lovely school with so many other lovely girls (not one of whom, including myself, ever acknowledged her presence or thanked her for cleaning up after us). She asked about my schoolwork with real interest and I showed off by dropping a few overly accented French words into my replies. She asked about my weekends at home and I exaggerated the comforts of the house on Jerome Avenue and the indulgences of an adoring family. I used too many gestures and spoke in a mannered voice, and Emily endured all of it with courtesy and kindness. I don't think I displayed much interest in her at all. I never asked was she happy or sad or did she miss her family back in England, never asked if she minded my loud presence in her room with the unlocked door. As the weeks passed, I found myself looking forward to that daily hour with Emily and I began to lose the affected voice and attitude. If Emily noticed the change, she never let on. She remained who she was, what my stepfather Barney used to call the genuine article, and there is no other person from that school I remember so well. I have had plenty of time to think about it and I realize now that what I came to feel for Emily was more than respect. She showed me what true humility and generosity of spirit were. I loved her and I didn't know it.

I practiced on the old upright until another, better piano became available. When I told Emily, she said she'd miss our afternoons. Then she nodded at her collection of figurines and asked me to tell her which was my favorite. I thought about it for a moment before I pointed at the little horse. Emily took him down from his place behind the blue duck and placed him gently in my hand. To remember her by, she said, and brushed a feathery kiss on my forehead. I was not an affectionate child and I never embraced anyone outside my family. I was uncomfortable with overt expressions of love and I squirmed when anyone displayed them publicly. It didn't matter to me how circumspect the behavior; a kiss on the cheek outside the house was enough to cause me acute embarrassment. I was the kid who never waved from the merry-go-round. But it seemed entirely natural that day to reach out and hug Emily. And when I did, she hugged back. There was no wave of expensive perfume when she came near; Emily smelled like Ivory soap.

I still have the little china horse. Some of the gold paint on his withers and ear tips is worn away. He has rested on kitchen windowsills, on mantels and bedroom dresser tops, in every place I've lived, and he's been picked up and nuzzled many times. For the past few years he has posted a steady, three-legged guard on my desk and every time I look at him, I think of Emily.

I was picked up at school every Friday afternoon by my grandfather, who required detailed reports during the drive home. He was particularly interested in the mandatory French courses; fluent in five languages, he was a martinet in all of them. Once, in reply to his question, I described a math class as "hard." My grandfather didn't say anything. He pulled over to the curb and stopped the car. Then he reached out, lifted up my left hand, and slammed it palm-down on the dashboard.

"*That* is hard. Mathematics is *difficult*."

He started the engine again and pulled into the flow of traffic. My hand stung but I said nothing. Pampy didn't tolerate what he referred to as "backtalk" from me or my mother, whom he still considered a child.

My mother came to visit me at school once. She wore white silk and her skin was deeply tanned. Her dark hair cascaded to her shoulders; the diamonds at her ears flashed fire. She had a radiant smile for everyone, and when she hugged me, I caught the familiar fragrance of Chanel No. 5. I was nearly speechless with pride; I had the most glamorous mother of all the other students. She didn't stay long, but in the dining hall that evening, several girls—most of them upperclassmen—asked if my mom was in the movies. When I said no, I could see they thought I was lying. I didn't blame them; she was a star to me, too, and I regarded her with the adoration of a fan.

I spent two consecutive summers in Los Angeles with my mother and her new husband at his vast, high-ceilinged apartment in a building that celebrated an Old Hollywood style of rococo architecture. My mother told me privately she had hated the original look of those rooms, with their heavily carved furniture and dark velvet draperies that blocked out the sunlight, so she hired a decorator and had everything redone in pale shades of gray and white, with sheer curtains pooling on honey-colored wood floors and the ebony Steinway, a gift from my grandparents, dominating the living room. There were two large guest rooms, each with a marble mantel above a nonworking fireplace, each with its own bath. I was given the room with casement windows that overlooked the rose garden and tennis courts five stories down. The decorator had transformed it into a magazine editor's idea of the perfect space for a growing girl: yellow and white striped paper on the walls, a four-poster bed, a wingback reading chair, and an antique secretary with garlands of yellow roses painted on the sides. It was a beautiful, sun-drenched room and there was no way to tell my mom, who was eager for me to like it, that yellow was my least favorite color because it reminded me of the headaches I had begun to experience.

She's so proud of this room and I want her to be happy. So what if there's so much yellow? I wouldn't care if the whole room was the color of raw egg yolk and there was only an old sleeping bag on the floor. My mother was thinking about me when she fixed up this room. And now I get to spend the whole summer with her. Lawrence doesn't matter; nothing else matters. I'm here with my mom.

Plans were made to fill my time away from school: a bus picked me up every morning and delivered me to a day camp on the grounds of a west side country club, where I was taught to dive without bending my knees and to shoot at targets from a prone position. On weekends, I was allowed to see a movie at one of the theaters Lawrence's corporation owned. If a dinner party was planned, I had my choice of sitting at the long candlelit table with the guests (and keeping still) or eating in the kitchen with Hattie, my mother's housekeeper. I always chose the latter; the kitchen, with its blue and white gingham curtains and old-fashioned pantry, was much cozier than the formal dining room. I thought Hattie was wonderful and I loved the stories she told me about her husband, Leland, who worked for the railroad and saw many instances of shocking behavior from the passengers. Hattie's stories were far more interesting than the muted conversations in the next room. I'd already heard about the time my mother, newly married to Lawrence, decided to tag along with him late one evening when he needed to put in some work at his office in the largest and most overtly palatial theater in the chain. A movie she wanted to see was playing there; she could catch the last show. Lawrence called ahead, a row in the VIP section of the two-thousand-seat auditorium was roped off, and he told my mother he'd come for her at the end of the film.

The final credits rolled; the stage curtain, hand-stitched with silver and gold threads depicting scenes from the court of Louis XIV, swept across the screen; the audience filed out; and my mother waited in her reserved space. She applied fresh lipstick and fluffed her hair. Lawrence would be leaning in to whisper her name any minute. When the house lights came up and the giant chandelier with its gilded cupids slowly descended to a height where the tiers of prisms could be dusted, she felt a pang of concern. She looked around: the only other people in the house were maintenance workers. She gathered her things and headed up the main aisle.

The hum of an industrial vacuum filled the five-story main lobby. Uniformed workers were cleaning the smaller but no less opulent chandeliers there, replacing burnt-out bulbs in the cove-lit murals, polishing the dozens of mirrors and massive walnut columns and fishing coins out of the three-tiered fountain with its white marble balustrade of elaborately carved dolphins at the head of the main stairway. My mother asked a member of the cleaning crew to call Mr. L. E.'s office (Lawrence's middle name was Eugene) and tell him his wife was waiting. The man looked at her, offered a placating gesture, and raced up the curving sweep of stairs that led to the mezzanine and executive offices. A moment later another man, this one wearing a suit and tie, appeared. He identified himself as the house manager, stammered a lengthy apology, and informed my mother that when Mr. L. E. had finished working, he asked for his car to be brought around and then drove on home. It seemed he'd forgotten he was married and that his wife was waiting for him.

My mother created a humorous story out of the incident and it was a big hit at dinner parties, but I would have bet anything Lawrence caught the worst kind of hell the night it happened.

I got along well enough with my new stepfather; we simply had nothing much to say to one another and I often wondered what it was he had against kids. Once, when I reached out automatically to take his hand as we crossed a busy street, he jerked away, then, relenting, wrapped his thumb and index finger loosely around my wrist until we were on the other side. It was the smallest of gestures but I never tried to touch him again and my dislike of him flourished in the climate of his chilly disdain.

Los Angeles in the fifties was like a different planet, a sprawl of land connected by a network of freeways that provided uninterrupted passage from the pristine streets of Beverly Hills to the dun-colored flats of the San Fernando Valley, from the neon-splattered main drags in Hollywood to Pasadena, where old money lived in understated splendor. If you didn't mind surface streets, you could pull onto Wilshire Boulevard where it began downtown and travel a straight shot to the ocean and the main artery of the Pacific Coast Highway. Los Angeles was drive-in movies and surfers and fast-food stands shaped like hot dogs; it was motion picture studios and prehistoric tar pits that oozed oily black bubbles. Its only weather was an unrelieved sun blazing out of a burnt-sugar sky.

Oakland had morning fogs and a sun that warmed but didn't sear. It had hills and a bustling downtown area and a lake for sailing, but the people who lived there didn't seem to think of it as a real city. The city was across the bay, connected to Oakland by a nearly five-mile-long bridge. Los Angeles was a hopscotch of interesting places, some of them Crayola loud. Oakland was home, the bread to L.A.'s circus.

After I went back to the house on Jerome Avenue at the end of that second summer, Lawrence and my mother traveled to Topeka, Kansas, where she rented an apartment and he signed himself in as a residential patient at the Menninger Clinic. He must have been thinking about it for some time, because my mom had confided to me that he was being treated by a prominent Beverly Hills psychoanalyst three times a week. She didn't say what his problems were and I was afraid to ask. But I'd read an entire shelf of his books on psychiatric case histories when I was in Los Angeles. I still harbored an intense dislike for Lawrence and I was sorry my mother was married to him but he didn't seem to be anywhere near as crazy as the people described in those books.

I went back to school and didn't think much about Lawrence or my mother. My grandmother was ill. Now when I went home for weekends, the house was silent and there was a nurse who walked on rubber soles and shut the door of the guest room where Nonnie lay in bed. My mother came back from Topeka and that night I heard what I thought was laughter through my bedroom wall. As I listened, I realized that the sounds were hard, rasping sobs and I felt a sudden chill; my mother, who never cried, was weeping for her mother. I couldn't allow myself to do that because I was gripped by an irrational fear that if I cried, it would kill my grandmother. And since a world without her was unimaginable, I controlled my tears and begged God to make her better.

We kept to the schedule: I was home for weekends and on Sundays my grandfather drove me back to school. Everything else was different; nobody laughed much now, and the big piano in the living room, the piano my grandfather had played every evening, was silent most of the time. Hotten took over in the kitchen, and although the meals were almost as good as those prepared by my grandmother, dinnertime was greatly changed: now the nurse took a place at the table with us. She was pleasant enough but seeing her there was an unavoidable reminder of how sick Nonnie was. One Sunday afternoon, my mother asked to come along on the drive back to school. It was a long, silent ride and at some point she reached out to switch on the radio. Pampy slapped her hand away from the dial and shot her a terrible look. She turned her head to look out the window and something dark inside me shivered with the perverse happiness of seeing him angry at her.

Nonnie died with her family around her. I was the only one not there, and beneath the pain of loss, I felt a horrifying sense of relief because I hadn't had to see her go.

Things happened fast after that. Uncle Henry moved to his club in Oakland. I came home from school to find that Loretta, the bright green parrot who had been the family pet since my mother was a child, Loretta, who bobbed her yellow-feathered head and spoke in Nonnie's voice, had been given to a family friend. It took the loss of the small creature my grandmother had cherished to unlock my tears. Hotten gathered me in and tried to explain: Loretta's presence and the sound of her voice brought up memories that were too painful for my grandfather to bear. Same with the house, so it was to be sold. Hotten would remain with my grandfather and they would find a smaller place in Oakland. Lawrence's doctors had recommended an indefinite stay at Menninger and I was to move to Los Angeles with my mother. Six months earlier, I would have been overjoyed. Now the only thing I wanted was to have Nonnie back. We were a superstitious family, vaguely afraid of anything supernatural, but I would have given anything just to see my grandmother's ghost.

It was very different, that summer in L.A. My mother and I were alone for the first time since our afternoon drives in Piedmont. She said no camp and devoted her days to me, and gradually, I began to feel better. She took me to the salon where she had her hair done and I got my first haircut from a stylist. We went on long drives around the city and sometimes she'd point to a particular home: "See that one with the tiled roof? Barbara Stanwyck lives there." Or, "That's Henry Fonda's house—aren't those rose trees pretty?" I'd crane my neck, hoping for a look at a movie star, impressed that my mother knew their addresses. It never occurred to me that she was simply pointing at random, trying to divert my attention from the loss of my grandmother.

We had long lunches at famous restaurants where my mother let me order for myself. One afternoon, when she lit a cigarette after the meal, I made a comment about how good it smelled. She looked over at me and smiled.

"Would you like to try one?"

I just looked at her, not quite able to grasp what she'd suggested. She held the pack of cigarettes toward me and I reached out hesitantly.

People at other tables stared as I pulled a cigarette from the pack and held it awkwardly for her to light. I took in a timid puff, hacked it out, and dropped the cigarette into the ashtray.

"Doesn't taste as good as it smells, does it?"

I shook my head and gulped down some water.

I heard a woman's laugh behind me; it withered into silence under my mother's unblinking gaze.

I loved those afternoons when we went to the great department stores on Wilshire Boulevard—places that seemed to shimmer with a glamour reflected by my mother—and picked out clothes together. I was thrilled when Mother, who often bought entire outfits shown by the models, asked for my opinion and listened as I gave it. I got a new wardrobe, as well. And not from Children's Wear; my mom led the way to the Junior Department and helped me choose clothes with a style and fit just right for a girl at the brink of adolescence. We went to the cosmetics aisle at Saks— marble floors and mirrored walls that echoed the lights of an Art

Deco–inspired chandelier—and my mother encouraged me to pick out my own cologne (although she was adamant in her rejection of my initial choice, a black-bottled fragrance called My Sin) and my first lipstick, a pale coral shade. As soon as we got home, I went into my room and put on one of the new dresses. I kicked off my saddle shoes and slid my feet into the narrow coolness of black patent leather pumps with 1½-inch heels. I dabbed on lipstick and blotted it with a tissue. I brushed my hair until it shone and placed a timid amount of the new, lemon-scented cologne at the nape of my neck and behind both knees the way my mother did, using the stopper from the bottle, which had a swarm of bees embossed on the glass. Then I walked slowly into the study, where my mother sat talking on the telephone. She told whoever was on the other end to hold on and then she looked me up and down appraisingly, taking her time. She gestured for me to turn around and sniffed the air, smiling as she caught a whiff of the cologne. She pulled a loose thread from the hem of my skirt. Then she nodded her head and, without looking away from me, spoke into the phone again.

"I have to tell you, my daughter is the most beautiful thing I've ever seen. She doesn't just look like a page in *Vogue*; she belongs on the cover."

I moved closer to her and she held out her cheek for a kiss.

We had early dinners with Hattie nearly every night. Sometimes we used the dining room; more often we sat in the kitchen. I always lobbied for more railroad stories and felt a stab of pride when my mother enjoyed them. We saw plays and movies and nudged each other during the best parts. When my mother laughed, I knew it was okay to be happy again. She told me about a flea circus she'd seen once in San Francisco: you watched through a big magnifying glass, she said, and saw flea ballerinas dancing in toe shoes and tutus; there were races with teams of flea horses wearing fancy bridles and pulling Roman-style chariots; there were even flea clowns, she said. I bought all of it until she raved about the false eyelashes and lipstick on the flea ballerinas' faces; then I shook my head and began to laugh, and my mother pretended to be greatly offended at my unwilling suspension of disbelief. I listened raptly when she told stories about herself as a teenager: going into H.C. Capwell, one of Oakland's biggest department stores, and riding the elevator as she played a ukulele and sang at top volume, getting off at every floor to continue the performance. She earned a title, "the Belle of Oakland," because of her popularity with boys and those few girls who were secure enough to claim her as a friend. She lived up to the legend by getting pinned to three fraternity boys in one year. She told me about her engagement to a young dental student and meeting my father, who had recently graduated from Georgetown, at a fraternity dance. She called off her engagement that evening, she said, danced every dance with the mysterious and handsome visitor, and married him a month later. I loved those stories because they provided a glimpse into her life and informed me to some degree about my father, but I was careful not to ask too many questions; my mother could shroud herself in her veil of mystery in an instant and you were on the outside again. But I'd never felt closer to her and I was afraid that if I went back to Piedmont, the wonderful sensation of intimacy would fade and disappear.

After I tossed out several broad hints punctuated with fervent promises of exemplary behavior, my mother spoke to Pampy and arrangements were made for me to transfer to a school in L.A. As a final vacation treat, she rented a cabin in Lake Arrowhead. We sunned ourselves on the shore, swam in the cold water, and went to dances at the lodge. And when no one approached me, my mother wrapped one arm around my waist and led me around the floor in the series of intricate steps we'd practiced at home. After ten days or so of delicious, uninterrupted privacy, a call came from the Menninger Clinic. Lawrence had died of a heart attack.

I looked at my mother to see how she would react to this news. *She's not going to cry. She's got her serious face on but she's not going to cry. Maybe she didn't like Lawrence, either, after they got married. I wish I could ask her but she'd never talk about things like that with me. I don't feel much of anything at all. I guess I'm sorry he died but what I really care about is how it's going to change things for me.*

Fifteen minutes into the drive down the mountain, I reached out and turned on the radio. My mother didn't say anything, but I knew she was thinking about that afternoon in the car with my grandfather. I looked over at her face with its flaring cheekbones and perfectly applied lipstick and was sure I saw the twitch of a barely suppressed smile.

Lawrence's death didn't change anything for me. We kept the big apartment in Hollywood and my mother finalized plans for my enrollment in the new school, a sprawl of Spanish Colonial buildings, tennis courts, and bougainvillea-draped cottages that had once been a luxury hotel. Now it housed a community of Dominican nuns and a small student body of girls ranging from grades seven through twelve.

It was my grandfather's decision that I be enrolled there; he had been raised a Roman Catholic in Belgium, but when his family urged him to study for the priesthood instead of attending the university at Heidelberg with his brothers, he fled to America. He never practiced Catholicism again, but he maintained the conviction that a Jesuit discipline was necessary for college-prep courses. I was beginning eighth grade.

I was fitted for uniforms and sent a list of things to bring with me and rules to be followed. One of the more mystifying items on the list was that no student was allowed to wear pullover sweaters because they were considered to be "suggestive." I wasn't sure what it was they were meant to suggest (or to whom) but my mother and I thought it was an idiotic rule and giggled about it. Still, at the beginning of the school year, she drove me up a narrow road to what was, essentially, a convent.

I was a boarding student at a Catholic school for the next five years. With the exception of my grandfather, my family was Jewish.

My grandmother and Hotten attended services at Temple Sinai in Oakland every Saturday morning and I went with them, as my mother had done before me. I learned my first prayers in Hebrew and had been given an award for perfect attendance at our synagogue's Sunday school, learning the same lessons about Noah's ark and God giving Moses the Ten Commandments that my mother learned. Now I was one of the few non-Catholics living at a school where a priest said daily Mass in the chapel and students recited the responses in Latin and learned Gregorian and Benedictine plain chant. I knew that if I wanted to be accepted, I would need to become (or pretend to become) somebody else. Without claiming to be Catholic, I recited along with the others, kneeled when the bell tinkled, made the sign of the cross, and prayed privately that my own God, the God of Israel, would not consider it a betrayal. Once, when my grandfather and Hotten visited Los Angeles, I asked Pampy if he still remembered the response to "*Dominus vobiscum*" and when he said, "*Et cum spiritu tuo,*" I experienced a rush of joyous gratitude. My grandfather may have been a lapsed Roman Catholic (he favored Christian Science reading rooms and only rarely accompanied us to temple) but he still remembered his altar boy's responses. He still belonged to the Church. The feelings of guilt I'd experienced every time I pinned a white veil over my hair, bowed my head, and repeated the Hail Marys of a rosary in chapel evaporated, and a great rationalization took over: the remaining shreds of my grandfather's Catholicism granted me the right to kneel and address myself to the Trinity with the same belief I held as a Jew. And, in my attempt to cover two religious bases, I managed a rudimentary understanding of both: In Catholicism, sin—a state the Church claimed every human is born into—was defined by category and absolved, first by baptism and thereafter by weekly confessions (with penances doled out by the priest) and an unyielding determination not to offend God again. In Judaism you worshipped, feared, loved, and were dealt with by the just but demanding God of the Old Testament. Ultimately, I constructed a private image of a stern but equally understanding and loving God who looked rather like my grandfather, only with a flowing white beard and a little more patience. It wasn't religious zeal that fueled my prayers at school, however; it was the fear of being an outsider.

I developed the requisite crush on an upperclassman during my first year, practiced kissing with a couple of my classmates (a great improvement over pressing my lips and the tip of my tongue against my own knuckles), and learned to whisper complaints about the same things as the other girls: the imposed hours for going to sleep and getting up, the food (which was actually pretty good), and the homework we had to do in study hall after class. When we talked about boys we made guesses about who our future husbands were, what they looked like, where they were at that moment, and what they were doing. It was thrilling to know there was someone you were destined to marry out there.

My first brush with raw sex took place when one of the school gardeners offered a jar of peanut butter to me and two other eighth graders as we dawdled up a shadowy flight of rustic, outdoor steps after classes. Peanut butter was a rare treat so we grabbed the jar and began to dig in with our fingers. The gardener, overweight and sweaty, watched us, taking in our obvious enjoyment.

"Man, that sure looks good."

We nodded our heads in unison.

"Mmm, I'd love some of that, only I can't because my hands are all dirty from working the soil. See?" He held up both hands, grinned apologetically, and watched us for another few seconds. Then he said, "Hey, here's an idea—how about you girls lettin' me get a little taste off *your* fingers? How'd that be?"

He looked at each of us in turn.

"C'mon, huh? My mouth's watering."

The three of us looked at one another. Then Maura Halsey shrugged, dug into the jar again, and offered up her hand. The guy lapped at the dollop of peanut butter and made a low, appreciative sound in this throat. He turned to Tyke Conroy; she held out her hand and he bent over it. When he got to me, he looked intently at my face all the time he was licking the peanut butter from my finger. The inside of his mouth felt hard, slippery, rough, wet. He worked his tongue down the bend and curve of my finger and when he fluttered the tip against the skin at the base, I felt a strange little tingle of excitement. He must have seen something, some slight shift of expression, because when he lifted his head, he winked at me as if I had become a silent acolyte in a dark and secret ceremony. Maura, Tyke, and I didn't talk much about what had happened except to agree that it had been creepy. We pushed the nearly empty jar of peanut butter under some discarded boxes in one of the trash bins and agreed not to mention it to anyone.

By the next year I was reading forbidden authors (Ayn Rand and Truman Capote in paperbacks I sneaked in after weekends at home; I thought *The Fountainhead* was overly dramatic but I loved everything Capote wrote) in the closet after lights-out and braving expulsion by sharing a vile-tasting blend of vodka and mouthwash smuggled in by one of my roommates, who left school the following semester to enter a Carmelite novitiate. Still, I managed to get the grades my grandfather demanded.

During one of my weekends home, my mother told me about Milton, a salesman she was seeing. She introduced us the next weekend. He was pleasant enough and he didn't peer coldly at me the way Lawrence had done, but still, I was uneasy. Milton tried too hard to make me like him: his one-size-fits-all-teenagers questions and his fake interest in any replies I gave made me feel like one of the prospective customers at his car dealership. When we were alone that evening my mother said she and Milton were talking about getting married and asked what I thought about it.

"I don't think you should marry anyone for a while."

"Don't you like Milton? He thinks you're very smart and that you have beautiful manners."

"Come on, Mom. He just wants to sell himself so I'll approve of him."

"He doesn't need your approval, miss."

"Well, he thinks he does."

My mother sighed dramatically.

"All right, Mary Léon, you've made your point. I won't marry him. But let me tell you something: I'll never forgive you for ruining my chance at happiness."

That was far too frightening a threat. Suddenly I was five years old again, riding next to my mother in her car, afraid to ask her why she left my father, afraid to cry because it might make her stop liking me. She married Milton a month or so later and by the time I made junior levels at school, they were splitting their time between a house in Palm Springs (which my mother swore was haunted) and a big white Colonial on the outskirts of Sherman Oaks. I missed Hattie, who had gone to live with her married daughter in another state, and I missed the big apartment where I'd been able to be alone with my mother.

This marriage, my mother's fourth, didn't last either. I have only a couple of vivid memories of Milton, one of which caused me to feel both humiliation and rage:

On one of my weekends home from school, my mother, her new husband, and I went to dinner at a restaurant in L.A. known for its mammoth portions of prime rib and Yorkshire pudding. The plan was to dine early and then take in a movie playing in Beverly Hills. I remember my mom was wearing a beautifully tailored suede suit and high-heeled d'Orsay pumps, but other than that, my only—and most indelible—memory is what happened inside the theater. Milton was a raging hypochondriac and one of his more annoying habits was to cover his mouth and most of his nose with both hands in any kind of crowd. So we were seated in the theater waiting for the feature to begin, my mother was in the middle between Milton and me, and he was sitting bolt upright in the seat, both hands clamped over the lower half of his face. The only way he might have been more uncomfortable, it seemed, would have been if the chair had been fitted out with electrodes. My mother leaned in close to him and snapped, "For Christ's sake, will you relax? You just ate like a horse. Now loosen your belt, sit back, and try to enjoy yourself." Milton did as he was told.

The lights dimmed, the audience came to attention, and the movie began. As always, I was transfixed by what was happening on the screen. Then the film ended and the house lights came up. People began their shuffle into the aisles, talking about the movie they'd just seen.

"Oh, my God! I'm *paralyzed*!"

Milton's shouted words rang out in the theater. People stopped talking and stared. My latest stepfather had gotten to his feet, forgetting about the loosened belt and undone zipper, and his trousers had slipped down around his thighs, inhibiting movement. My mother turned to look, got the picture immediately, and began to haul at the trousers, breaking the zipper in the process. This pushed her over the edge into helpless laughter. Milton tugged his clothing into place, buckled his belt, and drew out his shirttails to cover the broken zipper. For whatever reason, that made my mother laugh harder; she was bent over now in what she and I called "the forty-five-degree angle," clutching the back of the seat in front of her. I knew what that meant: she was trying not to pee, but dark stains were already spreading out over the amber suede of her skirt. I stood watching, horrified and unable to move. A ripple of laughter eddied through the theater as more and more people stopped to observe the tableau. Milton shrugged off his jacket and wrapped it around my mother's waist. Then he herded her past me and up the main aisle. People stepped aside to let them pass and that's when I sprang into action. I raced past my mother and Milton, darted around anyone in my way, sped through the lobby to the street, and headed for Wilshire Boulevard. The darkness of the street and the thought of making my own way home bothered me less than the scene I had just witnessed.

I don't care what happens. I don't care if I'm a zillion miles away from the house. Maybe I can just walk back to school. Maybe I'll end up in one of those parts of the city my mother is always telling me to stay away from. Maybe I can just stick out my thumb and hitch a ride. That would really kill the Belle of Oakland—she's always warning me about not ever daring to hitchhike. Well, I don't give a damn what she says or how I do it, I just have to get away from her and this guy who makes even that dead fish Lawrence look good, for Christ's sake.

I was striding up Wilshire, muttering insults aimed at my mother and Milton, when her white Cadillac with Milton at the wheel pulled up to the curb next to me, horn beeping. I turned and saw my mother kneeling awkwardly on the back seat so that her urine-soaked skirt wouldn't mar the leather upholstery. Milton leaned over to open the door on the passenger side and I stood silently for a few seconds, staring at both of them with undisguised contempt.

God, I loathe both of you, you're such phonies. You think you're such hot shit but you're afraid of germs and what people will think and if you're wearing the right shoes with some outfit as if your whole world depended on the choice. Maybe you were always that way—I don't know. I don't think so. But you're not the mother I remember, the person who didn't give a damn what other people thought, the mother I used to want to be just like. You're as much a stranger to me as this jerk you married so you wouldn't have to be alone.

"Get in the car this instant, Mary Léon. I'm in no mood for one of your tantrums." My mother's voice was ice.

I hurled myself into the passenger seat and stared silently out the window during what seemed like an endless trip back to the house in Sherman Oaks. A few years later my mother and I laughed about the incident, particularly when she told me that for about six months, at some point during every dinner party she and Milton went to, somebody would bring up the story about the guy whose trousers fell down at the movies and his wife who peed her pants all the way up the aisle in a Beverly Hills theater.

The final memory I have of Milton took place a couple years later when I was in my first year at the University of Southern

California. I'd chosen, with my mother's enthusiastic approval, to live in one of the dorms. The marriage was over and I was home for the weekend, watching from the small round window on the landing as he carried two suitcases from the house to his car. Mother was at the front door and when Milton neared the end of the brick pathway, she checked her wristwatch; closed the door with a soft, final thump; and turned to look up at me.

"Good, that's done. Okay, honey, if you get a move on, we can have dinner and make the early show at the Sherman."

She wasn't putting on a brave face to offset the pain of another collapsed marriage; she was simply being herself.

I enjoyed the freedom of living at a university: dances given by fraternities, reasonable curfews, smoking whenever you wanted, and at the top of the list, the dizzying new experience of going to classes with boys. Judith, my roommate at the dorm, was from a big family in Portland, Oregon, but in spite of the differences in our backgrounds, we grew close quickly. Within a week or so into our first semester, we decided that neither of us would pledge a sorority. Judith had been a popular member of a number of clubs at her high school and wasn't interested in repeating the experience, and I didn't want the insularity of being one of an exclusive group of girls again; living in a sorority house and following whatever rules were laid out for pledges seemed like a parody of boarding school to me. So Judith and I remained independents. We explored the campus together, took many of the same classes, and, in a burst of zany self-confidence, danced in front of the bronze statue of the Trojan warrior (the emblem of USC, known affectionately as "Tommy") at the center of campus. We borrowed each other's clothes, picked up each other's mannerisms, and were together so much we got used to hearing a single phrase: "We know you're sisters, but are you twins?" I was flattered because I considered Judith to be a true beauty and I liked the idea of having a sister, so we laughed and shrugged whenever we were asked about our presumed siblingship. We both liked the touch of mystery we were able to create but I think it was particularly enjoyable for me.

We met each other's respective families and I was invited to spend a month at her family's summer home in Oregon at the end of our freshman year. My family was immensely approving of Judith; Pampy spoke often of her intelligence, her exquisite manners, and his pride in me for having entered into a close friendship with her.

Judith and I talked about our plans for the future (which were constantly changing) and concocted coded nicknames and private jokes about the boys we thought were cute and the girls we tagged as nerds. We wondered what it would be like when we finally had our first sexual experience and framed scenarios with the kind of details we'd gleaned from films and novels. After the Easter break during our second year, the first question we asked each other was whether either of us had "done it" with a boy. We were both pleased to report that we had lost our rather cumbersome virginity—Judith with her boyfriend, the architecture student she would later marry, and I with a boy I was dating on a semiregular basis. When we got into details, I had to admit I'd been disappointed by the wham-bam of it all. I had expected to be swept away by the throb of passion she and I had conjectured about so endlessly; the reality of the act had been more like a rather painful series of full-body hiccups for me. Still, I counted it as the final step up to adulthood. I continued to do well in my classes, carrying the necessary units for a bachelor's degree in fine arts and seriously applying myself to every subject in order to gain the grades demanded by my grandfather. But, just as I had at convent school, I felt out of place in a university. As exciting as it was to be around boys, I was unsure of myself and awkward; if I wasn't being silent and watchful, I was talking nonsense, trying too hard to race across an entirely foreign landscape toward the easy, flirtatious camaraderie other girls, Judith in particular, seemed to enjoy so effortlessly. I watched her, my admiration laced with envy, as she drew in boys who seemed to want nothing more than to be around her. There wasn't any one boy I had feelings for; I'd be-come increasingly less interested in earning a degree and as time passed, my need to explore the world outside the confines of a uni-versity intensified.

I walked away from USC less than a year later, something I would not have done if my grandfather hadn't died suddenly. A ruptured aorta, the doctor said, and now Hotten would be coming down to live in L.A. in a small apartment near my mother. I was frightened by Pampy's death and surprisingly angry because I felt abandoned by the man who had been the strongest and most reli-able presence in my life. Pampy, who had always protected and loved me, who set the rules, who kissed my forehead and told me that good looks weren't everything, that I could be whatever I chose if I continued my education. Pampy, who called me his dar-ling and signed every letter with a blessing, was gone. I felt un-moored but I knew I couldn't discuss it with my mother; I'd become as expert as she at shutting off my emotions and I wondered if any kind of intimate exchange would embarrass her as much as it would me. In addition to the other feelings that threatened to drown me, I felt dungeoned up by school. I tried to step around it by plodding through much of the next semester but a fierce need to be on my own underlined the fact that in actuality, I *was* pretty much on my own. I'd lived at one school or another nearly all my life; now I was eager to get out there and live by whatever rules I set for myself. I knew that if my grandfather had been alive, I would never have dared to incur his wrath by leaving USC. But there was no one left in my family, not even my mother, who could ex-ert that kind of pressure, so I did as I pleased.

Mother had married for the fifth time and rather than go home to make an uneasy acquaintance with another stepfather who probably wouldn't last, I got a job at a department store in West-wood (working behind a counter until I was promoted to model-ing), moved into a studio apartment, and started to run around with men, only I was still calling them "boys" and hardly any of them were past their midtwenties. There was one much older man, a hotel magnate who lived in a High Renaissance fortress in Bel Air. He guided me through beautifully furnished, art-filled spaces, but the only detail that has stayed with me is a large walk-in closet near the pantry; this room was completely surfaced with a soft, tarnish-proof material that protected floor-to-ceiling shelves of table silver. There were flatware settings for fifty, tea services, trays, candelabras, pitchers, punch bowls, wine coolers, and chargers upon which dinner plates would be placed. It was a knockout display and I think it was his favorite thing in that museum of a house—not the silver itself, but the fact that it would never require polishing. The man was about the age my grandfather had been when he died, but he had the spirit of someone in his thirties and he spoke to me as a peer. We argued about movies, agreed on books, and enjoyed our times together. He kept a stable of tough little cow ponies and we went riding along trails in the foothills. He took me dancing at one or the other of his hotels and we were often joined by his friends and sometimes by his son and daughter-in-law. He gave an elaborate dinner and placed me in the hostess's chair at the foot of his near palace-sized table. There was a buzzer under the carpet near my right foot, he whispered, to summon the serving staff. During a lull between courses, he lifted his glass in a toast: "I know she's dog's years too young for me, but damn, I love to hear her laugh." I liked him, too, but I hadn't told my mom about this rather eccentric relationship. She would have homed in on Security (the word always seemed to be capitalized when she said it) and how I should make a try at snaring this wealthy man. I didn't want the wrangle that would have erupted. My mother and I were from different galaxies when it came to relationships: she'd marry someone, stick around awhile, and then casually move on to the next husband. She didn't seem to worry about Security: she never had a job, and she had the income from a blue-chip stock portfolio my grandfather had built up for her along with some property in Oakland; with the exception of whatever she received from Lawrence's estate, she never took money from any of her ex-husbands. I often wondered why she didn't simplify her life and take a series of lovers but I didn't have the nerve to ask. One thing I was certain about: I wasn't looking to settle down anytime soon, because I was living out all the dating fantasies I'd cooked up during my high school years in the convent. Then I met and was charmed by another older man, an actor known for his machismo presence in movies. He was at my place one evening when my mother and her latest husband came by for a surprise visit, a practice she had always claimed to abhor. The ersatz tough guy was so threatened by the sight of parental figures he left his leather jacket behind when he raced out the door. My new stepfather, Edward, picked up the jacket and flung it into the hallway and I got a lecture about young girls and their reputations.

My anger at my mother, her husband, and the actor (who never called again) simmered for a few weeks. Then it pinwheeled into something that might have caused real trouble: over dessert and coffee at a Beverly Hills restaurant, and with our hands clasped tightly across the table, I accepted an ardent proposal of marriage from the son of a well-known racketeer. I didn't love him; I barely knew him. It was our second date, and if he seemed overly enthusiastic about me, he was also a little drunk. I wasn't. I just figured it was as good a way as any to get back at my mother.

We were halfway to Las Vegas when I told him to turn the car around.

I didn't have much to say on the drive back to L.A. I stared out the window at the dark landscape and thought about what a Las Vegas wedding mill might have looked like: electric candles and soiled fake gardenias and a sleep-numbed official offering to sell us gold-plated rings before he droned the words that would lash us together. I thought about my grandfather and how disappointed and angry he would have been at all the mindless choices I'd made since his death. A quickie wedding to a stranger at some bullshit chapel of eternal regret would have been only the latest in a series of bad ideas. If I wanted a do-over, I needed to make some changes. I decided to move to New York.

Everything around me was changing, but I was only dimly

aware of what was going on. New words and phrases would enter the American lexicon: Counterculture. The New Left, associated with Students for a Democratic Society and mass college campus demonstrations against authority, racism, hunger, and an immoral war. The American civil rights movement, with its army of young Freedom Riders. Hippies. The overlords of national conscience would be Dylan, Cleaver, Hayden, King, and Bobby. America's taste for its young was on the rise but I didn't know it and I'm not sure I would have been concerned if I did. I was going back east to begin all over again.

CHAPTER 2

Me and Vincent at the Met

When people in L.A. told me they thought I came from New York, I was flattered without knowing why. When I asked what it meant, they'd shrug and say, "Well, you've got that New York thing." I don't know what they based their assessment on but I basked in it, assuring myself that I was more cosmopolitan than they thought. It didn't take long for me to learn how far I was from possessing the remotest trace of any kind of New York thing when I moved to that city. I was every bumpkin I'd ever read about. I craned my neck to gawk at buildings whose top floors were wreathed in morning mists. I ventured timidly onto the subway platform at Bloomingdale's after an eye-popping exploration of the store and let out a frightened yip because I thought the rumble of an oncoming train was an earthquake. I went to see a double feature at a movie house on Forty-second Street and fled in horror when a man sat down one seat over from me and began to masturbate beneath a folded raincoat.

When I gathered the courage to look for modeling jobs I realized how lacking in looks and sophistication I was compared with the other girls. They were like young warriors: cocky with the sure knowledge of victory on the field and at the same time, bored. They stood, hip-shot, with their heavy bags slung over one shoulder and their hair cut to fall in one piece, like a curtain made of heavy, expensive material. They smoked unfiltered French cigarettes and called each other "darling" and waited for the designer so they could point to the sample racks and say, "I want to wear that divine black with the cutouts, and the silk velvet, only without the jacket. I can carry the fucking jacket. Okay, darling?" They had that New York thing. What I had was determination. I went to a hairstylist I'd heard was a favorite with models. He looked at me, lifted my hair and ran it through his fingers, stepped back, studied me some more, and suggested that I adopt the helmet cut worn by silent-film star Louise Brooks. I'd seen her on TV when some channel did a tribute to the German Expressionists and I remembered how sexy—and cocky—Louise Brooks was. My hair was as dark as hers, and as straight. I could feel the soft tickle of the stylist's breath as he bent close to the back of my head and went to work. Long commas of black hair piled up on the floor. Finally, he stepped back from the chair, called over an assistant, and whispered. The assistant nodded his head and the stylist handed me a mirror. "You're a different person now," he said. "Now you look like a star."

I practiced a self-assured walk and stance in my room, watching myself in the mirror like a dancer at the barre. I brushed my hair and saw it fall into place in a single shining piece. I tried a lighter makeup, extended my eyes with shadow and liner, and was rewarded with admiring looks on the street. I landed a job as floor model at Bergdorf Goodman. It was grindingly tedious work but I knew I looked good in the clothes, and I enjoyed getting compliments from sophisticated New York shoppers. I wasn't planning to be there long; I was getting ready to take my shot.

I thought about that when I left the store at the end of each workday. I was no longer quite as intimidated by the city. Its air was sharp and bright and I took it in hungrily. I liked the wind that ambushed me between buildings; it held glittering motes of the success I was looking for. They landed on the ledges of office windows on high floors and dusted the awnings over the entrances of celebrated restaurants; they settled on the shoulders of men's topcoats and women's furs, slicked the surfaces of martinis made with ten-dollars-a-shot vodka. If you were young and ambitious, if you were a fast learner ready to make all the necessary changes, you could reach out and capture success in your hands.

My mother had paid a month's rent on a room at a famously staid hotel for women. It was as dull and repressive as a school in a Brontë novel but there was nothing antique about the leftover aromas of takeout meals and cigarette smoke that drifted through the hallways. Only the long-term residents, older women who worked as salesclerks or secretaries, connected with one another. They formed cliques, shared tables in the hotel dining room, and sat gossiping in the lobby. The younger tenants exchanged impersonal greetings in the elevators. None of us were interested in making friends in a place where we were all out-of-towners. We just wanted to move on and turn ourselves into New Yorkers.

Those first Sundays in New York were lonely. I didn't know many people so I carved out small routines for myself: mornings were spent reading the *Times*; I'd sit cross-legged on my unmade bed and pore over every section of the paper. I even read the sports pages and found myself enjoying columns about prizefights and baseball because the writing was so good. On Sunday afternoons, I treated myself to double-feature matinees and was reminded of those summers in L.A. when I went to one or the other of my stepfather Lawrence's theaters and sat, mildly embarrassed, in the center seat of a roped-off row. One weekend afternoon I took the subway uptown to Spanish Harlem and explored some of the streets there. I was fascinated by the sight of brightly colored clothing hung on lines outside stall-like shops. The shirts and dresses made me think of exotic birds. I breathed in the nearly palpable scents of foreign spices and listened to a mélange of dialects in other languages. New York was becoming an exciting challenge for me and I regarded it in much the same way a novice climber might assess his or her first mountain: imposing and dangerous, but there to be taken on. I placed collect calls to my mother every weekend and let the sound of her voice wash over me like warm, scented water. My anger at her had been replaced by a sense of yearning; I wanted to see her, smell her cologne, laugh with her again. I missed my mom.

One of the girls I'd developed a casual friendship with moved out of the hotel and into a small apartment on the West Side. She invited me over to see it, and if I was unimpressed by the sunless living room and a bedroom that seemed more like a walk-in closet, I felt a distinct ripple of envy. Patricia had nailed down what every young hotel resident craved: a place of her own. We spent an hour talking about my job at Bergdorf's and hers as a receptionist in a high-end hair salon while she pursued an acting career. We raked aimlessly through leftover gossip from the hotel. Then she checked her watch, said she had to dress for a dinner date, and asked if I'd stay and let him in if he got there before she was ready.

I opened the door to an older man with dark, fact-seeking eyes and a brush of mustache. He was wearing a very serious gray suit, and when he moved past me, I caught the familiar citrus fragrance of Guerlain's Cologne Imperiale. We introduced ourselves; he told me his name was David Merrick. I said Patricia was still dressing, that she'd be out in a minute. He looked at me for a few seconds and then asked if I was studying acting, too. When I said no, he came up with a puzzling question: what did I know about him?

"Well, I know you're wearing the wrong shoes with that suit."

A smile edged its way through his dour expression.

"I am? I don't think Patricia will notice, though. Do you?" He waved a hand in the direction of the bedroom. "Did she tell you I work in the theater?"

"No. She just said she had a date. Are you a director?" I had yet to see a Broadway show.

The smile twitched into a grin; it was clear my ignorance pleased him.

"I'm an attorney and I've produced a couple of plays. Now tell me something about yourself."

It was the beginning of a friendship that would last for decades, with David as a kind of distant father figure. His presence in my

life would fill some of the places in the void my grandfather's
death had created: I often looked to David for approval and he was
there for me when I needed him.

One Saturday, I woke to see rain sluicing down the window. It reminded me of the Bay Area and I thought about being sheltered
inside the warming light of a museum. I hadn't been to the Metropolitan Museum of Art, but I'd heard people going on about its
glories. Today seemed like the perfect time for a visit so I put on
my oldest jeans and a heavy sweater, pulled on a pair of scuffed
boots, and made my way over to Eighty-second and Fifth. I hur-
ried up the granite steps and through the Romanesque arches. The
Great Hall smelled of lemon oil and old, well-polished wood.

I wandered idly, standing for long moments in front of the
keyboards on clavichords that made me think of the big Steinway
in our living room in Piedmont, the one my grandfather played
every evening after dinner. I walked slowly through a series of perfectly reconstructed historic rooms, lingering in the seventeenth-
century Venetian bedroom with its testered bed and parquet floor
puddled with shafts of thick yellow light beamed in through mul-
lioned windows. Finally, I headed for the paintings galleries. I
moved past eighteenth-century wheat fields blazing under a white-
hot sun and candlelit studies by de La Tour. I stopped in front of
The Horse Fair by Rosa Bonheur; I'd grown up with a gilt-framed
reproduction of that image and I loved the heavy-hocked beasts
with their gleaming flanks and flared nostrils. I looked at paintings
by Caravaggio and Holbein and Thomas Eakins.

I was leaving the museum when I saw something at the end of
a gallery that made me turn back for a closer look. This was the
real thing, just as I'd seen it in books about great art: that limpid,
cloud-streaked sky with a creamy slice of moon sailing above the
pinkish haze that held a setting sun at its center. There, in the background, were the rolling, blue-streaked hills. And, rising up from a
surround of bushes, the narrow gathering of cypresses, blacks and
dark greens and grayish-browns laid on in thick swirls by the

artist, who had matched feathery branches to the pink-streaked shreds at a corner of the canvas. I took a few steps back and then moved in close until I was positioned directly in front of the painting. There was a deep groove of satiny brown paint at the center of one of the trees with a nearly invisible bit of grit trapped at the crest. More than anything, I wanted to reach out and touch that glistening ridge.

I looked around. The guard was giving directions to someone at the other end of the gallery.

I took another step toward the painting and leaned forward until the details swam before my eyes. I took off my glasses and pulled in a deep breath. Then I stretched out my tongue and let the tip glide across the rind of gray-brown paint. It was done in an instant and I turned and walked away from the painting and out of the museum. I felt the shining skin of that long-dried paint on my tongue all the way back to the hotel. I felt the memory of it that night. It was the first time I'd broken the rules so aggressively and that excited me. I was also intensely aware that touching the painting had provided me with a strangely sensual experience accompanied by the sting of loneliness for someone I liked well enough to get close to.

A few weeks later I met the first New Yorker who made me lean forward with real interest. I was having dinner with a man who had been a casual acquaintance in L.A. Marty, who worked in advertising, was a recent transplant to New York and, at the suggestion of mutual friends, called me. I accepted his invitation to dinner but midway through the meal I realized I didn't much like Marty. His main topic of conversation, one to which he returned constantly, was his pride at having snagged an apartment on a high floor of a rent-controlled building in the east seventies. He described the twelve-foot ceilings and classic moldings, lingered over the view, and raved about an ever-vigilant doorman. He seemed to take a rather perverse pleasure in assuring me I'd never find anything like it. I was getting ready to look at my watch and mention my need to get up early the next morning when a slim, dark-haired man approached the table. He greeted Marty and shook his hand but his eyes were on me. The irises were the same shade as the water at the deepest end of a swimming pool. Marty invited him to pull up a chair, and before we left the restaurant, each of us had learned something about the other: I realized quickly that John Calley was exceptionally intelligent and coolly funny. He mentioned that he was with NBC and I managed to insert the name of the women's hotel into the conversation.

He called and invited me to dinner a few days later.

I loved going out with Calley. He lived in a book-lined apartment in Greenwich Village and we often spent time there—making love, reading, listening to music. He introduced me to the works of Paul Bowles and to the double-bass jazz riffs of Howard Rumsey. We ate at small, clubby restaurants and saw movies at neighborhood theaters. He took me to what I considered exotic events, like the auto show, where he led me from exhibit to exhibit with the fervor of a seminarian at the Vatican museum. He owned a small Italian convertible with a ragged canvas top that was stuck permanently in the down position; I still have a vivid image of watching from the hotel entrance as Calley drove away through a drenching rain with water collecting on the floor of the car. He introduced me to his father, Jack, a salesman who talked like a character in a Damon Runyon story and seemed eager to impress a son whose intellect appeared to intimidate him. I laughed when John compared my cheekbones to those of a farm worker in the Ukraine and reached for his hand when he told me about sending away for mail-order dance lessons as an awkward and skinny teenager who babysat his younger siblings when his parents went out. We liked each other a great deal, maybe even loved each other a little. But I think both of us knew we weren't *in* love.

The studio apartment on the top floor of a slightly decayed brownstone in the high east seventies was perfect. There was a sofa that pulled out into a bed, a small kitchen behind pocket doors, and a tub with claw feet in a bathroom floored with subway tiles. The owner of the building, an elderly woman with a finishing-school accent and a manner that suggested a devotion to sighs, smiled indulgently when I asked if I might move in immediately. The indulgence, I would learn, went no further than the smile.

I could have the apartment on lease, she said, but when I brought out my checkbook, her right index finger went up in a not-so-fast gesture. She told me her most trusted tenant was an attorney; she simply couldn't make an important decision like this without his approval. I nodded to show understanding and she went on. It would be *greatly* appreciated if I'd consent to meet with him. She was *quite* sure it would all work to our mutual advantage—I *seemed* like such a well-bred young lady. She smiled again, brushed an invisible speck from her skirt, and waited for her delicately shaded words to sink in. I smiled back. I wanted that little studio and if I had to be looked over in order to get it, okay. It wasn't so very different from a go-see for a modeling job.

The landlady called the most trusted tenant and we made arrangements to meet for dinner that evening. I went back to the hotel and spent nearly an hour applying makeup that would accentuate my eyes without being obvious. I put on the black dress my mother said made me look like the daughter of a Sicilian banker, checked my reflection in the wavy mirror attached to the closet door, and tried out a guileless smile. I didn't need to dazzle this guy; I just wanted to sign a lease.

The restaurant had amber lighting and nineteenth-century hunting prints on the walls. The man whose approval I needed was waiting for me at the bar. He was younger than I'd expected, about thirty, and nice-looking, with dark hair that was just beginning to thin and intelligent, restless eyes. His palm was warm and cushiony when we shook hands and he asked me to call him by his given name. The captain bowed us to a corner booth and handed out oversized menus. Joel set his down without looking at it. Would I mind if he ordered for both of us? The steaks were great here. And how did I feel about a glass of wine?

As we waited for our salads, he offered me a cigarette and took one himself. Then he reached into his pocket for a chunky gold lighter and when he held the flame to the tip of my cigarette, he crooked his pinky finger so that it touched mine. It was the kind of corny gesture a guy might make to impress a woman. I began to relax.

We spoke in generalities and when I found myself admiring Joel's tough New York voice with its flattened vowels and hard-struck consonants, I forgot about his trick with the lighter. I liked the way he gripped his cigarette between thumb and forefinger, squinting slightly against the smoke. I looked at the curve of his mouth and wondered if he knew how to kiss.

When he asked me to tell him about myself it was with the inviting curiosity of someone out on a successful blind date. I talked about my family (editing out the litany of my mother's marriages) and boarding school and working at Bergdorf's. Told him about the hotel and the girl in the room next to mine who looked like a Charles Addams cartoon and typed all night. I was probably flirting a little when I said I hadn't yet been in a deeply serious relationship. Joel was a good listener and he laughed in all the right places. And if I couldn't read him, that was fine; it only added to my interest.

He signaled for the check, signed it, and, without looking up, told me he was going to recommend me as a tenant to Mrs. Phelps. Had she mentioned that he'd lived in the studio before moving to a larger apartment downstairs? No, huh? He seemed slightly disappointed, as if by not sharing that detail, the landlady had in some way disrespected him.

The night air was cool on our faces as we stood outside the restaurant. Joel looked at his watch. It was still early, he said, and asked if I felt like a walk before we said good night. I could take another look at the studio and he'd show me how to deal with some of those little emergencies that always seemed to happen at two in the morning. He smiled and spread his arms in the "What're you gonna do?" gesture of affectionate exasperation that most

New Yorkers share with one another from time to time. I faked it and nodded my head knowingly. I was beginning to feel at home. And I wasn't ready for the evening to end.

The apartment was even more charming at night. A floor lamp with a parchment shade cast a warm glow around the room and a faint aroma of floor wax reminded me of my grandparents' home on Jerome Avenue. Joel went directly to one of the tall, arched windows on either side of the sofa and began to fiddle with the catch. This handle was tricky, he said; on warm nights it liked to stick. I should take a look at it.

I wasn't expecting the kiss and pulled back from it. He looked surprised. My response surprised me, too. What Joel had just tried was what I'd been wondering about back at the restaurant.

"Come on," he said. "Don't be like that. It's just a little kiss."

I shook my head, suddenly uneasy.

He's not smiling anymore; he's pressuring me.

"Hey!" The single word sounded like a shot. "You were makin' with a little come-on all through dinner. And I didn't hear you saying no when I asked you up here. You acted like you liked me."

"I do like you."

That's a lie. I don't like him at all. This is a guy who has to get his way and if he doesn't, he shows a mean streak.

"Right. Okay. Now act like you mean it."

The flat New York voice had developed an icy edge. I took a step back and tried to keep my eyes on his. I felt a sudden itch of sweat at my armpits.

I'm scared now and I can't let him see that. I've got to keep calm and not panic. But he knows this room and I don't. I don't know how to get away from him. He has every advantage but please, God, don't let him hurt me.

When he grabbed my shoulders with both hands, I pushed him away. He reached out for me again and this time I made a sound midway between a gasp and a scream and he placed his cushiony palm across my mouth. We swayed in silent battle for a moment, then he gave a hard push and I felt the roughness of upholstery against my back and his weight on top of me. I smelled his too-sweet aftershave and, under that, the acrid odor of his sweat. He fumbled with my clothes and I heard a hiss of words—"bitch," "cockteaser"—and the soft snap of tearing silk. And then he was inside me, there on the sofa that was supposed to pull out into a bed.

It was over fast. He grunted and sat up, patting strands of hair back into place. When he leaned over and picked up my silk scarf from the floor, I thought he was going to hand it to me in an absurd gesture of courtesy and, childishly, I considered flinging it back at him. He didn't hand me the scarf: he held it up, sniffed it appreciatively, and wiped his penis with it.

Then he dropped it to the floor again, adjusted his clothes, and stood up. Just before he walked out of the apartment, he looked back at me and grinned.

Mrs. Phelps sighed and said I must have had a bad dream. She couldn't imagine *anyone* she knew behaving in such a manner, *least* of all her most trusted tenant. Then she delivered her indulgent smile.

I didn't report Joel to the police. *Hey, girlie, nobody forced you to go to an apartment with some guy you just met . . .*

I didn't tell my mother, either. Too embarrassing, and she would have ordered me back to L.A. But I didn't want to go home. What Joel had done to me was so crushing I could only allow myself to think about it a few seconds at a time. But it was my problem to be gotten over. I knew that dealing with it myself couldn't possibly be as awful as talking about any kind of sexual act (never mind rape) with my mother and Hotten. The thought of it made me shrink into myself. I was the one who had flirted with Joel and then followed his lead to the apartment I wanted so badly to rent; I wasn't about to relive with my family (who still thought of me as "the Baby") what had happened to me there. So I made do with a serious fantasy in which I sobbed out the whole story to my first stepfather, Barney. A call would get made and Joel would open his door one night to a man holding a gun with a silencer attached at the business end.

I found a doctor, who assured me I was not pregnant and that I didn't have a sexually transmitted disease. And I found another apartment. It didn't have the charm of the little studio but I didn't have to worry about the trusted tenant downstairs either.

I managed to bury what had happened in that part of the mind where unwanted memories drift as silently as sharks. Then, last year, someone asked if I thought date rapes ever really happened.

CHAPTER 3

Mack and Mickey

I was off the floor at Bergdorf's and being booked as a runway model through a high-profile agency when I met Mack Bing, a television director under contract to CBS. It was a blind date and when I opened the door to my apartment my first thought was that he looked like a bullfighter. He was tall and slender with one of those broken noses that make good looks better and pale green eyes that provided a startling contrast to his olive complexion and dark hair. I invited him in and offered a beer. I didn't drink, really, but my mom liked an icy Miller on hot days so Miller High Life was what I kept in my small refrigerator. Mack sat down, took a long pull from the bottle, and grinned at me. His teeth were very large and very white.

I like everything about this man: his looks, his smell, the way the hair at the nape of his neck is long enough to touch his collar. I like the way he looks at me: admiring but with an edge of amusement. When he asks questions he listens closely to my replies and then demands more details, as if he can't get enough of what it's like to be me. When he talks about himself there's a quality of holding back that makes me want to know more about him.

When I asked about his childhood and adolescence, Mack glossed over his relationship with his parents, who had divorced when he was six, and talked lovingly about his grandfather, who was still living, and the Dalmatians he'd trained to be show dogs. He told me about joining the navy at seventeen and he talked about his work, which he enjoyed. As the evening wore on, it became increasingly clear how much he resented his mother. This was an emotion entirely foreign to me—my mother had always been the most important person in my life; even when I was angry enough to feel a brief sting of hatred toward her, she was always the person most necessary to me, more essential even (and I always felt a pang of guilt when I thought about this) than my grandparents and Hotten. I told Mack (whose given name was Maximilian) about my mom and his expression darkened slightly at the mention of her marriages.

"Did any of those stepfathers ever try and touch you?"

I was surprised; nobody had ever asked me that question.

"God, no. My mother was really careful. When I was about twelve she was going out with some guy who was a judge and one night he took both of us to dinner. Afterward, we were going down the hall to our apartment and I was walking a few feet ahead of them when he made some comment about how shapely my legs were. My mom didn't say anything but that was it for the judge; she never even took his calls again."

"Did you and she ever talk about it?"

"What? No . . ." *I couldn't bring myself to tell her about being raped in that little studio apartment. How am I going to ask her about some man she was going out with admiring my legs when I was just a kid?* "We don't talk about things like that in our family."

And I don't want to talk about it with you, either. I don't ever want to know if you think, even remotely, that I got what I deserved because I trusted someone enough to follow him to a place I wanted to rent. The same way I trusted you enough to let you into this apartment.

Mack started to say something, stopped, reached out for my hand, and lifted it to his lips.

We never left my apartment that first evening. We talked for hours and then Mack leaned forward, placed his hands on either side of my face, and we began to kiss. When he touched me, his hands were firm but tender. When we made love he gripped my hair and tipped my head back so he could kiss my throat. He fell asleep before I did, curled around me on the tangled sheets. I pushed myself close against the curve of his body, knowing already how I felt about him.

I could love this man. I really think I could love this man. He makes me feel, I don't know . . . valuable.

I can't remember being apart after that first evening. We were each working, of course, but we had dinner every evening and slept together, either at my place or his, every night. He had a big black and white male cat he'd found on the street and he introduced me to him as if Myron was another person. On weekends Mack took me by the hand and we went exploring around the city. He pointed out things I hadn't seen before: the cobblestones on certain streets, the charming old mews houses in Greenwich Village. He showed me the Bethesda Fountain in Central Park and told me its great centerpiece, the Angel of the Waters, had been designed by a woman. He made me think of my grandfather, telling me I could reach whatever I went after if I worked at it. Mack was in his thirties; I was not yet twenty. He took the lead in everything: what restaurants we went to, what foreign movies we saw. And for the first time since the death of my grandfather, I liked being told what was right for me.

During the next few months we both tried to see past the mutuality of our attraction, past the bonds of background, religion, and shared priorities—we had both moved away from Republican backgrounds to become ardent Democrats—into the far reach of our prospects together. We didn't talk about it, nobody said the word "marriage," but the thought was there, hanging above our heads like a spiderweb on a high rafter. Then, during a trip to L.A. to visit our respective families, Mack asked me to marry him. Within hours and with his cousin, Jack (who had arranged for us to meet on that first date) as witness, we stood under an arch of dusty artificial orchids in a Las Vegas wedding chapel and recited our lines in front of a sateen-robed functionary with yellow hair swept into a gluey pompadour. The only difference in what I'd once imagined the chapel would look like and the thing itself was the genus of fake flowers and the fact that Mack had my wedding ring with him before we set out for Vegas. I looked at his oddly handsome face as we repeated the standard vows and wondered what our lives together would be like.

My mother gave us my grandfather's piano and Georgian silver wall sconces. Hotten's gift was a pair of beautiful antique ginger jars and Uncle Henry provided us with twelve settings of sterling flatware. Mack's mother, Florence (whom I found to be much more welcoming than expected), and his stepfather, Ben, gave us a dark green Jaguar. Ben owned a lavish men's clothing store in Beverly Hills, and the day before Mack and I were to begin our drive back to New York, he asked if we'd join him there. One of his best customers, who knew Mack and liked him, had expressed a desire to meet the bride.

I recognized the man as soon as he walked through the door; he'd been in the newspapers and on TV often enough. He had survived several attempts on his life, and he retained a battery of attorneys to engage in an ongoing and well-publicized battle with the federal government against charges that included racketeering and income tax evasion. He had outlived Ben "Bugsy" Siegel, Meyer Lansky, and Jack Dragna, an associate of my stepfather, Barney.

Mickey Cohen paused for an instant at the entrance to Ben's shop and two men appeared beside him. One of them held the door for Cohen before they ambled to a counter near the back of the room. Cohen greeted Ben warmly before he turned to face Mack and me.

"Thanks for comin' in. I like to pay my respects in person."

I noticed he didn't offer a handshake. Instead, he reached out and gripped the shoulders of Mack's jacket with both hands for a single brief contact. Then he jerked his head in my direction.

"Okay if I kiss the bride?"

He turned to face me and I felt something like an electric

charge shimmering in the space around him. I wasn't afraid but I was intensely interested in this man whose history was so ripe with brutality. He resembled a dark cupid with his round cheeks and baby's mouth, but it was the eyes that gave him away: they were the eyes of a guard dog, coldly vigilant, ready for the sudden move. Mack made the introductions and Cohen stepped in to kiss my cheek. But his lips didn't touch the skin; they came just near enough to give the illusion of a kiss and to allow me to catch a scent of mouthwash on his breath and see the thick black crescents of his eyelashes. He stepped back, still looking at me.

"You are one beautiful young girl. I hope you know you got yourself a good husband. A real mensch." He gestured at Mack. "I know this guy ever since he was a kid workin' here on school holidays. Even ran errands for me a couple times. Don't worry— strictly kosher." He barked out a short laugh and moved in close to Mack again, whispering. Mack nodded and Cohen handed him an envelope. Then he glanced over at the two men lounging against the back counter. He didn't snap his fingers, but the effect was the same: they came to attention and loped across the room to position themselves on either side of the glass doors leading to Rodeo Drive. Cohen made a small bow in my direction, turned, lowered his head, and charged out of Ben's store.

Later, driving through Beverly Hills, Mack took the envelope from the pocket of his jacket and handed it to me. There were fifteen new hundred-dollar bills inside and a small white card. The writing on the card was graceful, nearly feminine:

"All the best from Mickey."

When we got back to New York, David Merrick gave us a wedding reception in a private room at his favorite restaurant and teased me about having deprived him of his chance to give the bride away.

Mack returned to his job at CBS. I checked in with my agency, went out on go-sees, and hit the runways again. We decided to buy a house, found a small brownstone in the east fifties, and sold some stock I'd received as part of an inheritance from my grandfather to make the down payment. I cut back on modeling assignments to begin the work of furnishing a home. We moved in before the work started and it was like living in the lobby of an old hotel undergoing renovations. Painters and carpenters arrived at what seemed like dawn, and the sounds of hammers and power saws were like a dentist's drill near a live nerve. I walked through it all with my books on interior design, trailing samples of material and snippets of wallpaper, and I was on the phone to my mother almost daily, asking for advice about colors, fabrics, wood paneling. The more we spoke, the more I wanted to see her, and after Mack and I were settled in, books shelved, every platter and wineglass put away, each chair, table, and armoire in its proper place, I said I wanted to take a trip to L.A. Mack was busy with a new show so he told me to give his love to everyone and, if I had time, to call Mickey Cohen and ask how he was doing.

"Tell you something—if you got here a couple weeks later, I'da been gone already. It's like a good luck thing, you comin' to the coast now."

We were in Mickey's black Chrysler, heading toward his house in Santa Monica. Mickey and I were seated in the back. The same men who had been with him at Ben's store a year earlier were up front, with the older of the two at the wheel. Again, no introductions were made. They'd waited in the car when Cohen came to collect me at my mother's apartment in Brentwood. He had bowed over my mother's hand without touching it. His manner toward her was exquisitely formal, and even though he was probably older than she was, he referred to her as "Mom" when he thanked her for allowing him to cut into our time together. She was gracious enough, but I caught the familiar arch of eyebrow that signaled a breach of manners, and when I followed Mickey to his car, she stood looking down from the window.

"My fiancée Ginger's lookin' forward to meeting you. That kid's gone through plenty the past few months, believe me, and she never once made a move to walk out." He turned to look out the car window. "Goddamn government's got me in a vise." He went on to speak briefly about the denial of his final appeal on a conviction of tax evasion and the deal his attorneys had struck for him to turn himself over to the authorities to begin serving a lengthy sentence at Alcatraz.

"Same thing they did to Capone—couldn't get nothing else to stick." He glanced at the back of the driver's neck. "Abe, those guys still on our tail?"

"Yeah. Want me to lose 'em?"

"Nah. Let the bastards do their job." He looked at me again. "Feds. Don't let it worry you, hon."

"I'm fine. Really." Secretly, I was thrilled.

If I expected Mickey Cohen's house to be a monument to gangster excess, I was disappointed. He lived on a quiet residential street in a small, ranch-style house identical to most of the others on the block. (I would learn later that a more impressive home had been nearly leveled by a bomb.) The driver pulled into the driveway and hopped out to open the door for Mickey. The younger man opened the door on my side and extended his hand to help me from the car. He kept his eyes averted as I moved past him.

The interior of the house was sparsely furnished with blond wood furniture upholstered in a banana palm print. A console TV was set up at one end of the living room and a fieldstone fireplace looked as if it had never been used. The single personal note was a series of framed photographs of Cohen with a Boston bull terrier.

"That's Mickey Jr." Cohen spoke quietly. "Little bum's livin' with my sister now."

There was the sound of a door closing in another part of the house and a young woman walked into the room. She looked to be only a few years older than me and she was beautiful in the way you expect film actresses to be beautiful: pale, poreless skin, and blond hair that seemed to trap the light. She moved directly to Cohen's side, ducking her head a little to allow him to drape one arm across her shoulders as he introduced us. Her handshake was firm, her smile true. When she asked if I'd like something to drink, Cohen spoke up quickly.

"Bring out a couple Cokes and some club soda. And tell Jackie to order in some Chinese, huh?"

Ginger smiled, first at Cohen, then at me, and left the room. Cohen's eyes followed her until she was out of sight, then he looked at me again.

"I guess I must seem like a pretty thoughtless guy to somebody like you, but I'm used to callin' the shots without any fuss, see?"

There wasn't anything I could say that wouldn't sound like a smart-ass remark so I just looked at him and smiled. He didn't speak for a moment, then one corner of his mouth lifted and he grunted softly before speaking again.

"Cool breeze."

I saw Mickey Cohen and Ginger Nolan a few times during the three or four weeks I spent with my mother in L.A., and the drill was always the same: he picked me up at her apartment; the same two men waited in the black Chrysler; we were always tailed by the nondescript car. We went once to a small Italian restaurant in Westwood. The staff there responded to Cohen with great deference and we were seated at a back table, well out of the way of other diners who might be curious enough to stare. Mickey was unfailingly polite, but it was clear that conversation with him was filtered through an elaborate security system. New York, sports, politics, and Mack's job were acceptable subjects, but if I asked a question that veered too close to the personal, Cohen's defense reflexes went off, rising up in front of his smile like razor wire fencing. He remained cordial but I could almost hear the sound of a lock slamming home. I decided not to mention Barney and his relationship to my mother.

Mickey was at his most relaxed when Ginger was around. Behind the clinging outfits and jade-green eye shadow, there was an unspoiled quality about her that suggested a place separate from the shadowy empire inhabited by Cohen and his associates.

Mickey called and asked me to have dinner at his house the evening before he was to surrender to the federal authorities; there was something he needed to talk over with me. I didn't tell my mother about that aspect of the invitation. She just nodded her head and changed the subject. Looking back, I think it was something she must have learned during her marriage to Barney: don't ask questions if you think you might not like the answers.

Mickey Cohen, his two guys, and Ginger and I sat around a surfboard-shaped coffee table in the living room and spooned fried rice and garlicky shrimp out of takeout containers. There were soft drinks and whiskey, and for the first time, I saw Mickey pour a shot into his glass of club soda. The men did most of the talking and nearly all of it was about the past.

They told stories about friends, both dead and living, like the guy out of New York who had earned a fearsome reputation as an enforcer but suffered uncontrollable bouts of kleptomania. He was picked up at Macy's with a barometer stuffed down one leg of his trousers. Names like "Hooky Rothman," "Cockeye Bernstein," and "Bobby Dogs" were tossed into narratives like exotic seasonings. The telephone rang at intervals and the older man, Abe, would pick up. He'd listen briefly, cover the mouthpiece, and whisper a name to Cohen. Then Cohen might excuse himself and go into the bedroom to speak with whoever had called. If he shook his head, Abe would hang up without explanation. After we were done eating, I helped Ginger clear up and I was walking out of the kitchen when I heard Abe's voice.

"With respect, Mick, I think what you're doin' is meshugge. This girl looks like she's about fourteen years old."

Cohen didn't say anything. He smiled and reached out to pat Abe's cheek with the backs of his fingers. Then he looked over at me and nodded his head in the direction of the bedroom.

There were clothes in neat piles on the bed, on chairs, stacked near a dressing table that held a leather jewelry box and an assortment of women's perfumes. An open suitcase sat on an up-holstered bench at the foot of the bed. An arrangement of stuffed animals rode the pillows at the headboard.

"Gettin' rid of stuff before I go." He gestured at the suit-case. "Shove that thing over and sit down." I sat. Mickey looked at me for a few seconds, studying my face as if he were trying to de-cide something. The look made me uneasy and I wondered if I had offended in some way. I worried a small tear along the cord welt-ing on the bench and waited. Then he spoke again. "Listen, I'm gonna ask you to do a couple things for me—favors, understand what I'm saying? First off, tomorrow night's the first time Ginger's gonna be alone in the house and that'll be hard on her. She don't think so, but she don't know anything about this game and I'd feel better if someone was here with her. Think your mom would mind if you slept over?"

I hadn't realized how tense I was until I felt my shoulders relax.

"No, of course not. When are—"

"First thing in the morning." He picked up a dark blue polo shirt from the bed and refolded it. "Second thing's a little bit more complicated. I need you to take something back to New York with you."

I started to say something. Cohen held up one hand for silence.

"Let me finish, huh? There's a box. Not too big, fit in your pocketbook easy. There'll be something inside, of course. You don't need to know what, except it ain't gonna be a gun or a bomb or anything dangerous, you got my word on that. All you gotta do is take it with you, put it somewhere where it'll be safe, and forget about it until I send somebody to pick it up. You with me so far?" I nodded my head. He looked closely at me again, reading my ex-pression. "Now, I already talked to your husband about this and it's okay with him, but he says you gotta be the one makes the call seein' as you're the one's gonna do the job."

"Does he know what's in the box?"

"No. Better if nobody knows."

I wanted to tell my mom about what I was being asked to do but I could hear her response in my head: *Are you out of your mind? Of* course *you're not going to ferry some mysterious package across the country for a convicted felon. I won't allow it.*

Forget that I was married, forget that I could make a living, come to my own decisions. I decided to skip the inevitable scene and say nothing about Mickey Cohen's second favor. That night, lying in bed in my mother's guest room, I thought about him.

People see him only as a thug and a killer. But he's soft-spoken and almost courtly with me and with Ginger. He behaves in a respectful manner with those two guys who are there to do whatever he orders. He choked up when he showed me those pictures of his dog. Mack likes and respects him enough to ask me to call Mickey when I got to L.A. and he approved this mysterious favor. Maybe Mickey Cohen is a kind of paradox: a good guy inside the skin of a bad guy. Maybe. Anyway, this whole thing is pretty exciting. I feel like a spy.

So I made the argument for Cohen. There was no rationale for men like Joel, an attorney who smiled at me over dinner and lit my cigarette with a corny romantic gesture before he raped me in that studio apartment in New York. Joel and others like him, they were the bad guys.

Abe was alone and driving a different car when he came to pick me up the following afternoon. We didn't speak much during the ride to Cohen's house. I asked if Mickey had gone; he said yes; that was about it. This time he didn't pull into the driveway; he stopped the car at the curb and leaned across me to open the passenger door.

"You're not coming in?"

"Ginger's got my number, you need anything."

She must have been looking out the window because the door swung open before I had a chance to ring the bell. She was wearing a plain dark dress and flat shoes. Her hair was freshly brushed but her eyes were swollen and most of her lipstick was worn away. I dropped my things on a chair in the hallway and when I turned back, she was holding a box encased in a mummy-wrap of duct tape. The package was slightly larger than an ordinary brick. She handed it to me. Not quite as heavy as a brick, I thought, but close. I looked at Ginger and her shoulders hitched into a shrug. I buried the box at the bottom of my bag and we went into the living room.

Ginger settled herself against the sofa cushions and reached for a cigarette from a pack on the coffee table. Then she picked up a chunky gold lighter and said, "This lighter was the first present Mickey ever gave me." She lit the cigarette and polished the lighter against her skirt before she set it down.

"How did you two meet?" I was making conversation but I was interested, too.

"I was working as a cocktail waitress at a jazz joint on Sunset and Mickey would come in every so often and we'd talk—you know, just chitchat—and one night he asked me out on a date."

"Did you know who he was?"

"Oh, sure. I wasn't that much of a hick. But he was a really nice guy, you know? A gentleman." She pulled in smoke and sighed it out in a long plume. "I didn't tell my folks about Mickey the whole first year we were together. I just said he was in business and I didn't . . . well, I didn't tell them his last name. They still don't know what he does or that we live together. I feel kind of bad about that, but my dad's a wheat farmer and he and my mom are old-fashioned about a lot of things. I didn't even tell them about my job at the club; I just said I was working as an extra in pictures. They didn't much approve of that either." She smiled briefly. "But I notice they're going to a lot more movies lately. Anyway, I always go home for Christmas and the last two weeks in August." She spoke about being in the Midwest in late summer, the smell of the wheat and the wind moving through it, turning the field into "some big, alive thing."

The telephone jangled and we both jumped a little. Ginger looked over at the phone but she didn't make a move to pick up the receiver.

"Want me to get it? I can just say you're out."

She shook her head. "It's been doing that all day. There's another line in the bedroom if you want to call your mom." She crushed out her cigarette. "I'm going in to start dinner."

The bedroom curtains were drawn but I could see the piles of clothing from the night before. They were now wrapped and tagged. I spoke briefly with my mother and went into the bathroom. I was washing my hands when I noticed the lineup of partially filled bottles on the Formica countertop. They were in precise order with the tallest ones placed nearest the faucets. None of them were labeled. I picked up a bottle filled with an amber-colored liquid, unscrewed the cap, and sniffed. Listerine. Another one held a spice-based aftershave. I scanned all the bottles again and was able to identify most of them as either cologne or mouthwash.

Ginger was mixing salad dressing when I walked into the kitchen. She laughed softly when I asked about the unmarked bottles.

"Haven't you noticed how squeamish Mickey is about anyone touching him, how he never shakes hands? He's petrified of catching something. So anything he gets that's been touched by strangers, like those bottles, has to be dunked in boiling water before he'll go near it. Anything that can't be boiled, he sprays with disinfectant. There's a can of Lysol next to every phone in the house, just in case somebody else uses it. Mickey won't touch a receiver unless he sprays it first." Her smile faded. "God knows what it'll be like for him in prison."

An hour later we were seated in the dining room, eating chicken from Mickey Cohen's good china. Ginger had turned off the telephone in the living room and the uninterrupted meal had relaxed us. We were on coffee and cigarettes when the doorbell sounded. We glanced at each other across the table. Ginger looked vaguely frightened.

"Abe?" I whispered the word.

She shook her head. "We have a signal."

I pushed back my chair. "Stay here. I'll look out through the living room curtains."

The house was surrounded by television crews and reporters. Somebody saw the slight movement of the curtains; there was an instant flare of bluish lights and shouted questions peppered the air. I turned away from the tumult. Ginger was standing in the archway.

"Bastards. All they really want is to see me cry."

The reporters and TV crews were gone by morning. They left tamped-down flower beds, discarded coffee containers, and a foam of cigarette butts and fast-food wrappers in their wake. Ginger drove me back to my mother's place and told me she was planning to relocate to San Francisco in order to make regular visits to Alcatraz. Neither of us mentioned the package at the bottom of my bag.

The plane was over Oklahoma when I walked up the aisle to the restroom. I locked the door and the box was in my hand before the lights over the washstand stopped flickering. I looked down at the carefully wrapped package for long seconds. Held it up to my ear and jiggled it. Bounced it in my hands. Conscience was about to collide with unbridled curiosity.

The sharp edge of my mailbox key worked its way through the tape and sliced along the lid of the box. I lifted it carefully and set it on the counter. Then I peeled back a layer of cotton.

Diamonds. A river of glittering stones captured in a cardboard box.

I skimmed my fingertips across them. Round, square-cut, marquise, and pear-shaped gems. Different sizes, most of them unset. The largest, an emerald-cut solitaire the approximate size of a small stamp, shimmered in the vibration of the plane's engines. I stirred the diamonds with one finger, staring at their cold brilliance. Then I replaced the cotton, closed the box, and put it back in the bottom of my bag, making sure it rested firmly among the half-used matchbooks and stray subway tokens.

I asked the cab driver to make a single stop on the way back from the airport.

When Mack got home from the studio that evening, Mickey Cohen's box of diamonds looked the same as it had when Ginger handed it to me. The duct tape I'd picked up at the hardware store was an exact match of the original. Mack barely glanced at the package before he stuck it at the back of the wall safe built into a hall closet. He had only one comment:

"Okay. Now we forget it."

The next couple of years sped by. Mack was moving up the corporate ladder and suddenly it was the midsixties. Our daughter, Lisa, was born and I became a full-time, stay-at-home mom. I enjoyed all the small rituals of bathing and feeding and cuddling a baby. I made up silly little songs and kissed the satiny bottoms of her feet and wondered how she'd look in ten, twenty years. We found an antique rocker at a shop on Third Avenue and placed it near the windows in Lisa's room. I sat in the chair when I fed her, rocking as she drank hungrily from her bottle. When the gentle motion of the chair lulled her to sleep I continued to hold her, breathing in the faint, milky aroma of her skin, delighting in the small perfections of her fingernails and finely drawn eyebrows. And I tried to imagine my mother doing the same with me. I couldn't take hold of that picture. I could hear the spray of her laughter. I could feel the delicious skritch of her long fingernails chasing down an itch on my back. It was easy to conjure up the wonderful smell of her perfume. But when I thought about being held and rocked, kissed and comforted, it was my grandmother's face, her voice, and the feel of her warmth that came alive for me.

Most days I bundled Lisa into her stroller and we'd walk for a couple of hours, stopping now and then to window-shop along Third Avenue. When she began to walk, we'd hold hands and enjoy the sights and sounds on our own block. On weekends when Mack was home, the three of us would go to Central Park Zoo or we might sit out back and enjoy a picnic lunch while Lisa explored the confines of our small walled garden. There was one disappointing note: the house, as charming as it was, was too much to handle without the kind of help we couldn't afford. I loved the intricate patterns of the parquet flooring, the marble-manteled fireplaces in every room, the Dutch elm that shaded the garden. I'd miss the window seats that lent an added pleasure to long reads, but four flights of stairs with Lisa's room on the top floor tipped the scales in favor of getting out from under.

We sold the house and bought an apartment in one of the great old buildings on Central Park West. The fireplaces didn't work but it was on a high floor and nearly every window looked out over the park. An added bonus was the wall safe (Mack and I guessed wall safes were a typical home accessory in the city) located in a large cedar-paneled dressing room off the master bedroom. We settled in and it surprised both of us when we realized time had moved so quickly that Lisa was old enough to start preschool.

When Mack was offered a directing job on the West Coast, we agreed he should take it. The money was too good to refuse. I'd stay on in New York, hire a live-in nanny, and go back to work until Mack was comfortable enough in the new job to send for Lisa and me. I expected to miss him. But. But what? Our relationship was as placid as the surface of a frozen pond. We didn't have killer fights. We didn't even talk much, but when we did, my husband often seemed like a man checking his watch. Still, there were no instances of electric animosity arcing between us. Maybe that was it: there wasn't much of anything aside from our child (and good sex) going on between us. The consuming mutual interests that created our original attraction had burned themselves out. Not his fault, not mine. The marriage had simply rolled to a halt. So Mack went to L.A. and I went back to modeling. We spoke every week (Lisa, his work, my work, bills) and exchanged the occasional letter. And, in measures as small as dropped stitches, we stopped thinking of ourselves as a family and became separate entities with a child we both loved and a tundra of unspoken and misplaced feelings between us.

The box with Mickey Cohen's diamonds remained in the safe in the dressing room of our apartment. Mack got word to Cohen about his move to Los Angeles and a new routine was put in place: I'd get a call every few weeks, the caller would identify himself as "a friend from the coast," and we'd arrange a meeting.

No problem.

The first time I heard it, the voice on the other end of the line made me think of my stepfather Barney: street-hard with a core of warmth. He wanted to know when it would be convenient for him to stop by. I offered a couple of choices, we nailed down details, and the deal was done.

Three days later I opened the door to a middle-aged man in a black suit and tie. He looked like a slightly more conservative version of Abe, Mickey Cohen's guy in Los Angeles, and he was holding a box from the Carnegie Delicatessen. A few minutes later, over cheesecake and coffee and after some general conversation and a mention of greetings sent from "our friend in California," he got to the point: everything in good order around here? This had to be an oblique reference to the diamonds. I told him everything was just fine and offered to show him the package. He looked at me for a few seconds, shook his head, and took a small notebook and a gold pen from an inside pocket. He wrote quickly, tore out the page, folded it once across, and dropped it on the table next to his empty coffee cup. Then he stood up.

"I'll call you in a couple, three weeks." He glanced down at the fold of paper. "That's a number where you can reach me. If there's any kind of problem you can't handle yourself, something at work, say, or here in the building, maybe some guy gets outta line—*anything*—you call that number and leave word for me to get in touch. Then, whatever the problem is, it gets taken care of." He looked at me with coolly assessing eyes. "You understand?"

I understood. The implications were a little frightening to think about, but not since living at home with my family in Piedmont had I experienced a sense of such absolute security. I was alone again, this time with a child, but I had the promise of protection and a raging appetite to devour everything New York had to offer.

I never spoke directly with Mickey Cohen again. Two years into his sentence at Alcatraz, another inmate crept up behind him and slammed a lead pipe into the back of his head. Mickey never fully recovered from the attack and remained partially paralyzed. When Alcatraz shut down, he was transferred to the federal penitentiary in Atlanta, where he served out the rest of his term. He was released in 1972, returned to Los Angeles, and lived quietly until he died in his sleep four years later.

His most memorable quote: "I never killed anybody that didn't deserve killing in the first place."

CHAPTER 4

The Girls in Their Designer Dresses

I liked being on my own again. At night, when Lisa was asleep and the apartment was quiet, I found it relaxing, unlike the small talk that had seemed so unendurable when Mack was home. I was working enough to cover some of the bills as well as the nanny's wages but I wasn't so in demand I didn't have time to spend a few hours in the afternoons with Lisa and read to her at bedtime. She drew pictures for Mack and we sent them off to him. He timed his calls so they could talk to each other. I gave vague answers to her questions about when Papa was coming home because I didn't know what explanations to give. I was sure of one thing only: I would reinforce Lisa's love for her father in every way. That hadn't happened when my mother decided to cut my father loose. Every time I thought about him after their divorce, I experienced a rush of guilt. I was afraid to love him, afraid even to ask about him, because any time I misbehaved, there were tightened lips and references to how like my father's my behavior had become. From the fragments I was able to put together, my dad's singular offense had been that he was a quiet man who preferred to spend much of his time away from work with his books and the occasional round of tennis. Still, I began to identify bad behavior and the anger it incurred with my father. Now, with a child of my own and a determination to keep her father alive in her life, I felt a rush of unresolved feelings for the parent who had been excised from my childhood.

I called Information and spelled out his name to an operator in San Francisco. A few seconds later, I had a number. I dialed the first few digits.

This is my real father's telephone number and I'm scared to death. In a few seconds I'm going to be hearing a voice I can't remember and a man I haven't seen since I was three years old. What am I supposed to call him? What if he doesn't want to talk to me? What if he's dead? No, that can't be, they just gave me his number. If he was dead, I wouldn't have to talk to him, and Jesus Christ, that's a terrible thing to even think. I can't be that much of a coward but what am I supposed to say to this man? Do I have to say how sorry I am for not ever seeing him? It wasn't my fault but what if he doesn't know that? What if he starts crying? I couldn't stand it. Maybe if I start by telling him about being married and having Lisa, it will just go from there . . .

I dialed the last number, heard the first ring of the telephone on the other end, and was suddenly overcome with such a cold sense of betrayal toward my mother, toward my dead grandmother and Hotten, I slammed down the receiver before anyone could answer. The salt taste of tears was in my mouth. I was crying for myself and for the father I couldn't bring myself to speak to.

Placing that aborted call to my father cut deeper than I expected and I found myself crying hard at unexpected moments. A few days later I woke up with an odd feeling. I wasn't in pain and I didn't feel sick. But something was off. I went into the bathroom and looked at myself in the mirror. There was something about the way I looked—not *how* I looked, my face was the same as always, but the way I was seeing it. Acting on instinct, I held up one hand and covered my left eye; normal. I moved my hand across to cover the right eye: nothing, no vision at all. Instead of sight, there was only a solid field of brown. Not black, as I had always believed, but brown, the color of thick, dark chocolate. And it was impenetrable. I couldn't see around it or under it or through it. I was blind in my left eye.

I willed myself to keep calm as I brushed my teeth, washed my face, threw on clothes. There was no time to panic; I had to get myself to an emergency room. Lisa was still sleeping and I told the nanny I had to go out, I'd be back soon. I got a cab and asked to be taken to Mount Sinai Medical Center.

The ER was filled with people in various states of need and I was directed to sit down and wait. I wanted to yell that I'd just gone fucking blind, and how was I supposed to sit quietly like a kid at the principal's office? I didn't yell. I took a seat in a corner and looked down at my hands with my good eye. My hands weren't shaking and that surprised me, because I was more frightened than I'd ever been before.

What will happen to me if I lose half my sight? Will the other eye go, too? How do I tell my daughter? My mother will go into hysterics and ask questions I won't know how to answer. Why does it have to be the left one, the "good" eye? It has much better vision than the right. Should I call Mack and let him know what's going on? And if he doesn't drop everything and rush back from L.A. will I resent him forever? I don't know what to do . . .

Then, in the center of all that brown, a tiny pinprick of light appeared. Suddenly: light. I blinked hard—still there. I couldn't see anything but the light was really there and it was growing, like the widening aperture of a camera. By the time my name was called, I had regained nearly all the vision in my left eye.

The ER doctor aimed a bright light into my eye. Then he had me sit in front of a large black screen. He covered my right eye, placed a white pin at the center of the screen, and told me to look only at that pin. Then he told me he was going to move the beam of his handheld penlight and asked me to tell him when the dot of illumination disappeared. He moved the light several times, placing a red pin at the point where the light vanished at the lower right quadrant of my left eye. When he was done he uncovered my right eye and showed me the shape of the scar that remained after the hemorrhage behind the retina had receded.

"Hemorrhage" is one terrifying word.

"Have you sustained any kind of head trauma in the last few

days?" He was young, the doctor, and his manner was lightly casual.

This guy acts like he's never been surprised by anything in his life. That could be a good sign—maybe this happens to people all the time and it's no big deal.

"No. Nothing."

"Have you experienced anything particularly emotional that would cause you to cry a lot?"

I'll be damned if I'm going to tell him about that call to my father; he's not a shrink. I cried hard after I hung up the phone.

I told him yes, told him I missed my husband who was away working.

Well, that's a lie. But I was crying.

Then I had a question.

"Is this going to happen again?"

"There's really no way to know. It might. Then again, you could go all your life without experiencing another incident like this."

Great. Like Russian roulette with your sight, only you're not the one holding the pistol.

I decided to believe, to *know* it wouldn't happen again. I had too much to do and I needed both eyes to see everything as clearly as possible.

I thanked God with every tick of the meter on the drive back home. And I prayed it wouldn't happen again.

Lisa held out her arms for a hug, demanded to know where I'd been for so long, and asked if we could go to the zoo. I held her close, breathing in the smell of her, saying something about having gone to see a photographer. I decided to say nothing to Mack and my mother about what had happened. I knew how she would react and there was no reason to alarm Mack when he was so far away. There was something else, too, that kept me from telling my husband. Sometimes he had only one comment to unsettling news: "What do you want me to do about it?" I couldn't have taken that kind of response that day, not after having been so badly frightened. I decided to say nothing and move on.

I buried the temporary loss of vision in that beneath-the-surface place reserved for things I didn't want to think about. Friends were calling to invite me to the theater, to small dinners and big, rocking parties attended by celebrities of every stripe. I wasn't dating but an extra man was invariably provided. I began to enjoy a modest social life again. Lisa was healthy and happy, although she missed her dad. I tried to fill in for him whenever possible, but there was no way I could—or would—replace him in her life. Still, she and I had good times: we took walks, saw the occasional matinee, went shopping. Most evenings, we ate early and stayed in together. In spite of the separation from my husband (and maybe a little because of it) I felt good about myself.

When I went out, small dinner parties were my preference because they provided the most fun. A group of eight or ten people would be invited to someone's apartment or town house and as we ate and laughed and talked about what was going on in our respective lives, we'd all be looking forward to the invariable after-dinner games, the best of them instigated by Mike Nichols and Stephen Sondheim.

We met often at Adolph Green and Phyllis Newman-Green's duplex at the Beresford, a building that covered nearly a square block on Central Park West. Phyllis was, and is, a multitalented actor; Adolph and his writing partner, Betty Comden, were responsible for a number of Broadway hits and movies, *On the Town* and *Singin' in the Rain* among them. Other guests might include Amy and Milton Greene. Amy is as delicate as a Tanagra figurine and she is a force of nature. Milton was a greatly gifted photographer whose images of Marilyn Monroe are legendary. Cynthia and Patrick O'Neal were pretty much regulars. Patrick originated the role of the Reverend T. Lawrence Shannon in Tennessee Williams's *Night of the Iguana* on Broadway; Cynthia was, and is still, very smart and knockout beautiful, and took acting jobs when she felt like it. She felt like it when Mike Nichols offered her a small role in his film

Carnal Knowledge. When I saw it and complimented her on her performance, she laughed and said she'd used me as the model for her character. I didn't know whether to feel complimented or embarrassed; the girl she played, Cindy, was a real ballbuster.

My favorite after-dinner game was cutthroat charades. Teams would be chosen, and three-syllable words ("photoplay" was one example) would be broken down and acted out. We improvised costumes and went at it, arguing furiously over improbable words or who might be signaling tip-offs to their team. We usually ended game nights with something called murder, in which all lights were turned off, all draperies drawn. As I recall, a designated murderer would creep away and hide. At the count of fifty, the search would begin—in silence—and each time someone found the killer, they would have to squeeze into the hiding place with him or her and remain absolutely still. The fun heightened as more and more people struck pay dirt with a great deal of jostling and storms of smothered giggles. The last person wandering alone in the dark was, of course, the victim. After I moved back to L.A., I heard Mike Nichols brought Jacqueline Kennedy to some of the game nights and that she was an enthusiastic and fiercely competitive participant.

I loved going to the Beresford. There were only two apartments to a floor and the elevator opened to a small anteroom that separated the front doorways. Isaac Stern lived in the apartment opposite the Greens' and there were times I stepped out of the elevator to the high, pure notes of his violin, a continuous filament of music spooling out from behind his door. I often stood in that small space for long minutes, eavesdropping on a master before I rang the Greens' buzzer.

When the weather turned warm, invitations came in for me to bring Lisa for weekends at country houses. Those weekends were long and lazy and wonderful: days sitting around swimming pools or at the shore and evenings spent with people who either traveled in from the city or had summer places of their own. Nearly everyone was involved with the theater: there were composers, lyricists, photographers, actors, directors, and producers, all of them accomplished in their fields and unselfish with their talents; if a storm blew up, impromptu performances would be quickly arranged for the children. One memorable piece of theater involved Adolph Green as an operatically villainous Captain Hook delivering his signature solo (for which Adolph and Betty Comden had written the lyrics: "*Who's the swine-iest swine in the world?*") from the musical version of *Peter Pan*. This star turn was accompanied on the piano by Leonard Bernstein. Halfway through the performance, Adam Green (Adolph and Phyllis's son), four-year-old Lisa Bing, and Amy and Milton Greene's kids, Josh and Antony, wandered off to watch cartoons on TV just before Phyllis, swathed in makeshift veiling, made her entrance as the Mysterious Lady. There was a beat of amused silence, then the performers carried on for a group of grown-ups who were clearly more entranced than the target audience.

Midsummer arrived and with it, the fall and winter collections. The agency booked me for designer shows at Lord and Taylor, Henri Bendel, and Saks Fifth Avenue. I did the import collections (Chanel, Dior, Courrèges) at Ohrbach's and Bloomingdale's. There were days when I raced between showrooms in the garment center wearing only a tightly belted trench coat over my underwear. I walked runways for designers including Bill Blass, Donald Brooks, Anne Klein, and Oleg Cassini, whose chief designer, Bill Smith, a talented young guy out of Florida, was the first to call and book me. Bill and I had become good friends—we were introduced by Amy and Milton Greene at one of their parties—and it was Bill who put me back in the business I'd left for marriage and motherhood. Cassini, a determinedly elegant man with an international accent, had been chosen by Jacqueline Kennedy to design her wardrobe during her tenure as first lady. By the midsixties, his name was stamped on products as diverse as bed linens and sunglasses. When I met him in his showroom (gray silk on the walls and a herd of French Regency chairs and tables) in the garment district, he looked me over with minesweeper eyes.

"Are you wearing a bra?"

I hesitated and glanced over at Bill. He smiled and his eyelids lowered, like a cat's. I looked back at Cassini.

"I never wear one."

Cassini didn't speak. He walked me into the dressing room, pulled a wisp of black chiffon eveningwear off the rack, and requested that I slip it on and come back to the showroom. A few days later Bill called, laughing, to tell me Cassini had decided the new collection was to be shown braless.

We called each other "darling" and referred to ourselves (and were referred to by others) as "girls" despite the cresting wave of the women's movement. Many of us worked the same back-to-back shows. We sat at long makeup tables wearing short cotton kimonos from Chinatown or ratty scarves tied around our breasts. We squeezed out globs of white glue on the mirror in front of us for quick touch-ups on our fake lashes (a toothpick was the indispensable instrument for this) and set out foundation, powder, blushers and liners, lipsticks, anything we might need before and during the show. We studied our own faces in the mirror like duelists sighting down their pistols. The lineups of clothes and accessories, each change tagged with the model's name and the order in which she was to show it, were on racks behind each model's chair. Getting into the first change was easy; you could almost take your time. And there were dressers, one for each model at the big shows—people who worked behind the scenes and knew the clothes because many of them had made the clothes or some part of them—to zip, button, tug, and smooth, to brush away the vagrant smudge of powder, place the right pair of shoes in front of us, and offer a shoulder for balance. Once a show got under way, it was all about second-by-second timing and it was the dressers' responsibility to strip us of everything the instant we came off the runway; jam us into the next change; shove our feet into the shoes (or boots or sandals) that went with it; clip earrings to our lobes while we slapped on powder and fussed with our hair; slide on the

necessary bracelets, necklaces, belts, or whatever; then aim us either at the designer (who seemed to be everywhere at once) or an
assistant with a clipboard and a harried expression. He or she
would look us over, make a minute adjustment, and send us out to
show again. The air in the dressing room thickened with the smoke
from endless cigarettes kept going for that fast hit between changes
and the mingled odors of perfume and sweat. Things could get hot
in dressing rooms: during one show of winter clothes during the
dead of summer, I felt a heavy wetness trembling beneath my
Sassoon-cut bangs and pressed a clump of tissues to my forehead
just in time to staunch an avalanche of sweat down my face. Once
the show got underway, we worked in near silence, and everything
was geared to move along with military precision. The dressers
knew their jobs (generally thankless) and we knew ours: look cool
and unhurried and vaguely insolent every time you hit the runway.

By its nature, modeling creates an intimate atmosphere. We gossiped and laughed and shared cigarettes and makeup tips. If someone had a loose thread or a strand of wayward hair, another model
might reach out and fix it. With few exceptions (despite the urban
fashion myth about a model exchanging a rival's eyedrops with a
highly concentrated breath freshener), we were friendly without
being friends. We were competitors: for the favor of big-name designers and for the attention of the bookers who manned the phones
at the agencies. There was something else, too: an unstoppable itch
behind the ambition and the perfect moves, beneath the veneer of
supreme confidence. It was the sure knowledge that some fifteen-
year-old was boarding a bus in Passaic or a plane in Antwerp and
she was coming to New York to take your place.

There were models I enjoyed working with in New York during the sixties: Barbara Flood was and remains almost terrifyingly
beautiful. She moved along a runway as if she were crossing her
living room, and when she smiled, audiences must have felt they
were being let in on a delicious secret. Annie Marshall looked like
an elegant waif, all big eyes and scruffy red hair, but she had the

savage humor of a political satirist and a bawdy, room-filling laugh. Annie's sense of timing was superb; she walked out of one successful career and into another as personal assistant to Jack Nicholson, a position for which she was eminently qualified because she was used to celebrity: her father was Herbert Marshall, who often costarred with Bette Davis in such films as *The Little Foxes* and *The Letter*. Annie worked for Jack for over two decades. She raises orchids now and divides her time between her home in the Hollywood Hills and a house in Aspen. Judy Hinman was (to pull a critic's line about ballet dancers) a feather with muscle. Lydia Fields was like a very funny and rather wicked swan. Peggy Moffitt personified the term sui generis. Ellen Harth combined delicate features, porcelain skin, and black hair sheared off like a boy's with a Teutonic sense of purpose.

Sometimes a model would develop a passion for another model and if the feeling was mutual, a love affair would begin. The first time I was invited for a weekend at Fire Island by one of the girls I showed with, I was surprised and flattered. But her apparent interest flustered me and I blurted out the fact that I was straight. The other model looked me up and down and her lips curved into a lazy smile.

"So am I."

There were one or two models who used the clothes as props for a performance: one girl in particular seemed to feel that all other models existed only as her supporting cast (she was quite alone in that belief) and acted out each change as if she were the lead player in an English pantomime or an Ibsen play. If she showed a long dress in a somber color, she projected an illusion of such tragic boredom that one half-expected to hear piano chords followed by a gunshot after she dragged herself, hand to forehead, off the runway. If she wore schoolgirl ruffles, she turned in her toes, stuck a finger in her mouth, and simpered. My style of showing was to saunter along the runway, hips thrust forward, faking eye contact (I'm nearsighted and have never worn contacts) with random people in the audience. When I hit the end of the runway, I'd move into a slow turn before heading back. I never smiled. This rather austere approach was created not by choice (I would have loved to have been able to make all those fast little moves we called Dior turns in the sixties) but by a horror of twirling myself into some front-row celebrity lap. Runways aren't called catwalks for nothing. It was from a cat in a movie I filched my moves. The movie was called *Walk on the Wild Side* and it began with the camera tracking an alley cat on his late-night rounds backed by a bluesy soundtrack. That old tom ambled across fence tops and took corners as if his joints were oiled. He embodied sangfroid, he maintained perfect balance, and he never smiled.

Not all the shows took place in designer showrooms or on runways in larger venues. Awards shows (like the Coty) and important charity events might be held in a Broadway theater with extravagant showpieces from several designers. Those affairs were fun to work: a scatter of theater actors would be enlisted to show an outfit by a favored designer and the easy camaraderie backstage was infectious. I have a vivid memory of Lauren Bacall (whom I'd met at one of Adolph and Phyllis Green's small dinners) leaning over a balcony to call down an invitation to come up for a belt of champagne in her dressing room before the show. There was a full orchestra tuning up out front, a carpeted runway traveled halfway down the main aisle, and for those few hours it was like being part of a Broadway hit.

The Great Event was (and remains) the annual Metropolitan Museum of Art Costume Institute's Spring Gala, in which costumes from the museum's archives are shown by popular models to an audience of the celebrated, the privileged, and the endowed dressed in bespoke tailoring and bench-made Lobbs, couture gowns and the bluest of Winston's D Flawless. This was usually a one-change-only show because the antique clothes were so fragile they had to be handled with extraordinary care. The dressers, who worked in the archives, wore white cotton gloves to extract each article from its nest of tissue and the models knew they must stand as still as mannequins and allow themselves to be dressed entirely by others, like sixteenth-century royalty. No smoking, no food, no drinks in the dressing area. The drill for the show, as I recall, was one slow turn past the tables set up at the edge of the gleaming floor of the Great Hall, then maybe once around again. My single change, for which I had fittings at the museum the week before the show, was a floor-sweeping dress from the period following the American Civil War. Yards of silk taffeta the color of good port were draped across the front of the skirt and swept back on either side to form a bustle and a long train. The pointed bodice of the dress was constrictively tight, with a high neckline and sleeves that ended in a cascade of tiny pleats and ivory lace from below the elbows to the wrists. The archives had the original underwear (a waist-narrowing corset, pan-talets, corset cover, camisole, underskirts, and a roll of padding to plump up the bustle) and I wore it all, along with a pair of spool-heeled pumps dyed to match the dress. Kenneth Battelle, the cele-brated hairdresser whose clientele included Jacqueline Kennedy, was brought in to design the models' coiffures in styles that would com-plement the costumes. He made use of my eyebrow-brushing bangs but he pulled up the blunt-cut hair at the sides and pinned on waist-length falls that tumbled down my back from a thick, braided coro-net, to which the archivist in charge of the museum's jewelry attached a garnet clip from the same era.

Once we were in costume, there was nothing any of the mod-els could do but stand in place like slightly superior dolls waiting to be taken up and admired. One of the girls from my agency, a tall, blade-thin blond with whom I'd worked several shows, was wearing a bias-cut slither designed by Vionnet in the twenties. She gave me a fast once-over and told me I looked like Scarlett O'Hara at the end of the movie. Then she leaned in as close as she could get to all those furbelows and whispered something that would change the course of my modeling career:

"Rudi Gernreich wants a model who looks like a spy."

CHAPTER 5

The Lure of the Spotlight, the Look of the Mumps

I knew who Rudi Gernreich was, of course. He became an international celebrity—and something of a scandal, denounced even by the Vatican—in 1964 when he breathed life into the maxim that less is more by presenting model Peggy Moffitt in that one-piece topless swimsuit. His idea was to shock rather than charm and his great strength was the ability to do it with style. Gernreich didn't bend his neck to the rules; he made them.

He had not yet moved into his New York showroom when we met. Contrary to the unspoken rule of fashion, his studio was in L.A., where he lived; when he took his designs to New York, he booked a suite at the Gotham and showed there. I went to the hotel for the go-see and found that Gernreich was a broad-chested little workhorse of a man with a lion cub's face and intelligent eyes sparked with humor. He was dressed casually and entirely in black.

In order to look as much as possible like the spy he'd requested, I put on the trench coat I wore between shows and allowed my Louise Brooks hair to swing forward so that my face was partially obscured. I wore red lipstick and masked my charcoal-shadowed and outlined eyes with aviator-style dark glasses, which I slipped off at the last moment. Gernreich took it all in without giving away a thing and I wondered if I had overstepped myself. He asked me to try on a couple of changes; one dress, black silk with a print of brightly colored abstract flowers, was accessorized with long strand of marble-sized fake pearls. I turned slowly and stopped short in front of him. Then I swung the pearls once around my neck like a lariat and, without altering my unsmiling expression, let gravity take over. The necklace slid all the way down my body to land in a shining puddle at my feet. Gernreich's lips curved into something like a smile and he nodded his head in a slight motion.

Two other models and I showed the Gernreich collection in his hotel suite. There were no dressers; we helped each other while Rudi chatted easily with the pack of buyers and magazine editors in the next room. The atmosphere of desperate urgency that enveloped other shows was absent, replaced by a kind of calm, almost as if you could relax between changes. You couldn't, of course, but none of the models felt pressured. We got into our changes easily because that was how the clothes were designed: step into a dress, a skirt, or a pair of trousers, zip, done; shrug into a shirt or jacket, ready. There were no fussy accessories; that strand of oversized pearls, a few pairs of earrings, large plastic bracelets. White or black ballet tights with everything. The shoes were the classic slip-on Capezio patent leather pumps: not flats, but low heeled, with a tailored patent leather bow at the vamp. The shoes came in a variety of colors: black, red, orange, violet, poison green. The clothes themselves were unlike any I'd shown before: avant-garde, beautiful, unstructured, and wildly comfortable. And everything, from a casual skirt to a formal dress, had invisible pockets at the hipline. Genreich believed that comfort was an essential component of style. I wanted to own every piece I put on. And Rudi was as impressive as his designs: He possessed effortless charm and a biting wit, and he didn't seem to take himself—or fashion— too seriously. He loved his work but refused to become a martyr to it. I was sorry when he packed up the samples and left for home.

About a month after my first Gernreich show, I was invited to Amy and Milton Greene's anniversary party at their East Side town house. I spent the better part of the evening chatting with Jule Styne and his red-haired wife, Maggie. Jule had composed the music of countless popular songs and Broadway shows, among them *Gypsy* (with lyrics by Stephen Sondheim, produced by David Merrick), and now he was working on the music for another Merrick production: *Funny Girl* (lyrics by Bob Merrill, with Barbra Streisand starring as Fanny Brice). At some point in the conversation Maggie whispered something to Jule and he nodded his head emphatically.

"My wife just had a brilliant idea and I agree with her: we think you'd be wonderful in the show as a wisecracking showgirl. No singing or dancing. You'll just look haughty and beautiful and deliver a couple one-liners."

My mind filled instantly with visions of myself in a pink and amber spotlight on a Broadway stage. I'd be singled out for praise; there would be offers for bigger parts in other shows. Mack would be happy to move back east while I lit up Broadway; he and Lisa would come to a matinee and she'd be so proud of her mom; my mother, who disliked flying, would grab Hotten by the wrist and they'd take the first jet to New York. I called David and asked him to meet me for lunch. He suggested the Oak Room at the Plaza.

I couldn't wait to see the look on his face when I told him I'd been invited to try out for a small part in his new show.

He got a look on his face, all right, but it wasn't the one I was expecting.

Without raising his voice David let me have it: he had no intention of allowing me to posture on a stage while I entertained absurd notions of a second-rate acting career. I was to finish up this modeling nonsense and become what I was meant to be: a writer.

Writer? Writer? What the hell is David talking about? I love to read and we've talked a lot about books but I never once mentioned writing, never even thought about it. He's got to be thinking about someone else, some protégé who wants to write or some friend's daughter. But it sure as hell is not me. I'm the model, David, remember? If I can't show off on Broadway, then I'm

happy to keep walking runways until it's time to plan out the next
move. And I'll be the one who makes that decision, not you.

I found my voice and accused David of confusing me with
someone else, of being clueless, of being as sadistic as people said
he was, and above all, of displaying a stunning lack of feeling for
my dreams (I didn't add they were dreams hatched during the last
thirty-six hours), which, I insisted, had *never* included writing. He
laughed softly and signaled for the dessert cart.

My theatrical career ended over a slice of flourless chocolate
cake. I never figured out where David Merrick got the idea I
should be a writer. He was a master at manipulation and I can only
guess now that he was planting a seed because he liked the way
I talked.

Then Mack called and asked me to come to L.A. We could begin
the marriage again, he said, and it would be better for Lisa to be
with both her parents. I didn't say so at the time, but I thought
it would be better for me, too. New York was great—I liked my
work and the people I'd become close to—but I'd begun to miss
my husband and I hadn't expected that. He and I spoke a couple
more times about the possibility of a move and I agreed to leave
for the coast as soon as I finished up whatever shows I was booked
for. I didn't get to do the shows: I developed a case of mumps and,
with a face swollen to the approximate size of a Halloween pumpkin, languished in bed, read, watched old movies, and avoided all
reflective surfaces.

When I asked Lisa's pediatrician how I could protect her, he
told me to kiss her full on the mouth.

"That way we get the mumps over and done with."

Feeling like an abusive mother out of the tabloids, I did what
the doctor ordered and delivered a loaded kiss. Lisa was down for
a week with a mild case (small pumpkin) but I couldn't shake the
image of myself as the dreaded carrier of a disfiguring childhood
disease.

With matching mother-and-daughter mumps out of the way, I began to pack up for the move to L.A. Mack and I figured it might not be a bad idea to lease out the New York apartment for a few months and we agreed that the combination to the safe in the dressing room would not be part of the deal. I didn't mention my stillborn Broadway career.

CHAPTER 6

Where the Heart Is

I felt it on the drive from LAX to West Hollywood: L.A. was home because L.A. was where my mother was.

Mack had rented a two-story, well-furnished (once I got past the fireplace surround of gold-veined mirrors) apartment on a quiet street not far from where my mom and Hotten lived in separate apartments on the same block. We enrolled Lisa, who was touchingly happy to be with her dad again, in a private day school he'd researched. Then we picked up the routines of our lives together. Mack spent most of his time at the studio, and on weekdays, when Lisa was at school, I'd join my mother and Hotten and reacquaint myself with a city that was changing. I couldn't get enough of being with my family; my mother, for all her coolness, was the only person in the world who completely understood and got me, and Hotten's love was warmer than any sable coat I'd ever shown. I didn't miss the New York fashion world, didn't miss the high-powered evenings with people in the theater. I was home.

The West Coast seemed to be what the sixties were all about: San Francisco and L.A. had become gathering places for hippies. I'd only heard about them in New York and now I saw them in their natural habitat, grazing the Sunset Strip, holding sticks of incense that trailed wisps of sandalwood and patchouli-scented smoke, the girls with their waist-length hair and long, dusty skirts, the boys snake-hipped in their patched 501s, tie-dyed shirts, and hand-stitched buckskin jackets. They smoked hash and weed and dropped acid with fanciful names: Owsley (after the guy at Berkeley who cooked it up), Purple Haze, Orange Sunshine. I learned all this when I came back to L.A. I hadn't bumped up against illegal drugs in New York but I knew weed was marijuana and I associated it with dimly lit places where people listened to jazz and called each other "man." Acid was LSD, developed by a pharmaceutical company to cure migraines. My doctor in New York had prescribed it for me, a tiny yellow pill called Sansert that contained a measured dose of lysergic acid, the component of LSD. I took one each day for months and if it didn't cure the headaches, it succeeded in retarding the frequency of the attacks. But I had no idea about the hallucinogenic properties of lysergic acid and its growing popularity among students and dropouts, another term I was clueless about until I moved back to L.A.

I didn't want any part of drugs and was vaguely shocked at the casual attitude people on the West Coast seemed to have about them. Mack and I would go to dinner parties with people in the TV and film industries, and at some point a joint would begin to make the rounds. Mack and I always exchanged glances and he'd grin and shake his head and take another sip of his martini. He knew how to refuse something without looking like a prig and I tried to follow his example. I wasn't tempted to try marijuana or anything else, not because I was such a good citizen; I was just afraid it would make me sick.

Mack spent a great deal of time at work, but when he was home he gave Lisa the attention she needed. Sometimes he read to her. If he was watching some sports event on TV, she'd move in close and make room for herself in the curve of his arm. I watched them together and was happy; my daughter had waited for months to be with her dad again. Once the excitement of reunion faded, my husband seemed to have very little interest in me, and although I kept my mouth shut, thinking he needed to adjust to full-throttle family life again, it became increasingly clear that we were still mired in a relationship of cordial indifference. That wasn't enough for me. If the romance of a box of my favorite candy or a bouquet of unexpected flowers was done, okay—I could tell myself my husband was busy and I'd almost believe it. If sex was more about routine than passion, I could tell myself he was tired and distracted. There was no way to rationalize the mysterious telephone calls that kicked in when he was home. If I picked up, there was only silence and the arid little click of a set-down receiver on the other end. When Mack got there first, there would be a brief conversation consisting of a series of monosyllables from him and a sudden need for an urgent and unavoidable meeting at the studio. One night, after Lisa was in bed and sleeping, I confronted him.

"Hey, how about stopping the bullshit? And tell your girlfriend not to call here again."

"I don't know what the hell you're talking about. You're imagining things."

"Listen, here's the deal: if you don't insult my intelligence, I won't make you walk through fire."

I was putting up a front because I didn't want the pain to show. As always, I did my crying in private, but there was something else I kept to myself and it gnawed away at the edges of outrage: I missed the freedom I'd enjoyed in New York, missed my friends and the good times I'd had with them, missed the conversations that crackled with wit, the out-of-town weekends, the dinner parties and after-dinner games. I wanted to flirt again, be admired again. I'd lacked the courage to face it, told myself I didn't want to be like my mother with a trail of broken marriages behind me. That was bullshit. The truth was I lacked the courage to get out there on my own without the backup of a husband on another coast.

I spoke to my mother about the separation and impending divorce.

"I'm sorry, Mary Léon, but I don't think you're divorcing Mack because he was with another woman. I think you're divorcing him because you don't know what you want. I was the same way at your age. As it happens, this will be better for Lisa. She won't have to hear ugly words in raised voices and she won't think her mother was abandoned. If you handle it fairly, she can love her father without feeling guilty about it. Otherwise, she'll feel that caring about him would be disloyal to you."

I almost said, "Like the way I felt guilty for wanting to love my father?"

I didn't say it. It would have drilled through the wall that separated all the loving feelings I had for my mother from the memories that made me dislike her.

When Mack moved out it was inevitable that Lisa would wonder if she'd done something so bad it made her father leave us. I held her close and tried to convince her it was something that often happened when married people couldn't get along with each other.

"Now you listen to me: none of this is your fault in any way. You're the best thing that ever happened to your dad and me. We both love you more than anything in the world and that will never change. Not ever."

She looked at me with Mack's green eyes. Hers held an overlay of gray and they were shining with tears.

I told my daughter her dad and I still liked and, in a way, even loved each other. It was just that we needed to live in different places and both of them would be her home: during the week she'd be with me; on weekends she would stay with her father. I made sure she understood how much she would enjoy those weekends, underlining my support of the time she'd spend with Mack, remembering again how my own father had been cut off from me.

"You'll see, honey. This really will work out for all three of us."

Lisa swiped away the tears on her face and brought her head forward so her eyes were level with mine.

"Promise?"

I promised. And I realized it was true: this really was going to work out.

Mack and I agreed to an amicable divorce; neither of us was

willing to play the ugly game of That's Yours, This Is Mine. He
went back to New York to sell the apartment on Central Park West
and send whatever furnishings I wanted, as well as my books and
gifts from my family, back to me. John Calley, still a close friend,
offered to keep the piano with him until I settled in L.A. or decided to go back to New York. I'd lost faith in Mack's loyalty because he'd been the one who cheated on our marriage. If I'd
wanted to be fair, I'd have admitted to myself that I might have
done the same eventually. I wasn't thinking about fairness but I
knew I could trust Mack to make whatever plans were necessary
for the duct-taped package at the back of our safe in New York.
Years later, during the writing of this book, I asked him about
Mickey Cohen's diamonds. Mack told me "some woman" had
picked up the package shortly after our divorce and when I requested a few details, out of curiosity more than anything else, he
declined further discussion.

It was clear we needed to stay put in California; I knew it was important for Lisa to be with her father as much as possible and I
wanted to live near my mother and Hotten so Lisa could get to
know and come to love them. I wasn't worried about work. L.A.
wasn't a fashion center like New York, but Rudi Gernreich was
there and I knew I could find other modeling work through one of
the local agencies. I stopped worrying about being alone and realized the odds on being happy were pretty damn good for my
daughter and me.

I called Calley and he graciously arranged for the piano to
be shipped to Los Angeles. Then Lisa and I moved out of the furnished apartment and into a thirties Spanish Colonial–style building in West Hollywood that was filled with old-world charm:
built-in bookcases, bay windows, high ceilings. I could only afford
the rent on a one-bedroom apartment but there was a large dining
alcove off the living room and I decided to sleep in there and give
Lisa the bedroom. It was important that she have the privacy of
her own room with a door that could be closed . . . or even slammed.

Lisa loved her new space and we went shopping together for new furniture: a four-poster bed, a comfortable reading chair, a new lamp. We decided my dressing table from New York would work as a desk for her. I set up the rest of the apartment, polished the hardwood floors, arranged sofas and chairs, unpacked clothes and books, filled the shelves, set out well-loved objects, and asked my mom and Hotten to come over for final approval. Then I leased a red Mustang, signed up with an agency, and called Rudi Gernreich.

Lucky timing: Rudi told me Peggy had moved to London and asked if I was interested in taking her place as first model. Within a month I was reserving the greater portion of my professional time for Gernreich and a lasting friendship began. Over cigarettes and coffee between fittings at his studio in West Hollywood, and later at his home, Rudi described (in a surprisingly unaccented voice) a privileged childhood in Vienna, his father's suicide when Rudi was nine, and his initial forays into fashion at an aunt's shop, which became a kind of sanctuary. He told me about his first childhood images of sexuality: leather chaps with a strap running between the buttocks of street laborers' work pants and the white flesh of women's thighs above gartered black stockings. He talked about escaping with his mother from the German annexation of Austria in 1938 and landing in Los Angeles with few possessions and without money. To support himself and his mother, Rudi found work in a hospital morgue, preparing cadavers for autopsy. He was sixteen years old. He described his early days as a designer and his love-at-first-sight meeting with his life partner, Oreste. I enjoyed his stories and was flattered that he was willing to speak so openly with me. Being confided in by the man I was working for let me know I meant something more to him than just a body to hang clothes on. When Rudi met Lisa at his studio, they were instantly taken with each other. Rudi appreciated her good manners and natural charm; Lisa was impressed by the solemn way he shook her hand and told her she might be the perfect model for a line of children's clothes he was thinking about. She liked the idea well enough but the real thrill was the prospect of "going to work for Uncle Rudi."

When I took Lisa to her first fitting as model for Rudi's children's line, she behaved like the consummate professional, turning slowly as the pieces of muslin that make up original patterns were pinned together, lifting her arms to the precise degree requested, speaking only to answer Rudi's questions about comfort and fit. When she modeled the line to a big audience of buyers and members of the press, her smooth walk, perfect turns, and wide smile nearly stopped the show. I acted as her dresser and watched her work the runway from backstage, a mute Madame Rose to my child's first performance in a fashion show. The only missing elements in my role that day were a lope down the aisle and a strident "Sing out, Louise!"

The Gernreich children's line never took off—department store buyers weren't sure parents would go for violet and poison-green knit dresses with matching tights and kid-sized bathing suits with cutouts. But Lisa got to keep her samples and both Rudi and I let her know she'd been a great model. Lisa was pleased but told me privately she wasn't really interested in doing more.

"It's too boring, Mom."

When I repeated the remark to Rudi, he laughed and said he agreed with my daughter. I didn't; I liked being front and center in a spotlight, even if its beam was only momentary.

Rudi Gernreich found inspiration in everything he saw: on the streets, at the opera, on the pages of the history books he read with such avid interest. A pencil was as much a part of his right hand as the silver band he wore on his little finger, and he sketched designs the way a shark kills: quickly and with fluid ease. He saw women as Manchu warriors and brilliantly plumaged wild birds, as comic-opera guardsmen and splay-fingered Balinese court dancers, as veiled, black-legged Furies, Van Dongen paintings, and scowling, chalk-faced Mephistos draped to the ankle in quivering jet spangles. He looked to the future when he saw bare skin as a canvas upon which he might arrange a collage of geometric, multicolored decals. He looked at the body and saw the form upon which he could drop a nearly transparent slick of black jersey, slash out a plunging neckline, outline it with glove leather, and then, for sheer amusement, transect the curve of naked breasts with a series of tightly coiled industrial springs. He began an enduring love affair with the world press, swaggered center-stage, and twisted the arm of high fashion until it yelped out a squeal of sexuality. Gernreich was the bully boy who brought a flush of depravity to all those pallid sixties images: the pastel A-lines, the bouffant hairdos, the floor-length granny dresses. He reached out and twitched hemlines halfway up the thighs, cut peepholes out of sleeves and midsections and backs. He took knee-length, high-heeled boots and covered them with layer upon layer of speckled feathers, then added a matching shako and boa. Designs like this were made to be showpieces, suited only to a runway where Genreich's—or any designer's—commitment to their art would be on display. Working with Layne Neilsen on accessories, Rudi hammered jewelry out of dog tags, Ping Pong balls, and Lucite cubes and hung twelve inches of cascading, violently colored silk flowers from his models' earlobes.

To be one of Rudi Gernreich's models was to be a float in his parade. It was to become what was known, in old-style drama and opera companies, as Fifth Business. You didn't play the role of hero or villain, but you were essential in bringing about the denouement, or recognition. As a Gernreich model, you sat in overheated dressing rooms as Vidal Sassoon leaned in close to perfect a last-minute trim while an audience that included Andy Warhol and Edie Sedgwick, Brooke Hayward and Dennis Hopper (who would photograph me in L.A. and make me look beautiful with his incomparable eye and perfect timing), fashion critics, photographers, and Diana Vreeland, the doyenne of fashion editors, settled in for the first showing of the latest collection.

Working for Rudi meant seeing your photograph in a Russian fashion magazine and your likeness in a painting at a gallery in Munich. It meant posing for *Los Angeles* magazine with a pride of Southern California artists at the Los Angeles County Museum of

Art and seeing yourself on the cover of *Time* in December of 1967. It meant dressing behind a sheet in a drafty television studio in Philadelphia while Rudi struggled to make conversation with a dangerously high and overtly hostile talk-show host (cartoonist Al Capp) who hoisted his wooden leg onto the desk to display the artistic arrangement of tacks that held up his sock. It meant traveling to Mexico City and being photographed in any number of venues. At one of these, while waiting for the lights to be set up, I explored a couple of street vendors' stands and when I felt a soft stroking sensation on one arm, I looked down to see a tiny Indian woman peering up into my face and touching my skin as if she needed to assure herself that I was a living person and not some lifelike facsimile. Being Rudi's model meant slowly stripping off six layers of giraffe-stenciled clothing—everything from a face-shrouding hood and three-fingered, hooflike gloves down to matching bikini underwear—as you moved along a runway at the St. James Theatre to the brass-heavy overture from *Gypsy* while a full house of celebrities delivered a thunderclap of applause.

Finally, it meant moving into a place in Gernreich's private life.

It was a lifestyle the privacy of which Rudi guarded as zealously as he pursued publicity for his professional accomplishments. The central core, the humming dynamo of his personal life, was his relationship with Oreste Pucciani. Pucciani was himself a man of impressive note: professor of modern French literature and philosophy at UCLA, chairman of the French Department, undisputed authority on the works of Jean-Paul Sartre. Rudi and Oreste met in 1954, and by the late sixties their home in the Hollywood Hills was a dazzling walled fortress. The floors, designed by Gernreich, were constructed of burnished leather squares. The furniture was by Breuer, Le Corbusier, Eames, and Gernreich. There were paintings by Rauschenberg and sculpture by Bertoia. Later, works by Ruscha and Bell would be added to the collection.

Oreste and I clicked and that pleased Rudi immensely. Oreste wasn't particularly social and his manner of formal hauteur tended to intimidate. But the professor responded to my irreverent humor, displayed a surprising and infectious giggle, and urged Rudi to invite me up to the house at the top of Laurel Canyon for home-cooked meals. Once, when Rudi and I spent a weekend in San Francisco on a video shoot, we went to dinner at Ernie's, a fabled restaurant, now gone. The special that night was tripe. Tripe is true peasant food and I learned to love it after it had simmered for hours on my grandmother's stove. The captain at Ernie's, who recognized Rudi and took our orders himself, was so impressed that a fashion model was ordering the special he made sure I knew the main ingredient of the dish (tripe is the lining of a cow's stomach), and he was so delighted when I finished the bowl and began to sop up the tomato and garlic sauce with a heel of French bread that he came back with a second helping on the house. I finished that, too. A few weeks later, Rudi spent an entire Saturday cooking it up with a similar sauce and betting Oreste I'd ask for seconds and possibly thirds. He won the wager.

Sometimes the three of us would take weekend trips in Rudi's old work van. Once, on a drive up the coast, we stopped for an overnight stay at the Madonna Inn, a hotel with a live oak growing up through the roof of the dining room and a working waterfall in the men's room. Each guest room featured a different theme: a spelunker's cave, an 1860 Southern belle's retreat, a homesteader's log cabin. Rudi, Oreste, and I had connecting rooms; I was in the four-postered, rose-clotted plantation bedroom, while Rudi and Oreste were making do in something out of a von Stroheim film: black patent leather on the walls and an iron bed with an arterial red coverlet. The food in the tree-dominated dining room may have been forgettable but we were crazy about the Madonna Inn and its overwhelming commitment to the school of kitsch.

As the months passed and I grew closer to Rudi and Oreste, I realized that theirs was only the second completely fulfilled marriage I'd seen in my life. The first had been the lifelong union between my grandparents. When I spoke about it with Rudi, he was visibly touched. Then he reminded me that mutual commitment couldn't be hunted down; you had to stumble across it, recognize it, and then be willing to make your share of the concessions needed to make it work.

I was ready to make a few concessions but it didn't look as though I was going to stumble across anything like a mutual commitment. I went out with more than a few men. Most of them were easily forgotten but one or two stand out like the bright green plastic on exit signs: there was the Realtor I took on as a blind date after a married couple I knew wouldn't stop nagging me about his good looks, intelligence, and humor. This paragon took me to a great restaurant and then talked about nothing but wine for the duration of the meal. I was lectured on the glories of the vineyard (with a detour into something called noble rot) past the point where I said I knew little about his obvious passion except it was better if the bottle had a cork rather than a twist-off cap and past the point where I suggested it might jar me back to some level of consciousness if we switched to another subject. There was the dermatologist who, during a ride in a brightly lit elevator, leaned in to kiss my cheek but peered into my ear instead and said, "Good girl. Very clean."

These were perfectly okay guys; many women would have leaped—well, nodded, anyway—at a chance for a date with them. I wanted and needed someone who would find me interesting beyond whatever value they placed on their image of me as a successful fashion model. There was, however, a limit to the concessions I was prepared to make.

My mother accused me of being picky.

"Do you think every man you meet is going to offer you everything in a single package? You're lucky to have looks and wit, Mary Léon. You need to make the most of them and settle down with someone who will look after you and your child instead of wasting your time with long-haired nobodies."

She was talking about Jake, a teaching assistant at UCLA. He had long hair, all right, and he looked like an outlaw rock musician. I generally liked his conversation, although his habit of calling me "man" instead of my name was somewhat disconcerting. Jake reminded me of the hippies I saw congregated at the intersection of Laurel and Sunset, where cars with too much engine idled noisily at stoplights. Those people were younger and I imagined most of them living with their parents in the Valley, painting the walls of their rooms in Day-Glo colors and plastering them with peace symbol decals and R. Crumb posters of Mr. Natural. Jake had a house in Laurel Canyon and he maintained a solid relationship with his two sons from a previous marriage.

My relationship with my daughter was moving into a new phase. Lisa wasn't a little kid anymore; she was beginning to grow into the person she'd be: keenly intelligent with a sense of humor that tilted to the dry. I was pleased to see how kind she was—to other children, to adults, to animals. When, after a weekend with her dad, she came home with a tiny live lizard on a chain pinned to her sweater, it was her idea to set him free (and chainless) in the garden of a house near our apartment. When we talked about movies we saw together or one of the books I'd read as a child that Lisa liked, too, it was easy to forget she was only eight years old because she was so articulate and sensitive. We were becoming friends.

I kept on seeing Jake, probably to annoy my mother more than anything else, and it was with Jake I smoked my first joint. It was a rainy Friday evening and Lisa was with Mack. Jake had pulled together a fairly good dinner and now we were leaning back against Moroccan pillows piled in front of his fireplace. When he brought out a small plastic bag of marijuana and a packet of rolling papers, I started to say no, changed my mind, figured what the hell, and took my first hit.

I was surprised to find I didn't feel sick. The smoke was very different from regular tobacco: acrid and hard to inhale and hold in, but not unpleasant. It didn't make me feel any different, though. I wasn't seeing things and Jake looked and sounded normal. A Mozart piano concerto was going full blast on his stereo; I was familiar with the piece, it was one of my favorites, but I'd never heard it so clearly, never appreciated its exquisite nuance so deeply. I felt like I was sitting next to the soloist. When I told Jake, he laughed and I wondered why because I wasn't stoned at all. Then I figured he was probably very high and I was probably one of those people who weren't affected by grass. Natural immunity: that was it.

So Jake and I talked and laughed and I slugged down glass after glass of coolly delicious water as the smoke wicked moisture from my mouth. It seemed that everything we said was brilliant or funny or both. The fire became a work of art with preternaturally bright flames licking life into logs that glowed red and white in response. When Jake's fingertips stroked my skin I felt a ripple of delight. One thing was puzzling: the intrusion of some kind of foreign accent into Jake's normal speech pattern. This was punctuated, whenever he searched for a particular word or phrase, by a delicate lift of one index finger and the query "Mmm, how you say . . . ?" He sounded like a very bad actor playing the part of a non-English-speaking person. I convinced myself it was my imagination and decided maybe I was a little bit stoned after all.

It wasn't my imagination; it happened again the next time we got high. We were with a group of Jake's friends who lived, commune-style, in a rattrap apartment on the outside edges of Hollywood. A Jefferson Airplane album was playing at top volume and everyone was sitting cross-legged in a ragged circle on the splintery floor, nodding their heads in tacit agreement with "*Go ask Alice when she's ten feet tall*" as two or three joints made the rounds. I wasn't a fan of the band, preferring R&B to pop music. I looked around the crowded living room: colonies of spider plants and creeping Charlies dangled from macramé slings screwed into the grimy ceiling; unframed Escher prints were tacked up on the walls. A well-used hardcover edition of the *I Ching* lay open and facedown on a Formica-topped table next to a crumpled pack of Gauloises Bleues and an empty Chianti bottle with a candle stuck in the top. A sculpture of a dancing Shiva stood in a niche provided some thirty years earlier to hold one of those old candlestick telephones. I studied the eight or so people who lived in the apartment. The women (each one referred to as somebody's "old lady") sat unmoving as sketch models, their faces scrubbed clean of any trace of skin-praising cosmetic, their feet bare, their legs and armpits unshaven. The clothes they wore were thrift shop, their ornamentation gypsy (a style seized upon by young actresses and the wives of beads-sporting industry executives on the come). I'd borrowed liberally from the rubric of hippie fashion, too, pairing a couple of Gernreich's flowered silk shirts with my old 501s and often wearing a long cotton skirt with faded T-shirts, scuffed boots, and my mom's grudgingly lent silver and turquoise concho belt slung low on my hips.

The joints kept going, the music kept changing, and the men talked to each other, covering subjects from the ongoing war in Vietnam to the death of Otis Redding in a plane crash. For the most part, they ignored the women, me included, except for an occasional request for a neck rub or another beer. I was content to keep my mouth shut and watch the show. One guy kept pulling his shoulder-length hair into a ponytail, then shaking it loose a few minutes later, only to begin the whole process again in another few minutes. One of the younger guys made a great show of displaying his newly acquired tattoo of the Zouave whose black-bearded face was the emblem for Zig-Zag rolling papers. When my attention wandered back to Jake, he was talking, in that fake accent, about the need for everybody to move north of Humboldt County and live in . . . mmm, how you say? . . . tepees.

I had to admit it: my mother was right. I was wasting my time.

Three times a year, Rudi and I went to New York to show the fall/winter, spring, and resort collections. Lisa stayed with Mack's parents in the Valley and I called regularly to speak with her. She said she missed me, was enjoying herself with "Oma" (German for "grandma"), going out on shopping sprees and to Disneyland, but wanted to know when I was coming home. During the ten days or so I was in New York, I saw old friends, met a few new ones, and got around town a little. Now, years later, disparate memories pop up like spikes on a fever chart: going to CBGB and hearing a band called the Fugs play a song called "Coca Cola Douche." A party at Bill Smith's penthouse with long-haired, delicately boned young Frenchmen talking about Vietnam and putting on airs for the kid who played Cowboy, the birthday present/stud in *The Boys in the Band*, while a guy named Paulie, one of the first models to show up on billboards and in magazines as the Marlboro Man— leathery tanned skin, granite jaw, and shaggy, going-to-gray hair— clambered up on the coffee table, struck a bathing beauty pose, and announced that he was "Miss North Beach." Being part of a crowd at Elaine's restaurant, and Tennessee Williams, his voice syrupy with bourbon, murmuring compliments about the material of my Gernreich minidress ("My sister wore the *loveliest* things made of georgette . . ."). People talking about the "vitamin B_{12}" injections provided by a Dr. Max Jacobson, also known as "Dr. Feelgood," in a grubby office where Broadway stars, politicians, socialites, and the fashion elite turned the waiting room into an image out of Fellini. A maddening daylong itch lodged deep under the skin between my shoulder blades that surfaced during dinner at Max's Kansas City; when I reached back, finally able to scratch, the studied look of unflappable hauteur on my face morphed into an expression of such eye-rolling ecstasy that people at adjoining tables stared, slack-jawed. Late-afternoon cocktails with columnist Liz Smith and Bill Smith at his apartment; I admired her unaffected Texas drawl and warm, booming laugh. Dancing for hours with an actor named Raymond St. Jacques at a club called Arthur. Getting into the same hot-pink knit dress with its clear vinyl inset from throat to bikini line I'd worn on the cover of *Time* (at the newsstands that week) and going with Rudi to a performance of *Hair*, where we were invited to come up onstage during curtain calls. Rudi and I experiencing a terrifying and thrilling helicopter ride over Manhattan at dusk. Diane Arbus's tremulous smile when she asked if she could take my photograph after a show. I never saw any of the shots she took that afternoon. Appearing in *Basic*

Black, a short film conceived and directed by photographer William Claxton, who was responsible for brilliant shots of Rudi's models in each season's Gernreichs. The film starred Rudi's designs, worn by Ellen Harth, Peggy Moffitt (Claxton's wife), and myself. A few of us went, after the shoot and in full makeup, with Rudi to a dairy restaurant on Houston Street where the blintzes were so oil drenched I asked the waiter to extend my compliments to the mechanic. Being invited for a weekend at Fire Island and sharing a room with Joel Schumacher, who made me laugh so hard I wet my pants at a party on somebody's deck overlooking the ocean (Rudi once accomplished the same feat with me in a taxi on Fifth Avenue). Joel had not yet become an A-list film director but talent and ambition glowed around him like a second skin.

That was the New York I knew in the late sixties. Its frenetic pace was light-years away from the easy-does-it routine of L.A. and I appreciated the difference. I enjoyed being part of the New York fashion crowd and I liked being a recognizable model. After the shows and photo shoots were over for the day, I was free to do pretty much whatever I wanted and I took full advantage of it. My only concern was how much fun I could pack into the time I was away from L.A., where I had the responsibilities of a working mom. One hitch: I couldn't stop missing my daughter, the rest of my family, and my life there.

Coming home to L.A. after one of those New York trips was wonderful. Lisa was there to be hugged and held; I could breathe in the warm biscuit aroma at the nape of her neck until she wriggled away to open whatever small gift I'd brought back for her. My mother was there, her apartment a collector's Eden of Victoriana and antique Asian screens and porcelains, herself the center of a coterie of young men who adored her. Hotten was there, deceptively fragile with her sweet birdcall of a voice, always willing to cook a meal or fix a torn hem, unflinchingly ready to support (or defend) anything my mother or I chose to do. Uncle Henry took the bus

down from Oakland for holidays and birthdays and we'd be together as a family. He seemed never to change: still gruff when he
spoke, which was seldom, still smelling deliciously of cigars with
a hint of good bourbon. He never stayed long enough, it seemed,
before he went back to his life of card games and billiards at his
club and bus trips to Reno to play the tables for small amounts.
Then my mom and Hotten and I would go back to the routine of
having lunch on days I didn't work and spending an hour or two
excavating small treasures in thrift shops. My mother said Hotten's eye was so unerring she could spot a Fabergé Easter egg in a
landfill.

 Most evenings, Lisa and I would have early dinners together,
and then she'd sit in her hand-carved, child-sized rocking chair
from Amish country that had HAPPY DAYS painted on the backrest
in faded red lettering and we'd watch an hour of television before
she went to bed. I'd sneak glances at her face, illuminated by the
bluish light of the screen, and her unguarded smile always sent an
electric jolt of love through me. At those moments, I wished things
would never change.

 After Lisa was asleep in her room, I continued watching TV,
and when the late news came on—my only connection to what was
going on in the real world—I saw the demonstrations and the
protests ("Hell, no! We won't go!"), saw Vietnam veterans watching silently from the sidelines with impenetrable eyes set down in
grim, no-longer-young faces. When a pair of back-to-back slaugh-
ters at two separate locations on the ninth and tenth of August
1969 rocked L.A., word spread that a cult of outlaw hippies were
the killers. I thought about the dope-taking, acid-dropping hippies
milling around the Sunset Strip and an icy shudder eddied through
me. I thought about Jake's hippie friends living in that cramped
apartment, the women so calm and subservient, the men such clos-
eted chest-thumpers. I studied Julian Wasser's photographs of the
crime scenes when they appeared in *Life* magazine and was as
repelled and fascinated by them as I'd been by the glass-enclosed

spitting cobras in the reptile house at the San Francisco zoo when I was a kid. Mack, my mom, and I tried to keep details of the murders away from Lisa, who heard things at school and wanted to hear more. A temblor of fear rumbled through the city, weapons sales went up, and drivers weren't so quick to pick up teenage hitchhikers anymore. The insanity had hit home.

CHAPTER 7

Friends, Neighbors, and the Prettiest Girl in Town

Feminism by metaphor was often practiced in Hollywood at the beginning of the Me Decade: ingenues were dressed and coiffed by studio stylists for red-carpet events but some displayed a timid solidarity with their more radical sisters by showing thickets of unshaven hair at their armpits. LSD was still around, only now it had names like Window Pane and Blotter, and instead of a mellow trip, it got you nervous. People began mixing PCP, a horse tranquilizer, in with their weed and calling it angel dust. It just got you crazy. Janis died of a heroin overdose in a motel off the Sunset Strip in October of 1970 and *Laugh-In* was still the most popular sketch-comedy show on television.

Judy Carne was the "Sock it to me" girl on *Laugh-In*. She'd say those four words at some point in the hour-long ensemble show and a bucketful of water would douse her from off-camera. The phrase became so popular that Richard Nixon appeared in a cameo on *Laugh-In* during his '68 presidential campaign. He stared into the camera and intoned, "You want to sock it to *me*?" He didn't get the water treatment, though. I met Judy shortly before her final *Laugh-In* performance. I don't remember who introduced us; what remains indelible is Judy's wide smile and lack of pretensions. We shook hands and went out to dinner in a group, and by the time dessert was on the table, she and I were making plans to see a Clint Eastwood movie.

Judy was fun to be with; she had a lightning wit and a generous nature. She was from the north of England and suffered a somewhat sketchy education from years spent as a kid performer in
variety theaters around the country before she made the move to
America. She starred in three short-lived TV series before *Laugh-In*
and had been married briefly to actor Burt Reynolds. Judy was
forthright about her bisexuality but didn't push it. When we met she
was somewhat involved in a relationship with an Australian jazz
singer and they got together whenever the woman played L.A. Judy
was honest about her attraction to me, even taping a reel of songs
for my birthday one year. I remember Sly Stone's "(You Caught Me)
Smilin" and Leon Russell's "A Song for You" in the collection.

One of the strongest links between Judy and me was our affection for getting high. We smoked joints in the car, at the beach,
and in the stalls of theater restrooms before the feature went on. It
was Judy who introduced me to cocaine (which didn't do much
for me) and she was one of the first people I knew who had her own
stash. One morning, after I'd stayed at her house following a late
Friday night, I was awakened by Judy with a breakfast tray on
which she had arranged a plate of eggs and bacon, a glass of fresh
orange juice, a tightly rolled joint, and a small mirror with two
generous lines of what she called "wakeup toots."

I didn't keep grass (or any other illegal substance) at my place;
Lisa was at the age where very little escaped her notice. I did my
share during the weekends when she was with Mack, including an
unforgettable acid trip with Dennis Hopper, who had scored a
small flask of LSD from someone who worked at Sandoz, where
the formula had been developed. I'd stopped taking the small yellow
pills a couple years earlier because I didn't want a daily dose of lysergic acid stacking up in my brain, but I figured an infinitesimal
amount of the pure liquid wouldn't do any damage. It didn't, but
it produced a wowza of an effect. I didn't hallucinate an image of
the cosmos in a bathroom tile but it turned out to be one hell of a
Saturday night.

I never worried about doing too many drugs. I tried almost

everything (with the exception of peyote, because I heard it made you vomit before you understood the universe) on the weekends but I was always careful not to overdo: half a joint instead of a whole; two or three lines of coke instead of hit after hit until a whitish crust appeared around each nostril. I liked dope well enough but I liked maintaining control better.

I told my mom I smoked the occasional joint on weekends and left it at that. She signaled her disapproval with the usual "Oh, Mary Léon . . . ," and I countered with a predictable remark about her nightly intake of the barbiturate Seconal. She said my grandfather (who disapproved of women smoking anything, never mind pot) would have disowned me. She asked if I smoked around Lisa. Finally, she gave in and told me, for Christ's sake, not to tell Hotten or Uncle Henry and to *please* be careful; she didn't want to have to bail me out of jail for possession of an illegal substance.

"Look, you can't ask this guy any personal questions."

"Why not? Is he paranoid?" The dope smoker's catchall description; everyone was accused of paranoia at one time or another.

"He just doesn't like it."

Judy was behind the wheel of her mocha-colored Jaguar XKE and we were headed into Laurel Canyon for dinner at her new boyfriend's house. I knew he was in his late twenties and liked to cook. Knew his late father had founded Columbia Pictures. Anything else, I figured, I'd have to find out for myself.

Harry Cohn Jr. was delicately made and nearly movie-star handsome, with blue eyes and dark, curling hair. He was barefoot and faded jeans hung loosely on his hips. His black T-shirt was without a logo or message of any kind and his only jewelry was a slender gold wristwatch shaped like one of the melting timepieces in a Dalí painting. We shook hands and I looked around the small living room on the ground floor of the house. Comfortable-looking chairs and sofas were in haphazard disarray, the way children might arrange a room to suit themselves. A Tiffany lamp on a library table looked genuine. A large, nineteenth-century French circus poster dominated one wall. The dark brown aroma of roasting meat drifted in from the kitchen and the dining room table was set for three.

"Fifteen minutes to dinner," he said, and headed up a flight of stairs without looking back to see if we were following him. I wasn't offended by what might have been considered rude but I was intensely curious about such apparent self-confidence. I wondered if it was an act.

Cohn's house was something like an East Coast brownstone, with two rooms separated by a bath on the second and third floors. Unlike the living room, the office on the second floor was a model of geometric organization: a pair of Bauhaus-style black leather sofas faced each other squarely across a glass and steel table with copies of *Scientific American* set down in tidy rows next to a Steuben ashtray. An antique partner's desk anchored one end of the room; from here Cohn could survey his domain, then swivel his chair to look out the windows and see anyone ringing the buzzer at the gate of the high wall that surrounded the house. A Venetian mirror, so old that patches of the silvered backing behind the glass had worn away, hung between the windows. There was a celestial globe and built-in shelves heavy with books on photography, history, and philosophy.

Cohn opened a desk drawer and brought out three perfectly rolled joints. He lit one and held out the others to Judy and me. I glanced at her; the usual practice was for people to pass around a single joint. She grinned, dropped full-length onto one of the sofas, and held out a lighter. I sipped in a mix of smoke and air and sat on the sofa across from her. *Good grass*, I thought. We smoked silently for a while, then I leaned forward, rested my chin on one hand, and looked at Harry Cohn.

"Okay: I want to hear about Christmas Day when you were six years old."

Judy made a fake throat-clearing sound. Cohn didn't alter his expression of idle interest. He took a hit of grass, held it in, released it. Then he launched into a description of limousines rolling up the circular driveway of the family estate in Beverly Hills and uniformed drivers hustling around to passenger doors and extending gloved hands to movie stars under contract and actors trying to impress. He described the late-model Cadillacs and foreign sports jobs driven by directors and assorted studio executives. His voice was as impersonal as someone reading a book report as he talked about the ceiling-high tree trimmed by the Columbia art department a week before Christmas and his mother, Joan, in velvet and diamonds, handing out professionally wrapped presents while his father, the eternal autocrat, sat in a thronelike chair and waved his guests toward the buffet with his cigar. Cohn said he and his younger brother John fooled around with the elaborate toys they'd been given by people they didn't know, flipped through the new books, and kept out of the way as much as possible. He enjoyed the holidays, he said, because he didn't have to wear the uniform of the Black-Foxe Military Institute, where he had been enrolled in preschool at the age of three.

When we finished the joints (I'd pinched off the glowing tip of mine after a few tokes; too potent for one go) Cohn got up from behind his desk and went downstairs without speaking. I looked over at Judy.

"Let's give him a minute. He's breaking in some fancy new restaurant stove with eight burners and he doesn't know you well enough yet to let you watch him cook." She stretched out both arms, arched her back, and smiled. "I can't believe he answered that question about Christmas. I think you've made an impression, mate."

I got my first look at the family home, located on Crescent Drive directly behind the Beverly Hills Hotel, a few weeks after the dinner at Cohn's house in Laurel Canyon. There was a movie he wanted Judy and me to see: *Performance* with Mick Jagger. Cohn was friendly with the codirectors, Donald Cammell and Nic Roeg, and he'd made arrangements for it to be shown in the screening room his father installed during his reign at Columbia. The house was an enormous Mediterranean villa laid out on over an acre of gardens, lawns, and mature trees. The screening room was a perfectly preserved relic of the forties: bamboo-patterned wallpaper, thick carpeting, wall-to-wall screen, and three or four tiers of boxy leather armchairs, about four to a row, each chair connected to the next by streamlined stands with lights on dimmers, telephone jacks, and ashtrays. There was an enclosed booth at the back where a man worked the pair of side-by-side 35 mm projectors that eliminated any time lapse between reels. Cohn's mother was somewhere in the house but she never came to the screenings, which included new releases as well as European and Japanese classics. As a rule, it was Cohn, Judy, and me unless Lisa joined us for early dinner and a movie Cohn had picked with her in mind. He displayed sincere interest and affection toward my daughter and she returned the feelings. Sometimes I brought a date along but that was rare; Cohn generally preferred it to be just the three of us. It took a while but I finally figured it out: in his way, Cohn loved Judy. She was his match physically and she challenged him sexually. She was quick and she could make him laugh. I served another purpose: Cohn considered me a kind of peer, someone he could discuss films and art with. There was something else, too: an unspoken interest in expanding the threesome to include a bit of fun in the bedroom. Judy and Cohn didn't push it but the thought was there to be picked up on. I didn't pick up. I've never been interested in any kind of adventure that included more than one other person with me in a bed. Fine for others, just not for me.

At times Cohn allowed a mean streak to slip the leash. Then he'd say something subtly cruel, not necessarily about Judy but geared to slide past her, something he figured I'd hear and, presumably, appreciate. I didn't, because it was a snide form of bullying, and one evening when Judy was in another room, I called him on it.

To his credit, he didn't argue. And he stopped the bullshit.

I spent some time at the Laurel Canyon house on random weekends and met a few of Cohn's friends. They were independent producers, drug dealers, character actors, and experimental photographers. One guy, an editor at the Free Press, wondered if, as a model, I'd like to try to write a short piece on "the hostility of hot pants," a minor fashion fad. As a model, I declined. I didn't think hot pants were any more hostile than T-shirts with legends like HERE COMES TROUBLE.

Lisa and I loved our apartment in West Hollywood and we were both crazy about the young guys who lived in the units on either side of ours. Tom and Stephen, in 203, had been together for a couple of years; Tom worked in advertising and Stephen was finishing up his last year of classes toward a certification in interior design. He looked angelic with his long blond hair and delicate features but he possessed a wicked sense of humor that tempted me to join him in teasing the more serious Tom. One of Tom's clients was Baskin-Robbins, and when he asked Stephen and me to help him come up with names for new flavors, we suggested "Liver 'n' Onions" and "Trout Ripple." Glenn and Billy were in 201; they loved each other and shared a bed but were no longer lovers. They laughed about it and said they were far better at being friends. Billy was a fairly successful interior designer and Glenn (movie-star handsome in his midtwenties) was just starting a business of buying, collecting, and selling vintage film costumes and props. Lisa quickly became everyone's pet and she was welcomed in both apartments whenever she felt like a visit. For her, the sudden appearance of four young uncles in her life was something out of a magic show. Uncles, it turned out, who were funny and loving. Glenn became the person who resolved all arguments between my daughter and me and he provided a masculine point of view on the subjects of what dress Lisa might wear to a birthday party, whether she should be allowed to wear lipstick (the answer was "Not yet"), and how I should dress for a social event. He delivered the final word on everything. Lisa and I were in complete agreement about that, and when we had a beef, Uncle Glenn was called in to mediate. He weighed both sides of the argument, thought about it, and then handed down an opinion that was always fair.

The three units on the second floor at the El Mirador quickly unified into a very real kind of family. Stephen was happy to perform babysitting duties if I was working when Lisa got out of school. Glenn found wonderful vintage movie costumes in her sizes at the MGM auction and I got a beautifully embroidered pale green and apricot silk Chinese jacket from *The Good Earth*. Billy put up a ceiling-high tree each December and decorated it with strings of popcorn and antique ornaments and lights. On Christmas Eve, Lisa wore her black velvet dress and was allowed to work the switch that turned the tree into a glittering work of art. The presents under the tree were works of art, too.

When a 6.5 earthquake occurred shortly after midnight in February of 1971, Lisa and I raced from our apartment, burst into 201 (doors were left unlocked on our floor when we were home), and dived under the covers with Billy, Glenn, and Glenn's dog, Mrs. Craig, who was shivering with fear. Glenn got up, made hot chocolate with cinnamon and marshmallows, and sliced off a bit of chicken for Mrs. Craig. Then all five of us huddled close for the rest of the night.

When Lisa talks about those years at the El Mirador, she describes them as the happiest of her childhood.

I think it was Billy who introduced me to Richard, who was visiting L.A. for a few days. Richard was the most beautiful girl I'd ever seen. She was about twenty-three, tall and slender with tinselly blond hair, creamy skin, and a kitten's snub nose. Her voice was sexily husky, like Lauren Bacall's in *To Have and Have Not*, when she told me she was a transsexual. Richard still had male genitalia, she said, but she'd felt like a girl all her life. I liked her sweetness and honesty and respected her for keeping her given name. She was visiting my apartment one afternoon, and when Lisa got home from school, I decided we should tell her the truth. Lisa looked solemnly at Richard for a long moment; this was her first encounter with a man who was really a woman. Then she broke out her widest smile.

"You're so pretty I bet you have lots of boyfriends." And, before Richard could reply, she asked, "Would you like to see some of my movie costumes from Uncle Glenn?"

Simple as that: Lisa may not have fully understood the situation but she was ready to accept Richard for who she was.

That weekend I asked Richard if she'd like to go with me to a private club in Hollywood where we could have dinner and do some dancing. The club, called the Factory, was founded in 1967 by Frank Sinatra and Sammy Davis Jr., and I'd been given a free membership, along with several other models and young actresses. Richard loved the idea of going to the club and we spent Saturday afternoon at my place, putting on makeup and fooling around with our hair. I insisted that Richard borrow one of my Gernreichs—a close-fitting floor-length beige knit trimmed in brown glove leather with snap closures that allowed the wearer to opt for a plunging neckline and/or a thigh-high show of leg—for our date.

The Factory (the building had been some kind of factory at one time and you rode a freight elevator to the second story, where the club itself was located) was weekend crowded when Richard and I made our entrance. There was an immediate flurry of whispers as a beautiful, six-foot blond arrived on the scene.

We made our way to a booth, and within minutes an ant trail of guys, one after the other, began sidling up to Richard with requests for a dance. I watched and learned about gracious refusals that night: first a gentle smile, indicating gratitude at being asked. Then "Thank you so much, it's very nice of you to ask, but I really think you should know this about me: my name is Richard and I'm a boy."

The reactions were all pretty much alike: a narrowing of the eyes for closer inspection, disbelief, pause, then a bemused glance in my direction. I had only to nod my head.

Most of the men backed off but three or four persisted with a look at me, a look back at Richard, then a slow, negative shake of the head: *No way this chick is a guy.* Richard tried again.

"It's true. My name really is Richard, I really am a boy. I may not feel like one but it's what I am."

A couple of the erstwhile suitors were not to be swayed.

"So your name's Richard. So what? *Her*"—an indifferent jerk of the chin in my direction—"name's Léon and *she's* sure as hell not a guy."

Later, when Richard and I danced together, nobody tried to cut in but there were plenty of less-than-friendly stares. Word had sped around the club, with its girls in crotch-high miniskirts and patent leather boots, its guys in too-tight, bell-bottomed trousers and Jesse James facial hair, that a fucking drag queen was there among them, the real people. The would-be celebrities and the sprinkling of genuine star power couldn't seem to grasp the difference between a drag queen and a transsexual, but petty disapproval? They had that one down.

When I told Billy and Glenn about our evening at the Factory, their response wasn't one of outrage. They were used to the hostility of some straights and even a few gays to transsexuals. I wasn't and was furious. When I thought about it again, I remembered Richard's stoicism toward what had happened. The only people who reacted the same as I reacted were Lisa, who cried a few angry tears and wondered how people could be so cruel to such a gentle person, and my mother, who aimed a barrage of the swearing game's most forbidden four-letter words at the Factory's clientele.

Harry Cohn's getaway (aside from his mother's place in the Montecito area of Santa Barbara) was a ranch house in the desert on about two acres in the Joshua Tree Monument. The terrain there looked like the surface of another planet: arid stretches of land and tumbles of irregular, sand-colored boulders that Cohn and Judy liked to climb. They urged me to join them and I told them the only way they were going to get me on top of some thirty-foot rock was with a general anesthetic and a crane.

I often wondered, during those lazy dope-smoking, coke-sniffing times, why Cohn didn't try for some kind of career in the film industry. He had the connections and the funds to invest. He was intelligent and he had a talent for photography. But beyond taking stills on the set of Alejandro Jodorowsky's revered cult film *The Holy Mountain*, he seemed not to have the ambition and ruthlessness his father had possessed in such great measures. Maybe Harry Cohn Jr. was just too rich to care. Maybe he was afraid. Whatever the reasons, I didn't feel it was my place to haul out a psychiatric textbook.

So I remained an odd man out in their relationship. That was okay with me, but I wanted—and needed—to meet a guy I could connect with on every level. I'd talked about it with Lisa when she asked what "being in love" meant.

"It means you get to make love with the person who is also your best friend, the person you can share everything with."

I didn't mention that finding lovers was easy; meeting a man who would be both my lover and closest friend was another story. When Judy's relationship with Harry Cohn ended, I remained friendly with both of them, but I was closer to Judy until she sold her house and moved back to England. Cohn spent more and more time at his place in the desert, married a woman he met there, and fathered two kids. He drove into L.A. once in a while, always alone, and we'd have dinner at the Pacific Dining Car, a clubby down-town steak house. At forty, Cohn remained whippet-thin, but his good looks were evaporating at time-lapse speed. He was using more serious drugs and couldn't (or wouldn't) understand when I told him that I had quit doing anything and suggested he might try to cut back on his intake. His response was to tell me that he had it under control. He died of an overdose a few months later.

I didn't meet Victory through Harry Cohn but it turned out they were both part of a philosophical group called the Fourth Way (also known to its members as the Work, relating to "the work that must be done on oneself to wake from the unconscious state of 'waking sleep' from which most of humanity views reality"), founded by Greco-Russian mystic G. I. Gurdjieff in the early twen-ties. I met Victory at Glenn and Billy's apartment, where the cedar scent of Rigaud candles filled the air and a vintage Hermès scarf was displayed in a Lucite frame. She was seated in one corner of a sofa crowded by needlepoint pillows. This unsmiling, strangely attractive woman, with her long black hair and falcon's eyes, seemed out of place among the trappings of überchic, and my initial thought was she might be a gypsy, which intimidated me slightly. Then she smiled and patted the space next to her, and as we talked, I realized that this was someone as welcoming as she was intelligent.

She worked as chief accountant at a production company that filmed commercials, she told me, but her real passions were mysticism and astrology. I knew nothing about mysticism of any kind and I was profoundly ignorant of all things astrological. I knew I was an Aries, like my mother; knew Lisa was a Leo. Victory asked for the date, time, year, and location of my birth. I noticed she didn't make any kind of note and we went on to talk about other things.

Victory worked out my chart and told me facts about my background she could not have known. She also informed me that modeling wasn't what I was supposed to be doing: I was a writer, she said; it was right there in my chart—Jupiter, ninth house. My response was to tell her, with respect, that I thought she was nuts— I was doing pretty damn well with a modeling career, wasn't I? What did writing have to do with it? She smiled and changed the subject in the way people do when they realize the other person isn't ready to take in information. Within a month or so we were friends, talking often on the phone, going out for meals and the occasional movie. I learned that Victory was a vegetarian, not because it was a thing to be in the sixties and seventies but because she'd made a moral decision not to eat meat when she was in her early teens. She never tried to push it: I might order a steak or a cheeseburger when we went to a restaurant and she'd eat a salad or pasta without comment or attitude. She didn't push the writing, either, except to tell me she had a strong psychic sense that my degree of Scorpio rising was similar to that of Charles Dickens.

Yeah, yeah, yeah, I thought, and let it go at that. If I'd been a little quicker on the uptake, I might have saved myself some real time.

She talked about her beginnings in Chicago: left in a basket with her name pinned to the blanket that covered her, she was raised by a foster mother who assured the child that she would never escape the trailer park where they lived because she was too ugly, too stupid, and too stubborn. Victory was anything but ugly and she was far from stupid. She loved school and earned near-perfect marks in every subject. But money was hard to come by; Betty, her foster mother, wasn't about to hand out lunch money or an allowance. The kid wanted to read more than she wanted to eat lunch and when she was nine years old she walked into a small used book store and told the owner she couldn't buy anything but asked if it was okay if she just looked at the books. The owner said she was welcome anytime.

Victory had found a warming place. She sat on the floor and began to read—first a book on astrology, then she was drawn into studies of metaphysics. Nine years old. By the time she was eleven, she had a paper route at the trailer park and the means to buy hard-used paperbacks on the subjects she had come to love. The foster mother had been right about one thing, anyway: Victory was stubborn. But she was also unlucky: at fourteen she was raped by a resident of the trailer park who was AWOL from the air force. She didn't tell anyone because she figured no one would believe her. The guy was good-looking (Betty thought he looked like Elvis Presley) and popular; why would he have to rape some scrawny kid? After he was picked up by the military police, Betty would load Victory into her old junker once a month and they'd make the trip to visit him in the stockade.

Within two months of his release, Victory was pregnant. They married and rented a small house in a low-income neighborhood, and her son, Tom, was born six months after her fifteenth birthday. The marriage didn't last a year. Victory accepted ten dollars a month in child support, got a job at a manufacturing plant, worked part-time as a waitress, and moved to a cheaper place. Her ex-husband's family took care of Tom during the week.

Victory went to school sporadically but she studied on her own. Zen philosophy, the works of Alan Watts in particular, was added to her reading list. She made an appointment at the Chicago Institute of Psychiatry for psychological testing "to make sure I wasn't a whacko and that I could be a good mom." And she was, until the ex demanded custody of his son, saying, "I got people who'll come to court and swear to things you did, even if you didn't do them. Either way, you lose the kid. Count on it."

I heard those words, repeated by Victory without rancor or self-pity, and thought about how fair Mack Bing had been throughout our divorce proceedings, particularly where our child was involved.

"How could you let your ex-husband get away with being such a monster?"

"I didn't know how to fight him and"—she paused for a beat—"it wasn't like he knew what he was doing. He thought he was doing the right thing in the only way he knew how."

I wasn't then and am not now able to be that understanding.

Victory agreed to all his demands. It hurt like hell but she turned over her son to his father, swallowed her anger, and consoled herself with the thought that it was better to leave her child in a reliable environment with his paternal family than to take him with her on an uncertain road. She began saving for a move to L.A. It took almost two years but she made it before her twenty-second birthday (it was longer than that before she was able to reconcile with her son: Tom was in his thirties, still living in Chicago and a father himself, when Victory found him again.

She lucked out on her first job in L.A., working as girl Friday to the owner of a plant that manufactured doors. He recognized her innate intelligence and sent Victory to a city college, where she learned accounting. Then he stopped sending her out on errands and promoted her to the better-paying job of keeping the books. She never quenched her thirst for knowledge or her interest in astrology. When, in the mideighties, I told her I was beginning to write, she didn't gloat. She smiled, content that I was fulfilling the destiny she had seen so long ago in my chart.

CHAPTER 8

The King of Shitkicker Cool

"I see you like my newest acquisition." The host was genial enough but I thought it was pretentious of him to use such a formal word. The painting he was talking about, the one I'd been staring at, was anything but pretentious.

I nodded my head. "Yes, it's very beautiful. And I'd be very happy if you gave it to me."

It was clear that what I'd said shocked him. He looked at me blankly and then turned and began speaking in low tones to the person on his right. It was a small dinner party and a dull one. I don't remember who invited me along as his companion for the evening but halfway through the meal I knew this would be the only time we would be together under any circumstances. The single thing holding my interest was a painting on the wall opposite my chair, a pretty big painting, maybe three by four feet. The background was the color of chocolate pudding spread to a rich, shining finish. Placed dead center, in voluptuous black lettering, was a single four-letter word:

BOSS

I couldn't stop looking at it, didn't know who the artist was, didn't care. I only knew I'd never seen anything quite like it before.

If that painting belonged to me, it wouldn't be in the dining room. I'd hang it where I could see it first thing in the morning and every time I walked in the front door. That painting could put a smile on your face whatever your mood happened to be. And only a pompous ass would call it his "newest acquisition."

Years later I would learn that the genial host, a successful surgeon, paid two hundred dollars for *Boss* and doled it out in fifty-dollar increments, insisting the artist drive in from his studio at the edge of downtown L.A. to Beverly Hills for each payment.

A month or so after that dinner party, Rudi and I were posed on the broad flight of concrete steps leading to the entrance of the Los Angeles County Museum of Art. We were surrounded by tiers of artists, critics, and columnists, and I wondered what we were doing there. A few of the artists were standing or seated with one of their pieces from the museum's permanent collection: John Altoon, Deborah Sussman, Billy Al Bengston, Claes Oldenberg, Larry Bell, Craig Kauffman. Maurice Tuchman, the museum's curator of modern art, was there. Rudi and I were the only fashion people in that impressive crowd and I felt out of place and awkward. But Rudi was an artist, too, I reasoned, and as his model, in the same dress I wore on the *Time* cover, I could be considered one of his canvases. It was March of 1968 and we had all been brought together to be photographed for a cover story in *Los Angeles* magazine.

While the photographer fussed with tripods and reflectors, I looked around at the art and the people who had created it. The style of the big painting on the top step was unmistakable: a two-color background this time; dark blue on top with round, vaguely cartoonish letters spelling out a single word:

SPAM

The painting's title is *Actual Size* and the image on the lower two thirds of the canvas is a tin of the meat product hurtling through space. The artist (by then I knew his name was Ed Ruscha and that he was from Oklahoma) was seated, relaxed as a ranch hand with a bottle of Coors—legs spread, elbows on knees—in front of it. He looked like the actor Robert Mitchum if Mitchum were playing the part of Dick Hickcock.

I turned and whispered to Rudi. "Look behind you at the artist in front of the big Spam painting—that's Ed Ruscha. As soon as they shoot the picture, I want you to go over there and tell him someone wants to meet him. Say it's an admirer."

"What? I don't know him. I can't just—"

I cut him off. "Just do it for me, okay?"

Rudi looked back at Ruscha and the painting, taking his time. Then he turned toward me again.

"He's wonderfully good-looking. And the painting is beautiful," he said.

"Right. So will you please just go and get him?"

Ten minutes later Rudi was introducing me to Ed Ruscha, and while I was shaking hands and saying "Nice to meet you" and "I sure do like your work," what I was thinking was, *Oh my God, he's even better than his art.*

It was on. Of course he was married.

I don't know how he managed it. Didn't ask, probably didn't want to know any more than I wanted to think of myself as the villain in a clichéd scenario. I just wanted to be with this guy who was so different from anyone I'd been with before—so cool (before the word became a lazy and overworked catchall description), so easily himself, such an ardent and inventive lover.

We saw each other as often as possible, and possible was about four times a week. Ruscha would come to my place in West Hollywood when Lisa was at school or I'd go over to his studio, which was located at the back of a dusty courtyard on Western Avenue. He began a painting that would center the single word "unit" on a teal blue background—"unit" because that was how I referred to my car, mimicking the used-car salesmen I saw on late-night TV commercials who promised to put every customer in the unit of their choice. Ed planned to paint the word as a series of tiny, closely connected bubbles. When he finished the first letter, he called me.

"Listen, I'm about to go blind on these damn bubbles."

"So what are you saying? It'll just be a painting of the letter 'U' in perfectly rendered spit bubbles?"

"Well—yeah . . ."

"Well, that's one hell of a fake-out."

It was easy for us to find laughs together.

We arranged to meet up at gallery openings and other similar events, and as time passed, we met each other's friends. I took him to Toby and Bob Rafelson's home. Bob is an accomplished director (*Five Easy Pieces* is one of his classic films) and he was a partner in the company that provided financing for *Easy Rider*. Toby was the production designer on his movies. We went to Cass Elliot's house in the hills and to Harry Cohn Jr.'s ranch in the Joshua Tree Monument. Ed fell in love with the desert and would build his own place there some years later. We had dinner with artist Ed Kienholz and his wife at their house next to an unfinished tableau of a small pond with reeds, grass, and a covey of water gliders pontooning across the surface of the water. I met photographer Jerry McMillan, a high school buddy of Ruscha's from Oklahoma, who was working out of a second-floor studio in the courtyard. Jerry is a true artist and he took some beautiful and creative fashion shots of me. Ruscha introduced me to Joe Goode and Robert Graham, to Ed Moses and Larry Bell, all of them part of the emerging L.A. art scene. Mason Williams was another friend from Oklahoma and head writer on a popular and politically edgy TV show built around the Smothers brothers. Mason and Ed had collaborated on one of a series of paperback art books produced by Heavy Industries, a company founded by Ed. An early edition was called *Royal Road Test*: no text, just a series of photographs of an old Royal typewriter taken at different angles after it was tossed out the passenger window of a car traveling along a strip of desert highway outside L.A.

Ed's studio consisted of a large room with a concrete floor; another, very small room behind that; and a bathroom with a toilet and sink. The display of art on the walls was a picture of a Keene painting of a saucer-eyed child and a page torn from a magazine with a full-color image of Norman Rockwell's painting of a family gathered around Thanksgiving dinner. Ed admired the composition of the Rockwell; I can't remember what he liked about the Keene. The studio was furnished with a busted-down sofa, a couple of high wooden tables, and an old black-and-white TV. Ruscha liked to keep up with the news when he was working and he liked to watch prizefights. He was a great fan of welterweight Hedgemon Lewis and often went to see him in matches at the old Olympic Auditorium. During one ringside TV interview after a fight, Ruscha managed to position himself just behind Lewis's right shoulder. When the interview was shown again on the late news, Ed was ready with his camera and got a shot off the TV screen of himself with Lewis. He was so pleased with that picture he had a copy made for me.

We went out driving on the random Saturday afternoon (sometimes Ed took pictures for his books; the rear bumper of my Mustang appears on a page in *Real Estate Opportunities*) and there were times I joined him as he ran errands. One of them involved a visit to a printer, where Ruscha chose the font for the lettering on the cover of his boxed collection *Stains*. We left corny romantic messages for each other on our respective answering services. He was "the Artist," I was "the Model." One afternoon he took a small piece of paper, wrote something on it, and handed it to me.

> NAMES OF DRUGS OR TREATMENTS OF TODAY:
> IF VAN GOGH WERE ALIVE TODAY WE WOULD GIVE HIM A _____
> AND AN _____ AND HE'D BE DOING WINDOWS AT THE MAY CO.

He'd drawn a pair of arrows pointing from the top line to the blank spaces.

There were other spur-of-the-moment ideas, too: I still have a

sketch of a goose in profile wearing a sunbonnet with little cartoon puffs of air drifting out of its beak and the words "Goose
Breath" underneath.

I gave Ruscha a set of business cards engraved with a pho-
netic pronunciation (Ed-werd Rew-shay) in a smaller font under his
name and the legend "Young Artist." He took a boat ride off the
coast of Mexico and told me he looked at the hills along the coast-
line and thought about the curve of my waist where it blended into
the hip line.

Ed was wonderful with Lisa, surprising her with small,
charming gifts: a beautifully labeled tin of school paste from Italy,
a box of drawing pencils in imaginative colors. He never talked
down to her and he didn't try to win her over. So, of course, she
liked him. I introduced him to my mother (I didn't mention he was
married) and even she was drawn in. Ruscha was the same with
my mother and daughter as he was with everyone: always and completely himself.

A month or so after we met and the day before I was to go to New
York for two weeks with Rudi and the latest collection, Ruscha
asked if we could meet for lunch at Musso and Frank, a legendary
restaurant on Hollywood Boulevard where the martinis are made
according to an exacting recipe passed across the bar by F. Scott
Fitzgerald. My mother took me there often when I was a kid and I
love the unchanging look of the place as much as the good chop-
house food.

Ruscha was waiting for me in one of the high-topped leather
booths. There was a square package lying between the flatware
setting at my place.

"What's this?"

"Well, check it out."

I hadn't expected a gift, so I was surprised. When I tore off the
plain paper wrapping, I was stunned. The drawing was of a word
I'd swiped from a drag artist to describe the elaborate makeup I
wore for work:

slap

The lowercase letters (drawn with gunpowder and pastels, media Ruscha used often) were designed in the shape of a spiral of paper that spelled out the word. Where the "p" ended, a faint trace of pale pink trailed away from the last hint of dark shading that gave the letters their three-dimensional appearance. In very small writing, above the upper edge of the drawing and just below the tip of a shining rhodium frame, were the words "For Léon Love Ed."

I couldn't think of anything to say. I was overwhelmed, not only by the beauty of the work but by its personal message. After a short silence, I leaned over and brushed my lips against his cheek. Then I studied the drawing again.

"I don't know how to thank you for this. I'll take it with me to New York."

Ruscha nodded his head absently.

"Yeah, but you know, now I don't think it's enough. I want you to take something else with you. Something I'll need every day you're in New York."

I watched, pleasantly mystified, as he pulled out his wallet and flipped it open.

He glanced at me, took something out of the wallet, and slid it across the table. I looked down to see what it was.

His driver's license.

"Listen, I can't—"

"Just take it, huh?"

I picked up the license, put it in my bag, and took it with me to New York. I almost always recognize high romance when it's headed straight at me.

Ruscha had a proposition: Heavy Industries was getting ready to do another art book, the first to feature people. Would I be interested in playing the part of "the unattainable woman," one of four characters in a story called "Premium" by Mason Williams? Others in the cast would be a guy out on a formal dinner date, his driver, and a bellboy in a flophouse.

I was interested, all right. I'd known Ed for over a year and this was a chance to be part of one of his projects. I was used to being an outside element of his life and that really didn't bother me. I was with him as much as I wanted and he was always in a great mood despite a slightly possessive streak. He wasn't pleased when Ed Kienholz asked if he could sculpt my legs as the bottom part of a guitar, a component for a new project, and he didn't like it when Bob Graham mentioned me as a possible model for one of his exquisite small figures. Infatuated and foolish about it, I declined both requests. Still, I saw other men whenever I felt like it and sometimes we became romantically—if briefly—involved. I liked the arrangement because "freedom" seemed to be the key word. Maybe the word should have been "rationalization" but that occurs to me only now.

Most of the men I had one or even a few dates with seemed dull when I compared them to the subtle fireworks of Ed Ruscha. There was one young guy, John Steppling, who captured my interest. Initially, it was his looks that drew me in: he was as beautiful and as coolly aware of it as the callow young aristocrat Tadzio, the fatal object of desire in *Death in Venice*. The resemblance ended there. Steppling, long, taffy-colored hair framing his face, was slouched on a neighbor's sofa when we met. He was living any way he could and reading everything he could get his hands on. We began to talk, I invited him over to my place, and soon we were seeing each other on weekends when Lisa was with Mack. We talked endlessly about books and writers, went to double-feature matinees, waited in line for chili dogs at Pink's, and made leisurely love in my Victorian brass bed. It didn't last long; John drifted off and somebody told me he was in prison. Years later, when we connected again, he told me he'd done ten months out of a one-year sentence for robbery. By the time we renewed our friendship, Steppling had written a couple of well-received feature films, been awarded a Rockefeller fellowship, and was the recipient of a National Endowment for the Arts grant as a playwright. He lives, writes, and teaches courses on film in Europe now and we communicate by e-mail.

We began the photographs for *Premium* (subtitled "How to Derive the Maximum Enjoyment from Crackers") on a warm evening outside the main entrance of the Beverly Wilshire Hotel. Ed and sculptor Ken Price were both working cameras. Larry Bell, handsome in dinner clothes, smoked his signature cigar as he and I (wearing Gernreich's ruffled brown chiffon "baby dress" and huge black silk rose-petal earrings) lounged in the back seat of Mason Williams's immaculately restored Pierce-Arrow. Tommy Smothers, in a chauffeur's cap and jacket, was behind the wheel. Ed's directions were for Larry to behave attentively toward me, his bored and unresponsive date. When we were done with that location, we caravanned to a small hotel on a side street in Hollywood. More photographs: stepping down regally from the car as Smothers held the door; moving up the front steps, where an unimpressed canine resident slunk past us. Inside, Rudi Gernreich as a bellhop, unshaven and costumed in sagging, unzipped trousers and grimy T-shirt, led the way up a flight of uncarpeted stairs to the door of a room. End of first day's shoot.

A few days later, Ruscha, Price, Larry, and I were in the bedroom of Joe Goode and his girlfriend Casey's apartment in the Hollywood Towers (substituting for the hotel room) and Larry was urging me toward a bed covered with three kinds of fresh lettuce. I pulled back, unconvinced. Finally, he wheedled me into stripping off my clothes (modestly, back to camera, black lace panties kept on) and lying down in the salad (also modestly: I covered parts of myself with the greens). He stood over the bed, I held out my arms to him, and he turned, picked up a gallon tin, and proceeded to pour oil and vinegar dressing over me and the lettuce. Then, snapping his fingers as if he had forgotten some essential ingredient, he looked directly at the camera and mouthed the only printed word inside the book:

CRACKERS!

The final photographs are of Larry stopping at a convenience store to buy a box of Premium saltines followed by shots of him in a different and upscale location, taking off the tuxedo and lying back against a pileup of pillows on a bed. He is holding the box of saltines and eating a cracker with an expression of ecstatic fulfillment on his face. The unattainable woman, it is implied, remains in her place and in the salad back at the flophouse.

Days later, I was still finding bits of dried parsley from the dressing in the bath.

We did the whole thing over again as a 16 mm sound movie during the summer of 1971. That was when Ed introduced me to his younger brother, Paul, in from Oklahoma City for one of his regular visits. Paul Anthony Ruscha made a spectacular first impression: dark shoulder-length hair, an outlaw's mustache, and mirrored, aviator-style dark glasses. When he took off the glasses, his eyes were covered by mirrored contact lenses. Ruscha the younger looked like a fusion of Merlin and a rock star. We connected immediately when I told him I loved the mirrored contacts because they allowed me to look into his eyes and put on lipstick at the same time. After that we found conversation between us was like lobbing a tennis ball back and forth. Paul reminded me of his brother: they spoke in the same voice and had the same facial bone structure and beautifully shaped hands. But there was another, fiercer connection that shone through the normal bonds of siblings, and when Ed introduced me to their mother, Dorothy (who was visiting L.A.), I recognized her as the wellspring for their laconic humor and off-center viewpoints. Something clicked between Dorothy and me, because we were like girlfriends from the first handshake. She didn't seem to be interested in judging my relationship with her older son but she was wonderfully willing to poke a little gentle fun at some of his eccentricities. One day she and I had lunch together and it was one of those times I felt a bitter surge of envy toward Ed's wife, Danna; I wanted Dorothy Ruscha in my life as *my* mother-in-law.

When Paul moved permanently to L.A. in 1973, our friendship picked up again. We went out for meals and movies, gossiped and giggled, and sometimes, if he called from the studio, I could hear the Artist harrumphing in the background that "nothing could be *that* funny." Paul (married now to the beautiful Ulrike Kantor) and I still laugh about it.

Ed used money from a Guggenheim Foundation fellowship as funding for the movie version of *Premium*. The scenario was the same, only this time we shot the salad scene at sculptor Al Ruppersberg's studio over a Thai restaurant on Sunset Boulevard. The most indelible memory I have of that sweltering day, aside from the lack of air-conditioning, is the smell of the lettuce as it wilted under the blazing lights and cooking fumes from the restaurant downstairs. Still, we had great fun and this time I made sure the recipe for the salad dressing didn't include dried parsley.

Ed's and my relationship lasted for three or four years. I knew, at some point, that I was one of a cadre of young women forming concentric circles around Ruscha, and when I met someone else, a young film editor working with John Cassavetes, I began to go out with him. He introduced me to Cassavetes, who gave me a small speaking role as a degenerate gambler in his film *The Killing of a Chinese Bookie*. I continued seeing the film editor, and while it wasn't a serious relationship, my romance with the Artist dwindled.

Ed and Danna separated in the midseventies, and if he and I were no longer lovers, we were still friends. So when he called and asked me to spend some time with him, talking about the failed marriage and his feelings about that, I agreed.

He had a question: "Is it okay if I record what we say?"

"Hey. What do you think?"

So he and I took a long drive around L.A., ate at a diner, and talked nonstop with a tape recorder lying between us. We spoke about his marriage and his young son, nicknamed Frenchy. We talked about Ed's sense of betrayal at being left for another man and at some point in the conversation I remember asking what the hell he'd expected to happen when he fooled around so much with so many women. We bounced off random subjects, commenting on the architectural styles of buildings we passed (he liked my nickname for the Federal Building near Westwood; I called it the Out-of-Focus Building because of its blurred strips of night lighting) and the styles of classic cars we admired. We must have used up four or five reels of tape and Ed had them transcribed into a project called *The Separation Tapes*.

The evening didn't end with the final tape. Ed had one more favor to ask: would I be willing to come back to his house in Laurel Canyon and lie down with him in the bed he and Danna had shared?

So. He wanted a get-back. I thought about it for a minute.

Ruscha and I have lain down together more times than I can count and his being married never stopped me from enjoying it. To refuse him now on some tight-lipped moral premise would feel even creepier than fucking him in his wife's bed.

It wasn't as creepy as I thought, but still, it was strange to go into a room imbued with another woman's essence.

A day or so later, Ed called and said he wanted to bring something over to my place. I watched from the second-floor landing as he wrestled a very big canvas up the flight of stairs. When he turned it to show the image, I recognized it as one of his most iconic works: a perfectly rendered songbird magnified many times. I was struck by its beauty and staggered by Ruscha's gesture. But the wave of romance that swept over me a few years earlier when he gave me the drawing of *slap* and slid his driver's license across the table at Musso and Frank was missing. This was generous but impersonal, like the cherried-out vintage Corvette a grateful producer gives an actor when their movie tops the weekend grosses at the box office.

Ed didn't say much that day and we didn't talk about what had gone on at his house. He just asked for a hammer and hung the painting on my living room wall.

I loved living with that bird. Lisa sat on the floor and gazed up at it for hours. My mother was crazy about it and Hotten pronounced it the most beautiful painting she'd ever seen.

About a month later I got another call from Ruscha. He was damn sorry, he said, but he needed to get the bird painting back. I closed my eyes for a second and then looked over at the work of art that had given me and my family so much pleasure.

". . . Okay."

So that part of the get-back misfired.

"Is it okay if I come by for it later today?"

"Yeah. Sure."

What I was thinking did not include the words "yeah" or "sure."

Fuck you, Ed. And no, you can't come by for it later today. You gave me that painting and I love it and I'm not giving it back just because you're remorseful or scared or whatever.

I wanted to say all that but it was, after all, his painting and he had given it to me with the ardor of vengeance, not love.

He didn't arrive empty-handed. He had another large-scale canvas with him. This one spelled out the phrase "Listen, I'd Like to Help Out, But—" in uppercase lettering that marched in diagonal lines, moving up from left to right. Instead of paint, Ruscha had used ketchup for the letters against a colorless corn-syrup background. I didn't laugh but I sure recognized the irony implicit in the statement.

I see *Listen* first thing in the morning and every time I walk in my front door. The background was slightly damaged some years ago in a cleaning mishap but the painting still looks exactly the same as it did the day Ruscha schlepped it up the stairs to my apartment. And it still has the power to put a smile on my face.

CHAPTER 9

Ellen Naomi

The tug on my arm has pulled me halfway out of the kind of sleep provided by too much dope. The voice snaps me into full consciousness.

"Get outta that bed before I kill you."

A man is standing over me. I can see him clearly in the moonlight that falls in slits through the half-open blinds: he's about thirty, with long, uncombed hair and a tangle of beard. He's wearing stained jeans and his T-shirt is wet with blood. The thick, copper smell of it is streaming off him. From behind me, on the other side of the double king-size bed, I can hear the burr and wheeze of Cass's snores. She and I are alone in the house; three-year-old Owen is visiting Cass's sister, Leah. Lisa is spending the customary weekend with her father.

"I told you to get the fuck outta here. Now!"

I met Cass Elliot in 1968 at Cher's baby shower. She was still Cher Bono at the time and we became part-time friends after meeting backstage at a charity fashion show where Cher was one of the celebrity models. We enjoyed the random lunch together, strolled Rodeo Drive to look in shop windows, and had our nails done by the same manicurist. I visited the Bonos once, at the Bel Air estate they'd bought from actor Tony Curtis. It was imposing but there was a raddled, stopped-clock look about the place. A sweep of lawn was bearded with yellow and the tiled floors inside were uninterrupted by furnishings. Sonny and Cher were happily camped out in three rooms that dwarfed the stuff from their old house. They weren't worried about buying furniture; they wanted a child.

A year or so later, I pulled into the long drive leading up to the Beverly Hills Hotel behind a black Cadillac convertible with a personalized license plate that spelled out "ISIS." A parking attendant sprang to open the door and Cass Elliot stepped out from behind the wheel. She was wearing a full-length sable coat over one of the flowing caftans that had become her signature look on- and offstage. Another attendant took my car and I followed the parade that was Mama Cass as she waved and smiled her way along the porte cochere that led to the lobby. She was carrying a large package wrapped in pale blue and pink. I trailed her through the lobby and into one of the hotel's banquet rooms, where a crowd of women milled around looking for their place cards at tables set up in front of a dais where Cher sat, radiantly pregnant and surrounded by piles of fancifully wrapped gifts.

There's another, harder yank on my arm and now I'm sliding off the bed, scrambling for balance. My breath is coming in shallow gulps and I'm beginning to tremble. This man looks like one of the people who swarmed around Charles Manson. Manson and three of his women recently had their death sentences commuted to life terms for the murders of Sharon Tate and four other people at her home in August of 1969 but there are still plenty of Manson disciples out there. The only thing I know with any certainty is that I have to get out of this room.

Cass's place card was next to mine. She settled into her chair and shrugged out of her coat. Then she turned to face me, introduced herself, and said she'd admired a fashion layout I'd done for the *L.A. Times*. I said how much I liked her first solo album and the hit single "Dream a Little Dream of Me." The food arrived and as we ate shrimp salad Cass described a dinner party where the hostess passed around joints rolled in papers printed with the Louis Vuitton logo. I told her about the Rivers, a rich-hippie couple I'd heard about who, without a trace of irony, named their baby Moon. At some point we exchanged phone numbers but I didn't really expect to hear from her. Two days later she called to invite me to bring Lisa to her house for lunch and a swim.

Cass and her daughter, Owen, lived in a two-story house located near the end of an unpaved private road off Woodrow Wilson Drive in the Hollywood Hills. Cass had bought it from Natalie Wood and turned it into a mix of conservative family home and luxurious, incense-scented hippie pad. Silken banners billowed from windows and a big leather hippopotamus guarded a reading chair in the book-lined study. The wall around the fireplace in the living room had been given over to in-house graffiti. There were scrawled messages from Eric Clapton, Ryan O'Neal, Michelle Phillips, Don Johnson, David Crosby, Keith Allison, David Pearl, Graham Nash, and anyone else who wanted to leave their mark. Somebody (possibly Cass herself) had written, "The party don't start 'til Chuck Barris gets here," as a joke. The framed gold single of "Monday, Monday" from the Mamas and the Papas' debut album was displayed on another, unmarked wall. Soon after we met, Cass traded it to Bruce Johnston for his gold single of "Good Vibrations." Johnston, who played keyboard, had taken Brian Wilson's place on tour and was doing studio work with the Beach Boys.

Cass longed for romance in her life and she had a terrific crush on Keith Allison, the Paul McCartney look-alike who played bass with Paul Revere and the Raiders. Keith is an exceptionally smart guy with a pitch-perfect sense of the absurd. He was living in West Hollywood back in the late sixties, but the way he tells it now, he was "still reekin' of green from Texas." He drove a faded blue VW van outfitted with a Porsche engine and Pirelli tires ("Me and Ringo would cruise Hollywood Boulevard lookin' for girls in that old van") and his uniform offstage consisted of a pair of beat-up 501s, a long black velvet Johnny Cash–style coat, scuffed Lucchese boots, and a well-turned Stetson. Whenever he needed to make a late-night food run, Keith would strap a flashlight to the brim of the hat and ride his skateboard along Kings Road to the Mayfair supermarket. And despite the frightening matchup of cowboy boots and skateboard, he never fell: "Not even once, not even when I was stoned outta my mind." Keith's voice is still shot through with the languid drawl of a native Texan and he laughs softly when he recalls a steamy afternoon during the summer of '66 and driving along Sunset with the Byrds' "Mr. Tambourine Man" playing on KRLA. There were no FM stations back then; the only other music station was KHJ and both of them played back-to-back commercials between the songs. But it was nothing but music in between the ads and Keith could hear "Mr. Tambourine Man" blasting out of other car windows as he drove by. Then something came into his eye line: two teenage girls were bopping along the street in front of the Whisky, a rock club where the Doors, among other heavyweights, made their debut. Both girls were carrying tambourines and one was clutching a transistor radio, the iPod of the sixties. They were dressed alike in skintight, low-rise 501s and both were bare breasted.

"No bras, *nothin'*." There is still, years later, a trace of delighted shock in Keith's voice. "They got their T-shirts wrapped around their waists and them little fifteen-, sixteen-year-old titties pointin' north, and they're both keepin' time to the song with their tambourines." The two girls weren't attracting much attention, he says, " 'cause things was a whole lot different back then."

Well, not really. A police cruiser rolled past and a disembodied voice barked out over the loudspeaker: "Girls! Put your tops on!" Keith unleashes a full-throttle laugh. "I swear, since then, ever' time I hear that John Phillips song 'Young Girls Are Coming to the Canyon,' I think of them two little topless hippie gals on the Sunset Strip in the middle of the day."

I still have a vivid picture of Keith Allison's souped-up blue van. Every time he hit the red light at the corner of Sweetzer and Fountain, just below the second-floor apartment where Lisa and I lived, he beeped the horn in the opening riff from the Spencer Davis Group's "Gimme Some Lovin'."

* * *

Cass enjoyed bringing people together. She introduced me to a galaxy of musicians—including Keith—at the Troubadour, the legendary club where on any given night you might see Janis Joplin leaning in to talk to Harry Dean Stanton at the bar and Clint Eastwood or Dennis Hopper in the VIP section of the big room watching Steve Martin, Warren Zevon, Linda Ronstadt, Bob Dylan, Carole King, James Taylor, Steppenwolf, David Steinberg, and other musicians and comedians (some famous, some knocking on the door) perform. I saw an entire audience turn on Jim Morrison when he shouted drunken obscenities during the debut performance of Blood, Sweat, and Tears in the big room. Saw rock legends and movie stars sniff cocaine from the mandarin-length fingernail on the pinky of an actor out of John Cassavetes's stable of regulars. I did the same, every time I saw the guy. For young Hollywood, the Troubadour was Rick's Café in *Casablanca*: everybody went there, and when they did, they became Bogart, Bergman, or Dooley Wilson singing "As Time Goes By."

I'm at the foot of the stairs now, in the entrance hall. I'm shivering and barefoot, wearing only my underwear and a T-shirt. My car's parked a few feet down the brick path leading to the house, but the keys are upstairs in my bag. The nearest neighbors are maybe a quarter-mile away, down a dark, unpaved road. It's dark downstairs, too; a small lamp is making a puddle of light on the living room floor but that's about it. I stand still, listening, not sure what it is I'm straining to hear. It occurs to me, absurdly in that moment, that I have been listening all my life: to the political discussions at my grandparents' dinner table, to my mother's arguments with any of her husbands, to Lisa's baby monosyllables as they evolved into language. Terrible images are churning through my mind: Julian Wasser's unsparing photos of the bloody carpet in front of a flag-draped sofa where Sharon Tate and her unborn child were butchered. The words "Healter Skelter"(a misspelling of the Beatles' song) scrawled in Rosemary and Leno LoBianco's blood on the door of their refrigerator. I turn and begin to feel my

way through the dining room where Cass and I ate takeout a few
hours earlier. Smeared plates and crumpled napkins are still on the
table and the oily scent of leftover pizza hangs in the air. I need to
get to the kitchen; there's a phone in there. There are knives.

"If I wasn't here with someone, we'd be in the upstairs bathroom
right now with the door locked and your panties down."

Warren Beatty's voice was cashmere soft. Cass had introduced
me to him as her "best friend" before she drifted to the other side of
the living room, where Jack Nicholson and Michelle Phillips sat
talking to Julie Christie. Christie was the "someone" Beatty brought
with him to Cass's party that night and she was his long-standing
girlfriend. They had recently costarred in *McCabe and Mrs. Miller.*
I don't remember what I said to Beatty—he was too impossibly
beautiful, too dangerous. He was like a leopard stretched out along
a low-lying tree limb, lazily ready to reach down for anything that
took his fancy. We soldiered on with listless party chat for a while,
then he grinned and excused himself. A few minutes later I saw him
amble out of the kitchen with a bottle of beer and head for a group
that included John Phillips and Roman Polanski.

Cass and I formed a close friendship. We'd drive to the beach
and she would urge me to sing along with her: "Jeepers Creepers."
"I'm Gonna Sit Right Down and Write Myself a Letter." She loved
the old stuff and singing with her was like having a choir in the
back seat. I introduced her to my mother, who was notoriously
cool with new people. Cass broke through the ice and within minutes they were laughing at some politician's gaffe they'd both seen
on TV. Sometimes Cass would put on a pair of oversized dark
glasses and pull down a straw gardening hat until it rode at eyebrow level, and we'd take Lisa and Owen to a kids' amusement
park in Hollywood. I brought Ed Ruscha up to Cass's house one
steamy August night and he and I made love in the shallow end of
her darkened pool. Cass liked Ed and she admired his work. On
her birthday one year, he gave her a drawing that spelled out her
name in colored dots. Sometimes she'd hear about a recording ses-

sion; we'd show up and scarf down cold fast-food burgers and smoke weed in the control booth. We'd go to movies and be waved in because the guy selling tickets recognized Mama Cass. She would hire a limo and invite Keith, if he was around, and me to concerts, where we hung out backstage and whoever was on the bill would pay reverential court. I enjoyed those evenings with Cass. I relished the preferential treatment and I liked being flirted with by rock musicians who sometimes recognized me from fashion photographs they'd seen. The thing was, nobody ever flirted seriously with Cass. She was always cast as the good buddy who could be counted on for a sympathetic listen, a place to crash, advice on how to jump-start a career. She told me she hated being called Mama Cass and we began to refer to each other by our given names: hers was Ellen Naomi. We talked about books and guys and her unrequited love for Denny Doherty, whose tenor voice had balanced Cass's soaring contralto on the Mamas and the Papas' albums. I didn't ask about Owen's father, not from lack of curiosity but because there always seems to be an implied distance between stars and their friends, no matter how close the relationship.

I pick up the receiver on the wall phone in the kitchen and puff out a held-in breath when the dial tone buzzes. I dial quickly. There's a bread knife in the sink; the serrated blade is clotted with dried tomato sauce. I pick it up by the handle.

"Yeah . . ." David's voice is full of sleep.

A whimper squeaks up out of my throat but I manage to whisper where I am. He tells me to unlock the front door, he's on the way.

David Pearl is an ex–bronco rider from Texas, working now as personal manager for Don Johnson (known to all of us as Donnie Wayne—his full name) and Davy Jones of the Monkees, the kitsch knockoff of the Beatles. I met David at Cass's house and he lives only a mile or so away, down on the Valley side of Mulholland Drive in a house he shares with Johnson and, sporadically, Keith Allison. It would have taken too long to stammer out directions to

a voice on the other end of a 911 call. David's tough and he's smart.
He can take hold of a bad situation without breaking a sweat.

I aim a quick glance at the kitchen ceiling. Is Cass dead in
the double king-size, her long hair wet with blood? How will it
affect my daughter and the rest of my family if I am killed?

I have to unlock the door. I put down the knife; I can't handle
a knife. I feel my way back to the entry hall and slide the latch on
the front door. I need something in my hand, something I can strike
out with if the guy in Cass's bedroom comes looking for me before
David gets here. There's a halved rock on the hall table, a fist-sized
chunk of amethyst with a legion of crystals inside. I scoop it up, heft
it, wonder if it will stop this son of a bitch if I smash it into his face.

"I'm going to be a baroness!"

Cass sounded like an excited kid. She was about to be married
and wanted to know if I would be her maid of honor. Her future
husband was a young American journalist she'd met in London:
Donald von Wiedenman. *Baron* Donald von Wiedenman. He came
to her hotel for an interview, Cass liked what she saw, and things
rocketed from there.

I met the baron when Cass invited me up to the house shortly
before the wedding, and I don't think I was the only one of her
friends who tried to convince Cass to wait before leaping into marriage. She wouldn't listen to anything that sounded like "Wait and
see how it goes."

So I stood next to her at the brief civil ceremony in her living
room. The only other people there were Cass's mother, Bess; Cass's
sister Leah; and von Wiedenman's parents. Cass wore a black
dress from Biba in London, a gift from the groom, who was Elvis-
resplendent in blinding white leather. The marriage lasted about
a year.

I watch from the narrow window next to the front door as David
Pearl gets out of his truck and heads toward the house. There's a
revolver tucked into the waistband of his jeans. He opens the

door and I step into a slant of moonlight. He mouths a single word—"Where?"—and places one finger across his lips. I point up. He takes the stairs as silently as fog and I cover my ears because I don't want to hear what might come next.

What comes next is a slur of words followed by an angry shout and the crump of a body hitting the floor. Then David's back. He's got all my stuff and now he shoves it at me and tells me to dress fast, he's taking me the hell out of here. Cass is okay, he says, pretty wasted. The guy up there with her is Pic Dawson, an ex-boyfriend who broke into the house through the French doors in the study. He cut his arm on the glass, thus all the blood.

David tells me he slugged Dawson because the schmuck kept insisting the person he pulled out of Cass's bed was some guy who tried to kick him in the nuts.

David doesn't speak again until the truck is halfway down the private road. Then he tells me Pic Dawson was one of the initial suspects in the Sharon Tate murders. The first homicide investigators to arrive at the house on Cielo Drive saw three letters written in blood on the front door and thought they spelled out "PIC." Dawson had a record as a drug dealer and he was known to have made the occasional visit to the Tate-Polanski home. The word on the door turned out to be "PIG" but a lot of people, including Cass, were questioned about the multiple homicides that summer.

I was cruising along Sunset headed for a visit with a friend in Malibu. The car radio was tuned to KRLA, and when the DJ announced the death of a major pop star in London, I wondered idly about which of a dozen likely candidates had overdosed. Then I heard the opening bars of "Dream a Little Dream of Me." I turned off the radio and drove on for two or three blocks before I pulled over and let the car idle. I didn't cry, didn't yell. I didn't do anything. My hands were still on the steering wheel; I was still mildly thirsty for a drink of water. Everything was exactly the same as it had been a few seconds ago. Only now, in the space of a breath,

Cass was gone. Her heart had given out after a sold-out concert at the Palladium. She was thirty-two years old.

The velvet rope set up outside the chapel at Hollywood Memorial Cemetery held back a mob of shouting fans and tourists. I was with one of Cass's friends, a tough agent who used his shoulders to push our way inside. We sat silently as Cass's mother, sister, and brother were ushered to a screened-off section reserved, according to Jewish tradition, for family members. Everyone seated on the benches turned their head to spot each new arrival: Jack Nicholson. Peter Lawford. Helen Reddy. Cher and Sonny Bono. The Bonos were seated in the front row and Sonny turned to wave, pointing emphatically to an empty space next to them. Carol Burnett found a place on the aisle of the row where we were seated. John Phillips and Michelle arrived together with Denny Doherty in tow. John's and Denny's eyelids looked as if they were badly sunburned. Michelle's eyes were masked by dark glasses. Flowers banked the walls of the chapel and plunged forward to surround Cass's closed casket. A rabbi appeared and the insect-buzz of whispers faded away. He began the eulogy by admitting he had never met Cass Elliot. His remarks referenced her great talent and outsized generosity. After the final prayer, the rabbi suggested we remain seated to allow people from the roped-off section outside the chapel to file past the coffin. Then any of us who wanted to move through to an enclosed area in back could do so without interruption.

There was no way to avoid the interruption. An elderly woman with pastel-tinted hair and a camera dangling from a strap around her neck spotted Carol Burnett. The woman halted midstep, turned, and in a vocal pattern reminiscent of shows like *Hee Haw*, spoke: "Oh, Carol honey, I am so *happy* to see you here today and I just want you to know I watch your show ever' single week." She paused and smiled archly, unveiling a full set of blue-white dentures. "Don't *you* die now!"

Ellen Naomi Cohen would have loved it.

CHAPTER 10

Blood

The diary was lying open on Lisa's desk. I rarely went into my daughter's room when she wasn't home; she was coming up on her teens now and she was understandably touchy about her privacy. But we had forged an agreement: if she was at school and I was cleaning the apartment, her room was part of the battle zone. She spent much of her time in her room now. We'd have dinner around six and then she'd go back to her own space. I understood the need to be alone, and to preserve her sense of privacy, I always told Lisa the night before I was going to clean so she'd have plenty of time to put away all the stuff that was lying around, particularly anything she didn't want me to see. The deal was I wouldn't snoop around in drawers and she wouldn't leave too much of a mess. So far, and in spite of the inevitable arguments about misplaced articles, we were both comfortable enough with the arrangement.

Sometimes, when I was doing the housework, I'd experience a small wave of amusement at the image of myself in a pair of old jeans and a T-shirt worn tissue-thin, hair pinned back from my bare face as I scrubbed the toilet and crawled under beds to eliminate dust bunnies and whatever else had accumulated there. *The hotshot model,* I'd think, *oh yeah*. Other times I allowed myself a little dip into self-pity: *I'm a working mother and I'm raising an ungrateful kid who acts like I'm the bad news in her life and I haven't even got a life. How am I supposed to have one? I'm too busy being an unpaid servant. And what am I going to do when I have to stop modeling? Get a job selling greeting cards at Hallmark?*

I didn't give in to that kind of emotional blubbering often. Feeling sorry for myself was too depressing. And it didn't have anything to do with the reality of my life: *I'm still doing well at work and I've got the social life I want and if I'm not in love with some perfect guy who loves me back, too bad. My daughter is happy and healthy and if I'm no longer her whole world, if all we seem to do now is argue about everything from staying on the phone too long to helping out around the house, I've got to re-member she's going through some pretty big changes. Anyway, she still loves and needs me even if she is a pain in the ass.*

I worked the vacuum cleaner around the plush bear rug that had been one of Lisa's baby gifts and tried not to look at the diary. *She forgot to put it away*, I thought, *she's always in such a hurry in the morning.* She'd brush her hair with one hand and button her jeans with the other. She'd paw through the scatter of maga-zines and papers on top of the desk while she worked her feet into the pair of clogs she left under it the night before when she did her homework and wrote in her diary. Making the diary entry was the last thing she did before she got in bed. Her father had given her the small leather book. It had a lock and Lisa had worn the tiny key around her neck for a day or so before she put it and the book away in some secret place in her room.

She'd never left the diary where I could see it before and I won-dered if she was becoming bored with the ritual of writing down her thoughts each day.

But something else was going on, too: the desktop had been cleared. No lamp or papers, not a book or magazine. Even the enam-eled mug from Mexico, the one we'd bought to hold Lisa's pens and pencils, was gone.

There was only the diary, as carefully centered as a floral arrangement at a formal dinner party. I turned off the vacuum and moved closer to the desk. A single word was scrawled in large block letters across two pages of the diary:

BITCH

I can't say I was a single parent. My ex-husband was there for Lisa and, to a lesser extent, for me. But I was the one who made the rules at home, the one who said, "Either you take a sweater with you or you're not going at all." Or, "If you don't pick up your room, I'll simply assume you no longer want that stuff on the floor and I'll throw it in the trash." And, "Will you *please* stop using up all my perfume for school." I got to play the heavy five days a week.

I got to be the good guy, too. When Lisa brought home a scrawny young cat a few months past the cute kitten stage and swore it had been tossed from a passing car into her arms, I argued weakly, knowing she wasn't quite telling the truth, knowing I was going to lose this one and never mind my allergies to all things feline.

I noticed the cat didn't have a tail, noticed its eyes were a luminous shade of green. It leaped onto the chair where I was sitting, pushed its head under my arm, and started the small engine of its purr. Its gray fur felt the way whipped cream feels in your mouth.

"I already gave him a name, Mom."

"Unh-huh . . ." I didn't want to hear it. Hearing the name would be one more yank on the rug sliding out from under my feet.

"Dexter Dupont Bing." Pause for effect. "He really likes you. Listen to him purr."

I looked at my daughter's pleading eyes and wondered how I was going to refuse her a pet. It didn't seem fair. So Dexter moved in, Lisa got an affectionate buddy who would listen to all her secrets and not give them away, and I learned not to touch my eyes after I petted him.

As Lisa approached fourteen, her features began to take on form and dimension. Her hair was thick and dark, her eyes were starred with a fringe of lashes, her mouth held a promise of fullness. People who didn't know Mack said she looked like me. I thought she looked a bit like both of us but only within the framework of her own singular beauty. And she was smart as hell. But she was still a kid and there were times when she did dumb things. I couldn't keep her locked up in the house, couldn't insist that she come home directly after school. Home in time for dinner was the rule unless she had permission for a sleepover at a girlfriend's house. One afternoon she and her best friend, Karen, decided to hitchhike (a practice strictly forbidden by both Mack and me) over the hill to the Valley. They were standing at the curb on the corner of Sunset and Laurel with their thumbs out when a black and white sheriff's cruiser headed in the opposite direction slowed, made a U-turn, and pulled up in front of them. Lisa recognized the red-haired man behind the wheel and panicked.

"We're not hitchhiking . . ." Her voice scaled up in shrill reply to an unasked query.

The officer leaned toward the two girls. He was unsmiling and his eyes were pinned on Lisa's face.

"Listen to me: I don't *ever* want to see you out here again. I patrol these streets all the time and if I see you just once more with your thumb out, I call your mother."

The sheriff's deputy, Jim, was someone I'd gone out with a few times. He never told me about the incident but Lisa did, while I was writing this book.

Lisa and my mother (whom she called Margay, an early mispronunciation of Grandma) were great friends. My mom didn't slip into the mantle of stereotypical doting grandparent; she was as coolly remote with Lisa as she had been with me but she provided the same element of slightly forbidden fun. And, just as I had, my daughter adored her. They had their secrets and private jokes but I didn't feel left out; there was still that unassailable bond of love and humor between my mother and me and I knew how good it was for Lisa to be half of a closed society. Hotten took on the grandmother role, although she was far more interested in Lisa's talent for performing than she was in making hot chocolate. When Lisa sang or danced for her, Hotten beamed, nodded her head, and delivered her highest praise: "That's right, dear." She pronounced it "deah" and I can hear it as I write the word.

Uncle Henry still made his trips from Oakland to L.A. but as time passed they became less frequent. He was aging at an alarming rate: his gray hair had thinned and gone white and the faint fragrances of cigar smoke and good whiskey I'd loved all my life had disappeared. On the rare days he didn't shave, the stubble on his chin looked like a dusting of granulated sugar. He was too small now for the vested suits (with dark ties) he wore at all times, and his hands, which had been so squarely shaped and strong, seemed like small bundles of birds' bones. Uncle Henry, whose biceps had felt like river-smoothed rocks under his long-sleeved shirts. Uncle Henry, who worked as a bouncer at a waterfront whorehouse in San Francisco until he'd saved up enough money to buy a pawnshop. Who never married and had been my babysitter when my grandparents and Hotten went out to their weekly movie, who drew anchor tattoos on my arm with his gold fountain pen and took me to meet his buddies at the pool hall. Henry was sixteen when he found my fifteen-year-old grandfather, Léon, sleeping on the beach after he jumped the ship he'd hired on to as cabin boy when he left Belgium to escape a life spent in the priesthood. Henry brought the starving boy home to my German-speaking great-grandmother, Mary, and she took him in. Three years later he was married to Mary's eldest daughter, Fanny, playing piano at night in the whorehouse where Henry worked, and running messages for Sherman Clay during the day.

My great-uncle Henry detested the infirmities of age but he didn't complain. His most deeply felt regrets, I think, were that the great physical strength he'd taken such quiet pride in was gone and that he could no longer smoke his beloved cigars. He was ninety-six when he died, sitting on a bench waiting for the bus that would have taken him to Reno for one of his keno weekends. When my mother called to tell me Uncle Henry was gone, I felt a punishing sense of loss followed by helpless rage when she told me that as he slumped on the bench (dying or perhaps already dead) his

pocket watch, the platinum watch whose case bore the faint indentations of both my mother's and my baby teeth, had been stolen,
along with its finely wrought chain. The theft of Uncle Henry's
watch, something that was as intrinsic a part of our family's history as the man himself, was a hard blow to the wound of grief. It
is still painful to think of someone I loved so much made victim to
a thief as he sat dying on a bus stop bench.

I wish Lisa had gotten to know Uncle Henry better. He was
the last man in our small family and I think she would have loved
his shy, taciturn ways as fiercely as I did.

I got a phone call from Mack a few months after Uncle Henry
died. He'd been thinking about it, he said, and had decided it was
a good idea for Lisa to go to school in England. She wanted to go,
he said; they'd talked about it and she was eager to leave.

"Why didn't you talk to me before you decided all this?" I
was working at keeping the anger out of my voice.

"I'm talking to you now."

"No. You're telling me now."

"Jesus, are you going to start in?"

To hell with locking up the anger.

"Start in? Let's see . . . how about you should have asked
what I thought about sending my fifteen-year-old daughter away
for a couple of years, told me something about the school, sent me
a brochure. Kept me in the fucking loop *before* you got Lisa all
hyped up about it."

"Look, I'm sorry if your feelings are hurt. It's a private school
in London with a great curriculum and all kinds of international
students. She'll be living with a family whose daughter is enrolled
there. They're English, good people. What I called to talk about is
tuition and expenses. You make pretty good money modeling—
how much are you willing to chip in?"

"Hey. Mack. You made this decision without any input from
me, you pick up the tab."

Having the last word in this initial skirmish means nothing.

I've already lost the war. There will be many conversations before she leaves but Lisa will be going away to school because Mack told her she could. I'll talk to her and find out if she wants to be away from home for such a long stretch but I can't let her think I disapprove. I remember how excited I was to go to boarding school, but I had weekends and holidays with my family. Lisa will be thousands of miles away, and I'll just have to tell myself this is a great chance for her, a great adventure, and make her believe I really feel that way. But I'm damned if I'll help pay for it.

So, at the beginning of fall in 1978, Lisa Bing went away to school in London. She'd turned fifteen that summer. The day before she left we went out with my mother and Hotten to pick up some last-minute stuff. To save time, my mom suggested that Lisa and she could get some things while I stayed with Hotten to buy other necessities. That night Lisa handed me a gift-wrapped package; it was a photograph of her in a tortoiseshell frame. The next day, when Mack came to drive her to the airport, I tried not to cry (somewhat unsuccessfully), hugged her hard, kissed her forehead, and gave silent thanks because she'd left behind enough old clothes to allow me to catch her scent after she left. Still, I knew having time to myself was something I needed.

It was strange not to have my daughter talking endlessly on the phone in her room, playing her music too loud, sitting on the edge of the tub to watch me put on my makeup, and arguing with me about whose turn it was to fold the laundry. I thought about the times she sprawled next to me on my bed to watch a movie and the fun we'd had exchanging comments and criticisms, thought about how Lisa would ask me for a back scratch, the same way I'd wheedled my mother into scratching mine. I remembered her first date for a school dance when she was thirteen, the new dress and how she'd turned around slowly and looked so earnestly into my face, searching for approval. She looked beautiful and vulnerable and nervous and I felt the same jolt of love I got when she was six years old and I watched her in her little rocking chair, smiling at something on television.

I'd inherited a fondness for my own company from my mother, who never really wanted to live with anyone but herself, but this was different; a place inside me felt as if it had been scraped raw. I'd wake up every morning, and for those first few seconds everything was the same as always and my first thoughts would revolve around Lisa and what she might like for dinner or whether or not I'd said she could go over to a friend's house. Then I'd remember about not having to think about meals and homework and silly arguments about things that didn't matter, reality would hit me like a fist slamming into my chest, and I could feel a storm of tears building behind my eyes. I missed my wonderful, maddening Lisa.

CHAPTER 11

Zero at the Bone

The July 6, 1981, cover of *Time* magazine was a photograph of a martini glass against a stark black background. The glass was filled, not with clear liquid but with a white powder. A green olive was in the glass along with a short red straw. The legend beneath the picture read "HIGH ON COCAINE: A Drug with Status—and Menace." In his cover story, Michael Demarest described cocaine as the "All-American drug" and as "the caviar of drugs . . . at seventy times the cost of beluga." He wrote about head shops that sell tiny gold or silver spoons on matching chains and one-gram bottles of coke left as tips on tables in Aspen during the season. He told of cocaine used as barter for dental work, accountants' fees, even alimony. And he talked price: $60,000 for a kilo of 90 percent pure cocaine. A kilo weighs out at approximately two and one-fifth pounds, which breaks down to about 35.2736 ounces.

I read the piece with great interest because in 1981 I was in my third year of living in the Hollywood Hills with a successful midrange cocaine dealer. Nick Barbosa bought in bulk, twenty or thirty kilos at a time for $25,000 or $30,000 per kilo (if times were lean), which he split up, repackaged, and sold to the handful of dealers he worked with on an exclusive basis. He maintained a small place in the San Fernando Valley where he did most of his work, but he always pulled out a kilo or two to bring back to the Hollywood house, where he divided it into full-, half-, and quarter-ounce portions. These were reserved for private clients, people who were pretty much at the top of their respective games in the motion picture industry: actors, writers, agents, directors, and producers who preferred to buy their cocaine directly—and discreetly—from Nick, paying from $2,000 to $2,700 per ounce, depending on availability and quality. It wasn't unusual for some heavy hitter to come up to the house and spend the evening with Nick in the back bedroom he used as an office. They'd smoke some of his weed, always primo, and Nick would "customize" the buyer's newly purchased product, passing the solid cocaine chunks through a stainless steel strainer until they reached a powdery consistency. Then he'd extract small amounts and mix them with a cutting agent, usually a powdered baby laxative that was packaged in small blocks. This would be blended back in and the process repeated, with the buyer "testing" the result until any rough edges were smoothed out. The procedure often took hours. One evening a writer/director with a talent for persuading A-list stars to appear in his low-budget features got so coked up he was unable to drive home. I called a cab and he sat shivering in the living room, his jaw muscles clenching in rhythmic spasms, until it arrived. Then he stammered apologies all the way out the door and through the courtyard, seemingly unconcerned that he'd done up all the cocaine he bought that night.

Sometimes a personal assistant or trusted secretary would call, asking if they could come to the house and collect for their employer. Nick called these sales "quickies" and he preferred them to the time-consuming sessions spent blending some shot-caller's Peruvian flake. The quickie trade had its drawbacks, too: a harried assistant might call at an inconvenient time with a plea for help because her boss's client couldn't meet the deadline on his rewrite of a big-budget feature without an eight ball of pure.

I didn't like the idea of strangers coming to the house to buy Nick's product. There was no way to know if—or when—some assistant might decide to boast about going to a big dealer's place to score. When I tried to discuss it with Nick, he shrugged and grinned.

"Hey, beautiful, don't worry so much. Everything's under control."

Those days in the drug trade seem rather quaint now: men and women with the faux-hip paraphernalia that announced an allegiance to all things trendy—mirrors with the word "Coke" spelled out in the original cursive lettering, for snorting up lines. Two-and-a-half-inch-long silver straws. T-shirts with wink-nudge slogans: THINGS GO BETTER WITH COKE. People offered "toots" at parties as casually as they might hold out a pack of Marlboros. Nick didn't do business with these social users; he left that to the dealers he sold to. The coke crowd seemed to be everywhere: trawling for luxury items along Rodeo Drive and doing up a little blow in the dressing room, sidling in and out of theater restrooms for a quick snort in one of the stalls, at the supermarket buying bottles of the expensive brandy kept behind locked glass doors along with the single-malt Scotch and eighteen-year-old bourbon. That things went better with coke might not have been an unreasonable assumption if the gold razor blades dangling from chains around their necks were any indication.

I had met Nick Barbosa at Judy Carne's house and was drawn to him immediately. He was like the devastating but troubled older man in a romantic novel. At a time when the fashion for men's hair dictated long and unruly, Nick's was neatly cut, brushed back, and graying at the temples. He looked like a retired prizefighter who hadn't taken hits to the face, hadn't gone to fat. He dressed conservatively; no faded jeans or T-shirts, no Frye boots. A jailhouse tattoo between the knuckles and first joints on the fingers of his right hand spelled out "LOVE." Later, I'd see the others: dive-bombing bluebirds on his upper chest, a dagger inked to look as though it was piercing the skin above his heart, a rippling American flag on one shoulder, the name "Theresa" in fancy script on the other. His only jewelry was a watch. At a time when muscle cars were a mark of status, he drove a dark blue VW Rabbit. He spoke in the deep metallic rasp of a native New Yorker from a tough neighborhood (when *The Sopranos* began its run on HBO it was Nick Barbosa's voice I heard every time Tony Soprano spoke) and he used it to good effect: if he wanted to make a point, that voice did the work without any heavy lifting.

I called Judy about a month after Lisa left for London and asked about Nick. Was he as nice a guy as he seemed? Was he with someone? Judy laughed softly and said she'd give him my number so I could find out for myself. He called within the week and asked to take me to dinner. I suggested Chasen's, an old Hollywood restaurant as well known for its no-nonsense food as its celebrity clientele, for our first date. The front booths were always reserved for high-profile names, so I didn't expect to be seated there, but the captain must have noticed the heads turning as we walked past tables, because he seated us in a choice spot. And when Nick slipped a folded bill into his hand, he flicked a glance at it, his eyes widened, and he managed a small bow before he walked back to his station.

After we ordered our food, Nick sat back and looked at me. "Listen, we don't need to waste time with small talk, right? You met me at a customer's house; you know what I do. Now tell me what else you want to know. Talk to me." His eyes, the color of dark ale held against the light, were serious.

I needed a few seconds to think, so I took a cigarette from my bag and Nick held out a gold lighter. No corny gestures or flirtatious eye contact; he simply touched the flame to the tip of my cigarette and waited for me to speak.

"Tell me what you were like as a kid."

He laughed out loud. Heads turned again, movie people looking with genuine interest at someone more exotic than themselves.

"A kid, huh? Okay, I did a lotta little things that weren't so nice, but seein' you asked: By the time I was seven, eight years old I was stealin' change off the countertops at every store in Ozone Park, Queens. I was snatchin' ladies' pocketbooks off their arms and in the summer I'd go robbin' wallets on the beach. Take a towel, spot some guy's wallet layin' there, and when he ain't lookin',

My grandfather Léon M. Lang ("Pampy"). (Photo: Léon M. Lang)

My mother, Estelle Lang, at seventeen. The Belle of Oakland, and she knows it. (Photo: Léon M. Lang)

The Belle as the life of some party
Minneapolis in the '40s. (Photo: Léon M. L

My mother a few
years later at the beach.
(Photo: Léon M. Lang)

The "Baby" at three years old, on my tricycle in Piedmont. Several family members were off-camera and at the ready in case I plunged to the pavement. (Photo: Léon M. Lang)

3 years 11 mos.

..., the little reader, in front of our house: ...oks over dolls, always. (Photo: Léon M. Lang)

Posing against my will in the backyard while wearing a costume I loathed. The sullen look on my face says it all. (Photo: Léon M. Lang)

A Gernreich strapless slick of silk jersey with big '60s earrings and even bigger '60s makeup (Photo: Dennis Hopper)

Gernreich knit with matching mid-thigh stockings, very sexy. When I moved, there was a
sh of upper leg. (Photo: Dennis Hopper)

Rudi and me. I'm wearing one of the bird outfits with a headdress. This one is a pheasant.
(Photo: Dennis Hopper)

m proud as a peahen in her mate's plumage. (Photo: Dennis Hopper)

Matching shirt and bra by Gernreich. The vaguely sluttish expression is courtesy of t
model/author. (Photo: Dennis Hopper)

udi fiddling with chairs, while I worry if my hair looks all right. (Photo: Dennis Hopper)

This formal dress was in luscious shades of pink and amber. The silk taffeta made a gr[e]
swishing sound when I moved. (Photo: Dennis Hopper)

Gernreich giraffe with very long arms. Even the underwear was giraffe-print.
(oto: Dennis Hopper)

Another Gernreich animal print: dalmatian this time. (Photo: Dennis Hopper)

...is wonderful black-and-white georgette dress reminded me of serpent scales. Rudi was a ...ster at praising a woman's body. (Photo: Dennis Hopper)

Me, lying on a stone bench in a park in West Hollywood in the mid–1970s. (Photo: Sam Sh

The women of my life:
Lisa Bing, Estelle Lang,
and Ethel ("Hotten")
Morris, during the late '80s.
(author's photo)

Hotten with parasol. She was
in her nineties when this was
taken. (Photo: Lisa Bing)

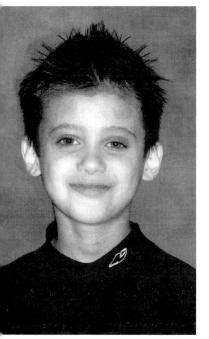

My grandson, Dominic
LoRusso, at nine years old.
(author's photo)

Me and Bobbie in the backyard. (Photo: Mark Pickell)

drop the towel over the wallet, pick the whole thing up together, and keep movin'." He smiled, deepening the dimples on either cheek. "I was always gettin' smacked as a kid. My mother would give me a beatin'—sit on me and smack me. Then, by the time I was nine or ten, I'd sneak outta the house and stay out late with my friends. I didn't have no latchkey, see, so when I'd get back, I'd holler up to the front window—'Ma!'—and she'd lean out and say, 'Sfatcheem!' which is like a little Italian curse, nothin' bad."

"Where was your father?"

"Yeah, well, he spent a lotta time at this little social club in the neighborhood. They'd play cards, guinea ball, stuff like that. A few connected guys went there: the Eboli brothers—Patsy, Frankie, and Lulu. Vito Genovese was there almost every day. He came to our house, too. I'd see him sittin' with my father in front of the big radio in our living room, the two of 'em with their heads together, talkin' soft with the radio on loud. It was a tough neighborhood, Ozone Park. Mostly Italians from the old country, like my parents—old Italian heads, old-fashioned ways of thinking. They'd say somebody was a 'Jew bastard' or a 'nigger fuck' and not think nothin' about it." Nick repeats these words without embarrassment or prejudice. They were simply phrases he heard growing up, and while it was clear he did not approve of them, he wasn't making apologies either, and I liked that about him. He wasn't trying to impress with some kind of hastily pulled-together correctitude.

The waiter wheeled a cart to our table and performed the small ritual of making a Caesar salad. Nick and I watched silently, and when the salad was equally divided onto chilled plates and set down in front of us, I looked over at Nick again.

"More."

"What 'more'? What you wanna hear about? How I started in fightin' when I was eleven or twelve? Lots of times I'd be fightin' for people who was getting picked on. There was this one Polish kid, a redhead, we had about three fights. *He* was tough. But I never got beat up. I was lucky."

No, I thought, *not lucky. He was tough and you were tougher.*

Years later, when I spoke to him about this chapter, Nick told me what he was thinking that night over dinner at Chasen's: *What the hell am I gonna tell this lady ain't gonna make her see me like an animal? She's got class, she don't need to hear about all the bullshit I had goin' on at school, all them girls I disrespected. She don't need to know how me and Sonny Florio was hitchin' rides on freights until he fell off and how I ran and the cops yelled, 'Come back—your friend's dyin' here!' so I go back and Sonny's only burned a little, he's fine, but I get arrested and sent to Lincoln Hall Reformatory because I'm only thirteen. I guess I could say I was pretty good in there, did good in sports, and that would be true. But hell, I ran away after a year and got caught and they give me more time. That's when I started workin' in the chapel, kinda like an altar boy, but how am I gonna tell her about the priest—well, not a priest, more like a brother—who used to give me blow jobs? He kept comin' on and that was fine with me. I never thought nothin' about blow jobs. The best one I ever got was in the pen from a guy who took his false teeth out. And I can't tell her about the times when I was goin' out with Theresa before we got married and I'd need money for the show or a dance and I'd take a little walk through the park and guys would pay twenty bucks to give me a fast blow job because I was a good-lookin' kid. I was never rough on gay people, though. I hustled 'em, but I never hurt 'em."*

I don't know how I might have reacted if Nick Barbosa had told me those things over dinner that first evening. I might have been shocked but they probably wouldn't have made much difference. I liked Nick, liked the rough edges that reminded me of Barney, and I was as drawn to his otherness as the people around us who kept glancing at him over the rims of their wineglasses. Soon we were seeing each other nearly every night and within three months he and I moved into a three-story duplex with an extravagant view of the city. By then I'd heard all about the safecracking and the stints at Elmira Reformatory ("Reformatory, *ugatz.* That joint was like Sing Sing"). He told me about the job he got at eigh-teen, working as a collector for one of his father's friends, a loan shark. The job didn't last long; Nick didn't like hurting people so he turned to safecracking. When I asked about guns, he said he "never worked armed," that carrying a gun was "too good a way to get killed." He meant it, too. There was never a weapon in the house in the Hollywood Hills.

"You know, you don't have to work no more."

Nick's voice was soft, almost apologetic, as he spoke those words. I was touched by his earnest concern but I'd decided to quit modeling before we moved in together. Rudi and I had spoken about it a few times: getting out at the top of your game. On the oc-casion of his fiftieth birthday, he was convinced he had entered the category of old age. He'd been labeled an enfant terrible who kicked down the doors and changed everything about fashion and now that was over, he said, because he'd turned fifty. I thought that was silly and told him his talent was as fresh, his ideas as out-rageously young, as ever. But still, something struck home: I rec-ognized how important it was for a model, whose main asset is her dewy insouciance, to step off the runway and away from the cam-era before others began to wonder why she was still plugging away after ten or fifteen or however many years. When I told Rudi I was done modeling he said he was sorry because he felt it was far too soon for me to give it up. But, he said, he understood: I'd wisely bought into the foolproof theory of quitting while ahead.

Without the daily activities of motherhood, and with the freedom of being jobless without having to quickly figure out my next career move, I was able to relax, to sleep later in the mornings, to see more of my mother and Hotten in the afternoons. I intro-duced Nick into the mix over dinner at Musso and Frank. I'd told my mom about him, glossing over his real line of work by com-paring him to her second husband. He was a "businessman." *Like Barney, Mom. You remember.* Of course she remembered and there wasn't much she could say about it. Hotten liked Nick for the same reasons she'd liked Barney: he was attentive and charming, he behaved like a gentleman, and he was as loving and generous toward me as Barney had been with my mother. Hotten didn't care what a man did for a living as long as he didn't drink or gamble to excess and as long as he was good to my mother and me. The same rule applied now, to Nick Barbosa. I kept it simple for myself and employed the old "I won't think about the dealing part now, I'll think about it tomorrow" gambit.

Tomorrow seemed a long way off.

Hotten was wrong about the gambling. Nick liked to play the horses and he bet big. He didn't go to the track often but his younger brother Johnny, who worked for him, came to the house every morning with the racing form. Johnny was a less handsome version of Nick and he was a *shtarker*—Yiddish slang for a big man whose physicality could threaten. He seemed to idolize his older brother, although he had a sense of play that allowed room for teasing. I liked Johnny and was always pleased to be hugged gently and respectfully by him. After the usual exchange of embraces and kisses between the brothers, they got down to business.

Nick studied the racing form and marked down his choices and the amounts he wanted to bet. Then he'd hand it back to Johnny along with an envelope stuffed with cash. For bets on football games and races at tracks in other states, there was a bookmaker who was contacted by pay telephone.

If I asked Nick how he'd done on any given day, the answer went one of two ways:

"Won a few."

"Lost a few."

Nick never volunteered an amount and I never had the nerve to ask, but I had a pretty good idea the figure was in the thousands. His mood didn't change; neither did the expression on his face. The only way I could tell he'd had a big win was when he'd press a fat roll of bills into my hand and tell me to buy myself something nice.

One afternoon, after complaining about the T-shirts I wore to bed, he went to Neiman Marcus and bought a dozen sets of

lace-edged silk underwear from Paris and at least that many night-
gowns and negligees in different colors. In a gesture reminiscent of
Gatsby's romantic toss of colored shirts for Daisy Buchanan, Nick
covered the bed with a frosting of pastel lingerie. I still have
some of the stuff, but I've gone back to the T-shirts for sleeping.
There were other gifts, too: jewelry, perfume, a new black BMW
he took in trade. But as a rule, Nick simply peeled off a couple
inches of twenty-dollar bills from what he called his "working
money," placed the stack in my hand, and told me to buy myself
something nice.

I began to learn a new vocabulary: "shy"—for "shylock"—a
loan shark; "vig"—for "vigorish"—the weekly interest, always ex-
orbitant, tacked on to the original loan; "on the arm," credit extended to a dealer for the large amount of cocaine ("product") he
ordered from a distributor, who got it straight from the "kitchen,"
the place where the coca leaves are boiled down to a paste and
molded into solid form. It was a matter of honor (and good business) that the debt be settled within twenty-four hours. Nick spoke
a Neapolitan dialect and I figured out what some of the words
meant by their placement in speech. "*Stugatz*" seemed to be a riff
on "balls"; "ugatz" meant "my prick" and was used in a variety
of ways, all of them negative. "St'a t'a zite" (*stai zitto*) meant "shut
up." "Do the job" was a way of saying "kill." I learned that "connected" meant mob affiliated and that "mushad" (*muciata*) or
"*mush'a-mush'*" translated into a feeling of slight depression. "*Stunad*" meant stupid, as in "He's an okay guy but a little *stunad*."
And, finally, "*mamaluke*": an oaf. Nick gave me his definition of
responsibility, too:

"You gotta be responsible. You gotta be moral. If you step in
it and take a bust, that's your responsibility. But you don't squeal.
Never. Somebody gets caught, it's like, 'What, you gonna squeal on
me? You got unlucky. Take what you got coming, that's all.' Because you gotta have honor. That's your *word*—you don't ever
break your word. And unless somebody comes at you, you don't
hurt nobody."

Everything he said rang true. And it reinforced my rationalizations about living with a criminal.

Shortly after Nick and I moved in together, I had one of the migraines that hit me five or six times a year since I'd reached adolescence. I had only enough pain medication, prescribed by my doctor in New York, to last through one attack and I used it when the aura—the visual hallucination of flashing lights—began. Nick had never seen anyone go through a headache that was like a thorn pressing behind one eye and he felt helpless: beyond drawing the blinds, shutting off the phone in the bedroom, and not smoking anywhere near me (the smell of smoke—any smell—intensified the nausea), there was nothing he could do. The next day he asked why I didn't have more medication on hand and I explained: the only thing that really worked was an opium derivative I'd learned to inject in one thigh when I was married and living in New York, but it was a triplicate prescription, difficult to get. Despite Nick's trust in me, he listened carefully and watched me closely as I spoke to see if I was telling the truth or just wanted to get high.

The man who came to the house the following day was about forty. He was skeletally thin and his face was pitted with scars left by what must have been a bad case of acne. His eyes didn't connect with anything directly; he seemed to be observing something terrible in the distance. When Nick introduced us he bowed slightly and shook my hand as if it were made of a rare, friable material.

"Renzo here is gonna take you to get that medicine you need."

The man, Renzo, nodded gravely. "We're drivin' into Beverly Hills. You ready to go?"

Thirty minutes later we were seated in the oak-paneled office of a well-known internist. The doctor was immaculately turned out and nervously eager to please. When he began to ask the stock questions about migraine symptoms, Renzo cut him off.

"Hey! This is a classy dame. She don't need no fuckin' headaches. Now stop your bullshit and give her the medicine she's askin' for."

I went home with ten single-dose ampules of the drug I'd

requested (three ampules was the standard prescription from my New York doctor) and a strand of plastic-wrapped disposable syringes. I never saw Renzo (or that frightened Beverly Hills doctor) again.

There were postcards and letters from Lisa every week or so. She liked her school and was enjoying her time in London. There were weekend bicycling tours and trips to museums and a boy she liked. She wanted to know about Nick so we called her and I made introductions by phone. His way of making a living wasn't mentioned but they talked for a longer time than I expected. Then I took the receiver again.

"Mom, he seems like a pretty good guy. And it sounds like he's crazy about you."

"I guess. I really miss you, honey."

"Me too. Are you happy, Mom?"

"Sure I am. Everything's fine here. Listen, I love you."

"Love you, too. 'Bye."

My daughter was so eager for my happiness. I felt a sharp thrust of guilt; I was focused on Nick's honesty and innate fairness of character and I kept skirting the issue of how he made his living. He was a coke dealer, and if I wasn't complicit in his work, I was delighted to spend the money he made at it. I pushed those thoughts aside, as I would many times during the years I lived with him.

Nick had a grown son, Anthony, who lived in L.A. and was in the wholesale jewelry business. Anthony had the same striking good looks as his father but he was without the streak of ruthlessness that Nick kept under control most of the time. His son was soft-spoken and polite and Nick adored him. They often discussed Anthony's mother, Theresa, who was still married to Nick, although they saw each other only on those rare occasions when he went to New York. Nick loved and respected Theresa, but the marriage represented everything he was committed to keeping out of his life: the Catholic Church, the old neighborhood, and, most urgently, the bindings of formal vows. Anthony understood this and he seemed to be genuinely fond of me. I provided stability without stress and was clearly more interested in his father than I was in the cocaine he sold. Aside from his business dealings, Nick and I maintained a fairly normal existence: early dinners, favorite TV shows, the occasional night out. I knew he had a temper but I never saw it until I overheard a frightening dialogue one evening when I was in my dressing room getting ready for a dinner with friends. One of Nick's associates was in the office with him, door closed. There was the soft buzz of conversation, then the pitch of Nick's voice got louder.

"Hey! Get smart with me and you're lookin' for trouble. *Don't.* Believe me, it ain't worth it."

I didn't hear him speak again but the office door opened a short time later and I heard Nick's footsteps behind whoever it was he was showing out of the house. I finished dressing and didn't mention what I'd overheard. But I realized how scary Nick could be if he thought he was being crossed, and it gave me the same dark pleasure I'd felt years earlier when my grandfather slapped my mother's hand away from the car radio during the drive back to my school.

I had lunch dates with Rudi every few months. He seemed quieter each time, happy to see me but less inclined to talk about new ideas for designs and more ready to tell me what was going on in his private life. He was thinking about a line of gourmet soups with his name on the label. He and Oreste had gotten a couple of dogs. The only time I saw him display even mild excitement was when I showed him a beautifully drawn tattoo of an eagle just above the tricep of my left arm.

"Darling, it's wonderful! If you'd had that done when you were with me I'd have designed dresses with cutouts to show it off."

But Rudi's decline moved on inexorably. He closed his studio and went to work on the line of custom soups. When I saw a newspaper photograph of him wearing a chef's toque and stirring a cauldron, it made me think of a captured soldier with his hands held over his head in the classic gesture of surrender.

We had one or two more lunches together but there seemed to be less and less to talk about. The gourmet soup line wasn't successful, and while Rudi tried to behave as if he wanted only to retire from the spotlight, it was clear he felt passed over and irrelevant. He died in 1985 shortly after designing one of first thongs. He called it the pubikini and it was his final hurrah.

Every once in a while, some kind of new equipment would arrive at our place: television sets, stereos, speakers. Everything was always delivered by a young guy named Eddie who played up a slight resemblance to Al Pacino in *The Godfather* and had a distinct New York accent and a penchant for flashy cars. Eddie was likeable and easygoing, and one day when he dropped off a video player, I asked where all that stuff came from. He looked slightly surprised. Then he shrugged and grinned.

"Fell off a truck."

"Off a truck without breaking and you were there to pick it up? How is that possible?"

He looked at me oddly for a moment.

"Aw, you know what they say—right time, right place, huh?"

"What?"

"Hey . . ." Eddie's smile was gone and suddenly he didn't look so easygoing.

The nickel dropped and with it, the last of my naïveté—or, more likely, the final shreds of denial about any of the other unlawful activities I was benefiting from.

One weekend we flew to Vegas for what Nick said was a sit-down with a couple of people. There was a car and driver waiting at the airport, a top-floor suite at one of the hotels on the Strip. I don't remember which of the big places it was, but Cher was headlining in the main room. I thought about sending her a message and decided against it. Too complicated.

I was in the bedroom dressing for dinner when the phone rang. Nick picked up and, a few minutes later, opened the door to three men. They were all dressed casually but they might as well have been wearing dark suits and ties. I watched from the bedroom as each of them delivered the standard kiss and embrace, then Nick raised the TV volume and chairs were placed in a tight semicircle in front of the screen.

I closed the bedroom door.

Two hours later, after a room service meal we'd ordered up when the three men left our suite, Nick and I were downstairs in the hotel casino, a timeless, windowless space filled with the rise and fall of voices, the click and whir of gaming tables and slot machines.

"Here, sweetheart." Nick handed me a stack of twenties. "Have yourself a good time and don't worry about losin' it. Just come find me and I'll give you more. I'm gonna play awhile now."

He turned back to the craps table. I'd never played anything but bridge at school and a few hands of poker with friends in New York. I positioned myself out of Nick's eye line and watched him play. When I felt I had the basics of the game, I turned in the cash he'd given me for $2,500 in chips and found another table.

I placed my bets the way Nick did: chips on various combinations of numbers. If I won, I let it ride; sometimes I doubled up. I was completely clueless about what I was doing but I was caught up in the thrall of throwing winning combinations and hearing the cheers of people who were betting with me. I knew I was betting big and winning large amounts but it was the excitement that got to me, the rush that builds in the blood and chews away at reason.

I won $36,000 worth of chips over the course of a few hours and gave back nearly all of it the same night. I haven't gone to Las Vegas since. Money isn't money there; it's stacks of plastic discs. And gambling fever is far too contagious.

Nick and I were often invited to dinner parties in the Hollywood community. Cocaine was much in fashion in the eighties and it was considered a mark of cachet in some circles to include your dealer among the guests. Nick and I didn't attend many of these affairs because it seemed to us that the actors, the agents, and the young moguls were too much like naughty children, giggling nervously behind their hands at the sheer proximity to an actual criminal. If they imagined an aura of imminent danger and palpable threat around Nick, they were pretty sure it wasn't going to wash over them. What probably remained was the persistent notion that their existence was being tainted in some essential but entirely pleasurable way. Looking back at those years, it was very likely the same for me. I found it easy to take or leave the cocaine; the real high was being with an outlaw. It was like having a wolf as a pet, a fearsome creature that would allow me to rub his unprotected belly and scratch his ears as he lay on his back grunting with pleasure. But still, a wolf, ready to tear apart anything that threatened his (or my) well-being. It was a big part of my attraction to Nick and to hell with worrying about whether or not I was being tainted. When I think about it, maybe it was the wolf that should have worried.

The rare occasions when real players in the drug trade threw a party were quite different from the industry dinners, where hard feelings seethed beneath the breezy conversations. One memorable event was the wedding reception of one of Nick's friends, a guy responsible for much of the marijuana smuggled into Southern California. The ceremony was performed at a church in Malibu and there had been a brisk exchange of champagne toasts on the lawn for relatives and friends. Then the families were sent home and it was time for the real party to begin: a convoy of cars wound its way into the foothills above Malibu and to the groom's newly purchased home, a glass and steel conceit balanced on the lip of a promontory that overlooked the ocean. There was more champagne, Dom Perignon this time, in crystal flutes. Cases of vodka, single-malt Scotch, and Rémy Martin were stacked in cases behind a bar where guests helped themselves; no bartenders or caterers at this celebration. A conventional wedding cake was centered on the dining room table and a sideboard against one wall held platters of lobster salad and bowls of Iranian Gold caviar nestled in ice. Expertly rolled joints on silver trays were set out on every table in the living room.

People settled themselves on sofas and chairs and a short line formed at the door of one of the bedrooms, where the coke dealers were laying out generous samples of their product. I made myself comfortable in the alcove of a window seat. I'd been sitting there for ten minutes or so when a somberly dressed middle-aged man approached me.

"I just want you to know ain't nobody here deserves more respect than your friend, Nick." He paused and then spoke in whisper: "I'd kill for that guy, ba-boom."

There was nothing I could say to that. "Thank you" seemed highly inappropriate but I managed a weak smile and felt a surge of relief when he did an about-face and moved off.

A few minutes later a barrel-chested young guy wearing a vintage Hawaiian shirt sat down next to me. We chatted about the wedding and the view, and then, because it was that kind of gathering, I asked about his specialty in the trade.

"Me? I smuggle diamonds." He laughed softly.

And I laughed with him.

The reception lasted three or four hours. Nobody got drunk or greedy with the drugs. The stereo was kept at a reasonable volume. It was a civilized event but if a net had been dropped over the house in Malibu that evening, most of the Pacific coast would have gone dry the next day.

When I told Nick about the "I'd kill for your friend, Nick" man, he shook his head and his lips compressed into a narrow line.

"Some people like to talk big, make everything into Italian opera."

He lifted my hand and kissed it.

"That guy was out to impress you, makin' like the Big G . . ." Nick pronounced it with a hard G and mimicked the man: " 'I'd kill, ba-boom . . .' *Ugatz*. People who really do the job don't talk about it. I learned that when I was a kid back in Ozone Park."

Whenever friends came to the house in the Hollywood Hills, Nick would offer food, wine, coffee, and cocaine. Nobody ever took a pass on the coke. Nobody said no to a second, third, tenth offer. People who refused a cup of coffee because the caffeine kept them awake jumped on the free ride and snorted up line after line of cocaine. It annoyed me because I felt that whatever act someone was putting on in their life, it was easily seen past when they were around coke. Sometimes it got to me and I'd ask the person who was really going at it if they *ever* had enough. Nick was hurt when I did that; he viewed my outspoken annoyance as a lack of generosity and manners. Maybe he was right; it was his cocaine, not mine, but I figured if I said no to an offer of blow nearly as often as I accepted, then others might show some degree of restraint. It was as naïve as believing stereos fell off trucks.

When Larry DuBois moved into the other half of the duplex, it was inevitable that we'd meet in the shared courtyard. He introduced himself by his nickname, "Butch," and explained that it was after a great-grandfather who rode with Butch Cassidy's Hole-in-the-Wall Gang. Our new neighbor, Butch, was a tall, lanky guy in his late thirties, a nonpracticing Mormon from Salt Lake City who'd come to L.A. to work with Hugh Hefner at *Playboy* as a staff journalist after a similar stint at the Playboy mansion in Chicago.

I liked him immediately. He spoke quietly, had a sense of humor, and there was the spark of true intellect behind his eyes. I realized, in that initial conversation, how lonely I'd become. Not for company—I was happy with Nick and enjoyed being alone when he went out of town—but for conversation with someone (other than my mom) who kept up with what was going on in the real world. Nick wasn't much interested and I hadn't bothered with the newspapers for months. Most of my information came from the nightly news on NBC. I'd become a fixture in Nick's life and while I was enjoying the perks mightily, I'd locked myself away behind them.

I invited Butch over to meet Nick a few days later. As usual, cocaine was offered up along with the coffee. Our new neighbor did up two lines, commented on the fine quality, and politely refused more. I hadn't observed that kind of restraint in a long time.

Larry DuBois steered me back into what was going on outside the cloistered existence I'd chosen to share with Nick. He began leaving copies of the *Los Angeles Times* outside the front door, sometimes with a note suggesting one article or another. I'd read the paper front to back, and when Butch was around, we would talk about the issues. We exulted when Ronald Reagan appointed Sandra Day O'Connor as the first woman justice to the Supreme Court and were outraged when he cut funding for school lunches and allowed ketchup to be counted as a vegetable. We worried about friends in both of our lives who had been diagnosed with a virus that seemed to have appeared out of nowhere with a single purpose: to attack the human immune system.

Nick liked our neighbor and was happy—and probably relieved—that I'd found in Butch someone who was less intrigued by cocaine than he was involved with discussing current events, books, and movies with me. Larry DuBois was going out with a beautiful young woman but he stepped into the spot of a close friend for me.

David Merrick called whenever he came to L.A. and Nick and I would have dinner with him. The two men formed a friendship based predominantly on their mutual affection for me, with a few lines of cocaine thrown in as bonding material. I always enjoyed listening to the interplay between the street-savvy ex-convict and the Broadway producer (and attorney; he'd earned a law degree before taking on show business in order to construct the language of his unbreakable contracts) whose reputation was that of a cold-hearted son of a bitch. Despite the differences in their backgrounds and educations, Nick and David connected fully with one another. But if I'd had to bet on which of the two men was more ruthless, my money would have been on Merrick.

David met Jerry Wexler, cofounder of Atlantic Records, at our place. I'd known Jerry since the late sixties, and his outgoing personality and raked-gravel voice provided an interesting contrast to Merrick's restrained approach. It was fascinating to watch these two heavyweight-division titans engage one another. Jerry's speech pattern was New York street with an overlay of the Delta and a trickle of Yiddish slang. David spoke like a lawyer with a sub-rosa sense of humor. Their combined intelligence quotient had to have been stratospheric and their mutual respect was evident from the first handshake.

Nick was out of town during one of David's trips to L.A. and I invited him to the house for a casual dinner. When he arrived I told him we'd be joined by my neighbor, Larry. David's back stiffened immediately.

"Who is this fellow? What does he do?"

"He's a journalist. But you have my word: Larry DuBois doesn't want a thing from you. He's not that kind of writer."

"We'll see. But be assured, I'm not going to talk to him."

David hated the press and valued his privacy so zealously that he once told me he wanted his obituary in the *New York Times* to avoid any biographical data or listings of his theatrical accomplishments. He said he wanted only a simple statement of fact: "David Merrick died last night. So what?"

I called a gourmet deli and ordered up a spread. When Butch arrived, David extended his hand for a listless shake and then sat mutely in the big armchair in the corner, looking like a disapproving cleric in his black suit and tie. Butch ignored the chill, plopped down next to me on the sofa, and began to talk about something that had happened in Washington that week. I'd read the newspaper reports, was able to add a few comments, and felt a surge of accomplishment, like a student who has gotten a high mark in a difficult subject, at my reentrance into the real world. David listened closely, nodding his head from time to time. Then he leaned forward and, for the first time, looked directly at Butch.

"Where did you go to school, Larry?"

Butch told Merrick about graduating from Stanford and being accepted to the Woodrow Wilson School of Public and International Affairs at Princeton. David gave a curt nod and asked what Butch considered his most intriguing piece of journalism. Butch described a two-part series he'd authored with another writer for *Playboy*. The title was "The Puppet and the Puppet Master"; the subject was the relationship between Howard Hughes, the Nixon administration, and the CIA. (It wasn't mentioned that evening but I learned later that the piece had been given a Sigma Delta Chi award from the Society of Professional Journalists).

Now Butch and David were speaking only to each other and David was saying how terrible it was to have had to announce the death of director Gower Champion to the first-night audience of *Forty-second Street*. On an earlier visit, David had told Nick and me he was planning to use his own money to finance the show, something he hadn't done with any of his previous productions; when the show was a hit, David wondered aloud if it wouldn't be better to teach his young daughter how to survive in an increasingly hostile world rather than to leave her a fortune.

I made coffee, opened another bottle of wine, and listened to the back-and-forth for an hour or so. Then I excused myself and headed for bed. I could still hear the hum of conversation punctuated by bursts of laughter when I turned out my reading light.

"You didn't tell me you were a writer, miss." "Miss" was a nickname Butch had come up with for me.

"Maybe because I'm not one."

"Not according to David Merrick. He talked plenty about you as a writer."

"Oh, please. I don't want to hear this bullshit. It's bad enough he's got some kind of fucking thing about it. I don't need you hocking me, too."

I figured that was the end of it. Butch had other plans: he waited a month or so and then handed me the manuscript of a book.

"Hey, miss, do me a favor and read this. A woman I know

wrote it and I can't be objective enough to give her an unbiased response."

I was flattered to be asked to give an opinion about an unpub-
lished manuscript so I sat down and began to read. I knew what I
thought about the writing by the middle of the first paragraph but
I staggered through to the end of the book because I'd promised
Butch.

"So what do you think?" The expression on his face wasn't
giving away a thing.

"I think my marketing list reads better than this."

"Really?" He mentioned a major publishing house. "They're
bringing it out next year."

And he let me sit with that information.

Lisa came home from England a beautiful young woman—slender,
delicate, but with an undeniable sensuality and an individual style.
She was heading into in her late teens now and being away from
home for so long had allowed her to develop an independent streak.
She wanted to spend time with me, with my mother and Hotten,
with the friends she hadn't seen for so long, but she wanted to live
apart from all of us. I wanted her with me, wanted to tell her how
impressed I was that she hadn't come back to the States with the
phony international accent of broadened A's and clipped consonants
so many short-term expatriates acquire. I wanted to nuzzle my face
at the back of her neck the way I'd done when she was little. But
she'd grown up while she was in England and I realized I'd have to
disengage from my daughter as the child I remembered. This was
another person entirely, one I'd have to reintroduce myself to and
accept. I didn't have to like it; I just had to do it.

She liked Nick. His business as a coke dealer wasn't mentioned and she didn't ask how he made his money, but my mother
told me Lisa and she talked about it. Lisa wondered if Nick was
some kind of racketeer and my mom (who believed he was because I'd compared him to Barney) advised her to leave it alone; he
was good to me and I was happy, so why ask questions? I didn't

like mysterious gaps in the dynamics of family relationships—I'd
had enough of that as a kid—but this was necessary: if my daughter didn't know about Nick's unlawful activities, she couldn't be
tied to them. She was in and out of the house in the Hollywood
Hills but she elected to stay with a girlfriend she'd known before
she went to Europe. She wasn't ready for college yet, she said; she
was thinking about becoming an actress and, to that end, she got a
job waiting tables to pay for classes and to contribute her share of
the rent and expenses.

"Oh man, you should've seen her. She did a monologue from
Shaw's *Saint Joan* and just fucking—sorry—she just nailed it. When
she finished, Stella Adler turned to that whole audience of people
trying out for acceptance at her studio in New York and said,
'Ladies and gentlemen, *that* is an actress.' " Lisa's boyfriend, Rocky,
a young actor she'd met in class, was nearly stammering with excitement. "She's *in*. Adler's taking her as a student."

Lisa sat next to him on the sofa, her eyes riveted to a placement of small objects on the coffee table. She was embarrassed,
joyful, maybe even slightly confused by all this.

I'd seen Lisa perform at a theater in Hollywood. She played
the ghost of a young girl who died at Auschwitz, and when I
watched her onstage, I saw how she'd channeled a great sprawl of
disparate talents into acting and I was happy that Stella Adler, legendary teacher of James Dean and Marlon Brando, had recognized
it as well.

I looked at my daughter.

"So how do you feel about all this?" Lisa had barely gotten
home and now we were talking about another absence.

"I want to go, Mom. I really do. I can get a job waiting tables
in New York. "

"Okay, honey. But let's sleep on it and talk more tomorrow."

Nick had remained silent during the conversation. Now he
spoke up. He would pay for airline tickets and cover all of Lisa's expenses for at least a year in New York, more if she wanted to stay

on and continue her studies. And he offered a round-trip ticket for Rocky to go along and help Lisa get settled in before classes began.

After Lisa and Rocky left, I tried to build a rickety, not altogether sincere argument. Nick looked at me with cold eyes.

"Hey! Stop the bullshit. You know I make a lotta money so let me do something worthwhile here. Your daughter's a good girl, she deserves a break."

About three months after Lisa moved to New York, I went east for a short visit. I traveled by train because I wanted time to think, to make sure I'd be able to handle whatever feelings might come up when I saw her. And I wanted to be alone for those few days, comfortably isolated in a compartment with a number of books I'd been planning to read.

Lisa seemed happy and well settled. She liked her classes at Stella Adler's studio, she said, and was eager for me to meet her new boyfriend, another acting student. Nick had provided me with more than enough cash to take them out for meals at good restaurants and to leave Lisa with a few extra bucks before I left. I returned to the West Coast much relieved.

Six months later Lisa was back in L.A. and reluctant to talk about her studies with Stella Adler. But it was clear that any thoughts of a career in the theater were finished. The talent was there; the ambition had blazed itself out. Something else was going on, too: I felt a new and disturbing distance between my daughter and me but when I mentioned it to Nick, he shook his head.

"I don't see it, hon. I think she's just trying to adjust to being back here."

I accepted his appraisal because I wanted to. What I didn't want was to think my daughter liked me less than she did before she went to New York.

Lisa stayed around for a short time and then announced she was going to move to Colorado for a while. As far as I knew, she didn't know anyone in Colorado, but I didn't want to try to

exert my influence one way or another. Lisa needed time and distance to sort out her life, just as I had when I left L.A. for New
York to begin a career as a model. When I kissed her good-bye and
wished her luck, there was no push of relief in my voice. I liked it
better when my daughter was close by even if there seemed to be a
widening gulf between us.

I didn't have time to ponder what I'd done to alienate Lisa, or
if I'd done anything, because, suddenly, there was only Hotten
to think about. Hotten, who taught me how to read and then pa-
tiently fed me breakfast or lunch because I was too engrossed in a
book to feed myself, who held my hand to steer me across a street
even after I reached adulthood; Hotten, whose love for her family
was absolute and unwavering, was suddenly ill and in the hospital.
She was there for less than a week and then she was gone. My
mother and I stood by her bed and told her how much we loved
and needed her because we knew she'd stay if we asked, just as
she'd done with everything else we asked her for all our lives. This
time she couldn't.

My mother called to tell me Hotten had died during the night.
We mourned separately. I cried hard when I was alone and tried not
to when I had to tell Lisa that Hotten was gone. My mom said she
wept only once: when she went into the small apartment where
Hotten had lived for so many years, for the task of sorting out her
belongings. My mother told me the mundane stuff like dishes and
cooking equipment wasn't so tough, but clothes that still held the
memory of floral-scented cologne were very difficult. It was the
little things that brought on Mom's tears: photographs of the family, all neatly pasted into scrapbooks; the antique Chinese figurines Hotten collected; the green, star-shaped candle I gave her
one Christmas when I was a kid and that she never lit; the little tray
woven in the shape of a ladybug; her two-tiered sewing basket. I
still have the scrapbooks, the tray, the sewing basket, and the figurines, but somewhere between Hotten's apartment and mine, the
little star-shaped candle was lost.

Nick was wonderfully gentle and supportive, but he and I

were breaking up by mutual consent. With the aid of a backward glance, I think the adventure of living outside the law simply wore thin. He gave me enough cash to keep going for a while and I was happy to accept it. When a friend who knew I'd been living with a cocaine dealer suggested I try a meeting at a twelve-step program, I went with her and continued to attend meetings on my own. Within a few months I figured out that everything I heard in those rooms applied to me: I might not have been addicted to drugs but there are all kinds of addictions; mine was to the lifestyle the sale of drugs provided.

I'm not sure if it was the loss of my beloved Hotten or the end of my relationship with Nick, but I sensed a kind of tectonic shift within myself: for the second time I wanted, and knew I needed, to make some serious changes.

CHAPTER 12

Fuck You—*I'm* Your Future

Butch was still living in the other half of the duplex. His girlfriend, a flight attendant, was gone much of the time so he and I had continued our practice of going over the papers, and now that Nick was gone, we added watching the evening news reports together. We saw Ronald Reagan define the Soviet Union as "the focus of evil in the modern world" and read about the terrorist bombing of the U.S. embassy in Beirut that caused the death of sixty-three people. We were amused when "Just Say No" became the slogan for Nancy Reagan's program to combat drug use and surprised when Chicago drivers began paying $3,000 for cellular phones to use in their cars.

One evening, after the six thirty news, we drove down to Hollywood Boulevard for a fast meal at the counter at Musso and Frank. It had been a warm day so we decided to walk after we ate, and as we covered the blocks, I noticed little knots of teenagers standing around on corners and lounging on the sidewalk in front of shuttered shops. They were all wearing clothes that could have used a wash, and a few of both genders sported Mohawks dyed in throat-clenching colors. A boy with tattoos scrolling up his arms had a large safety pin jabbed through his upper lip with a slender chain connecting it to another pin stuck through his earlobe. One or two of the girls were holding on to frayed ropes tied around the necks of skinny dogs.

I asked Butch about these groups of wasted-looking kids.

"Most of them are runaways scrounging for change and living in squats."

I'd never heard the word used as a noun. "What are squats?"

"Abandoned houses, condemned buildings. Anywhere they can find a place to sleep for two or three nights. They probably tell themselves they're living the good life out from under their parents' fucked-up values."

I looked at a boy who couldn't have been much older than sixteen take a large gray rat out of the pocket of a ragged jacket. The rat allowed itself to be stroked for a minute, then it skittered up the boy's sleeve and perched on his shoulder, grooming its face and tissue-paper ears with its front paws. Its long, naked tail curled around the back of the boy's neck and hung down like a bizarre organic earring.

"Those kids look interesting . . . ," I said. I nearly added "Somebody should write something about them." But I stopped myself from saying it out loud.

Somebody should write about these wasted kids but I can't imagine myself doing it. I've never taken a writing course in my life and the only stuff I've ever written are letters to family and friends, those damn blue-book essays at USC, and a few little stories for Sister Leticia. I wouldn't know where to begin as a real writer and I sure as hell wouldn't know how to walk up to these scary-looking kids and ask them to talk to me.

Then, as if somebody else was choosing to argue:

You got straight As on the essays and stories. You read all the time, you know how to separate good writing from bad, and you sure as hell know how to ask questions. Now all you need is a notebook, a pen, and the nerve to go up to those kids, tell them you want to write about them, and ask why they're choosing to beg for money and looking to crash anywhere they find a floor. Thank God my Lisa is who she is. She'd never walk out on her future.

Butch's voice cut through my thoughts.

"You're miles away. What's so absorbing?"

"Huh? Oh, I was just thinking about Lisa."

He nodded his head. "Yeah, you got lucky with her. The parents of these kids must be going through hell."

The duplex in Hollywood was too big for one person and a cat so Dexter and I moved into a fanciful, Walt Disney–inspired cottage in Silver Lake, a community to the east of Hollywood. I was sorry to give up my proximity to Butch but our friendship had reached the stage where distance would make no difference in closeness.

Lisa returned to L.A. after nearly two years in Colorado. We'd kept in touch while she was away, and now that she was back, there was a slackening of the strain I'd sensed and a return to the affectionate bond between us. It felt good to laugh with my daughter again, to smile at her and have her smile back at me. We talked about what she wanted to do but she hadn't settled on a career course and I didn't want to push her. She got a job as cashier at an upscale restaurant, bought a car, and moved into a small, sun-filled apartment in Hollywood. She invited me to dinner one evening and we talked and laughed, and I was impressed at how much of a home Lisa had made for herself. When I told her about the homeless kids on Hollywood Boulevard, she listened with real interest and it was her response that got me thinking seriously about writing about them. Stronger than all my resistance and fears of failure was a need to make my daughter proud of me.

I asked around and a young guy I knew slightly from twelve-step meetings told me about a group of kids living in squats around the boardwalk in Venice. Without saying anything to Lisa, to Butch, or to my mom, I put a notebook and some pens in my bag and drove toward the beach.

They were lounging on the sand between the Venice boardwalk and the ocean, a clutch of eight or nine scruffy kids, none of them older than eighteen. I walked up to them, introduced myself, and mentioned the name of the guy who had told me about them. A scrawny, heavily tattooed boy wearing a black head rag with a skull pattern, ragged 501s tucked into worn-out camouflage boots, and a stained tee with the circular emblem of the Germs was the first to look up at me.

"Right. So what're you looking for?" I couldn't see his eyes behind the mirrored lenses of a pair of knockoff Ray-Bans.

I said I hoped they'd speak with me because they represented expanding tribes of teenagers who were turning away from a society that must have disappointed them so badly they were choosing to ignore it. Told them I wanted to write about them because I was interested in what they thought but couldn't guarantee what I wrote would get published. I offered to buy lunch for anyone who would allow me to interview them.

The boy looked around the group. Nobody said anything for a minute and I could hear the MDC song "Business on Parade" racketing out of a radio farther down the beach. Finally a girl with piebald black and yellow hair done up in dozens of random spikes nodded her head and looked over at the boy with the mirrored sunglasses.

"Zane. Dude! Take off those shades a minute."

Zane flicked the glasses high on his forehead and twisted his mouth into a gargoyle's grin. His eyes had retreated into their sockets and the flesh around them was stained a festering reddish brown.

"Hepatitis," he said. "Caught it swimming around the pilings at the Santa Monica pier. Rad, huh?"

I drove down to the Venice boardwalk every day for the next three weeks and talked to homeless teenagers. A few of them were squatting in the basement of an apartment house that had been in an advanced state of decrepitude for years. The basement was dank and smelled of mold, unwashed bodies, and the rotting blankets and sleeping bags scattered around the cement floor. Two or three bongs clogged with dark brown water and surrounded by discarded fast-food wrappers were lined up against one wall. The people who lived there called it the Dungeon. Other kids were squatting in a place known as the Madhouse, a decaying two-bedroom cottage owned by somebody's father, who had taped clippings about various rehab programs to the grime-scummed refrigerator. A homeless surfer kid named Adam, who prided himself on being "the most lovable asshole on the beach," thought the Madhouse was "gnarly because the par-tay goes on all day, every day." Sometimes the par-tay would go off the rails: Adam told me about a boy called Turtle getting killed over a quarter gram of coke, his body found in a Dumpster. I learned that Dumpsters were also used as squats, as were carport lockers, vacant movie houses, and the back seats of cars. The girl with yellow and black spiked hair, Molly, had a job washing dishes in a diner on the boardwalk and she was sleeping in the Olds Omega she'd driven from her home in Baton Rouge to L.A. That worried her some, a girl alone in a car, but she'd tried the Dungeon and it wasn't for her. She said she bailed from home because her parents didn't treat her like a real person.

"Mostly I'm looked down on, but if anyone ever takes the trouble to get to know me, they realize I'm not just some dumb kid with weird hair."

Molly jerked her chin at a group of other kids lounging on the beach.

"Apathy, that's the big one, you know. No politics, no reading, nothing . . ."

When I asked Zane how he viewed the world, he launched a rant: the world was a blind suicide, just barely hanging on, and he was angry—at the Rockefellers, because they funded the first methadone program on the street and he went for it, a poison that ate through your bone marrow and left you soft and lazy and impotent; at Kerouac and Rimbaud and Ginsberg, for prodding him awake with their words and then abandoning him to work it out any way he could. Mostly, he was angry with himself.

"You know what Nietzsche says, don't you?" Zane's voice was hoarse. " 'The dog-type man ends up sleeping on the beach.' "

When I asked Zane what he thought about the future, he rasped out a sound meant to be a laugh and said he never thought he'd live to be *this* old. He was eighteen.

I saw an outpouring of graffiti in Venice during that summer of 1985: ANARCHY CREATES A FREE SOCIETY and THERE'S A NEEDLE IN YOUR ARM THAT LEAVES YOU BREATHLESS and IN ALL YOUR DECADENCE PEOPLE DIE. The title of this chapter is one of the statements I saw spray-painted in large, angry letters on a wall near the Dungeon.

When I finished the interviews with the kids in Venice, I sat at the dining room table in front of the IBM Selectric a friend had given me when he got a computer and sorted through my notes. There were scribbles in margins and starred sentences, cross-outs and underlinings. There was no particular order to anyone's quotes (other than who said what) or to my own observations. The notes couldn't have been more chaotic if I'd shredded them. And I had to make everything cohesive if I wanted to take readers into the world of squats and Dumpsters and eighteen-year-old boys with cavalier attitudes about life-threatening illnesses. I looked down at Dexter; he stared at me with unblinking eyes and began to groom himself.

I allowed myself a moment to think about not going forward. I wasn't used to hard work, and the easy stuff, the interviews, was over. I was going to have to do some sweating now, but suddenly and very strangely, that didn't seem so frightening, because a single clear thought let me know I would put my notes in order so I could write about those kids and that whatever I wrote would be good enough to get published.

I put everything else aside and concentrated on those three weeks in Venice. I told my mother I had a cold, knowing it would keep her from wanting to see me because of her fear of catching anything from anyone (she wouldn't even allow me to touch the magazines in doctors' waiting rooms when I was a kid). The phobia didn't stop her from cooking up a four-day supply of chicken soup (one of the few dishes she made to perfection) and leaving it at my front door. I worked every day for three or four hours, stopping only when I felt a lessening of the razor edge of focus. By the second week I knew I could take off a few hours to be with my mom but I still wasn't ready to talk about writing. I proofread at night and the next morning I'd type in every correction and retype the last page I'd finished as a warm-up exercise. It took about six weeks and as many bottles of Wite-Out before I had something I considered good enough to show. Then I called screenwriter Jeffrey Fiskin, a man I didn't know very well but whose work I admired, because I still wasn't ready to bring Butch into my first effort if it failed. Jeff told me he'd be happy to read whatever I'd written and give me an opinion. I had the pages copied and sent them off the same day. Then I waited, reading my untitled article obsessively, agonizing over typos I'd missed. Jeff called within the week and said he'd like to show the piece to someone who worked at *Los Angeles* magazine. I was staggered by his offer and asked again and again if he was sure it was good enough to be taken seriously. Jeff laughed and told me, for perhaps the fourth time, that he was absolutely, without a doubt sure.

The woman on the other end of the line identified herself as an editor at *Los Angeles* magazine. She sounded young.

"This isn't quite right for us but you might try showing it to the people at the *L.A. Weekly*."

I stammered a fast thank-you and looked up the number of the *Weekly*.

When I told the receptionist I had a piece (professional journalistic noun courtesy of Jeff Fiskin) on homeless kids in Venice and asked if the *Weekly* was interested, she told me to hold on, she'd ask the news editor. A minute or so later a man's voice came on. He introduced himself as Eric Mankin and suggested I send the pages over; he'd read them and get back to me.

"Listen, I live only a couple blocks away. I can bring this over right now so you can read it and tell me what's wrong and I'll fix it. But you have to read it in front of me. Okay?" The words rushed out of my mouth, fueled by a mix of fear and chutzpah. To his great credit, Eric Mankin restrained himself from telling me to get a grip.

Less than an hour later I was sitting in Mankin's office in the warehouselike space that housed the *L.A. Weekly* staff. I picked at my cuticles and tried not to fidget as I watched him read through my work. Go-sees for modeling jobs were a finger-snap compared to this, I thought. His eyes swept across the lines; he flipped back to check something, smiled, and went on to the end. Then he squared the pages and looked across his desk at me.

"If you give me five hundred more words, I'll put this on the cover."

Just like that. The cover. I went numb for a second. Then I regained enough composure to ask a question.

"How many pages would I have to write to get five hundred words?"

He couldn't hold back the grin but his eyes, behind the lenses of his wire-rimmed glasses, were kind. He looked like a rock musician with his thick, unruly hair and easy slouch. I guessed he was somewhere in his midthirties.

"Five hundred words make two pages. Cover stories are five thousand words, give or take."

He stood up and walked around his desk to hand me my pages. I thanked him, got up, and headed for the door.

"Hey, Léon Bing."

Shit, he changed his mind.

I turned to look at him again.

"Don't you want to know how much we're going to pay you?"

"Oh! Well, yeah . . ." I was embarrassed at being such an unprofessional yahoo.

"Five hundred dollars. Acceptable?"

"Yeah!" I was having trouble getting my mind around the fact that I was going to be paid anything for something I'd written.

Eric held out his right hand and I went back, brushed past the hand, and gave him a quick hug. *What the hell*, I thought. As my friend Victory says, might as well go the whole hog plus the postage.

* * *

I called my mom the instant I got home. She squealed with excitement. "See? See how you can do anything you put your mind to? I'm so proud of you, darling. Now say a little thank-you prayer." She'd probably guessed the truth about the phantom cold but she didn't mention it.

I called Lisa.

"Mom! You're a writer now. That is so great." Our old closeness really seemed to be back. That was when I sent up silent thanks.

A few days later, after I handed in the two pages Eric had asked for, a call came in from Howard Rosenberg, the *Weekly*'s photo editor. He told me he liked the piece enough to shoot the pictures for the story himself. We went to Venice Beach together and I found him to be very smart, deadpan funny, and an ace with the camera. An unexpected bonus was his resemblance to Daniel Day Lewis.

Eric edited the piece himself, explaining each tweak and cut to me, pointing out places where I'd overwritten, showing me why certain passages were good. And he provided a great title: "Slow Death in Venice." The day the *Weekly* hit the stands with my story on the cover (August 23, 1985) I drove up to my old address and put a copy in front of Butch's door, just as he had dropped copies of the *L.A. Times* in front of mine. When I called David Merrick's office in New York, his principal assistant told me that David had suffered a massive stroke and was not expected to regain all of his faculties. I sent a copy of the piece to his New York apartment but I was never able to communicate with David again. He died in April of 2000, wheelchair bound, in England. Whatever reputation for ruthlessness he earned on Broadway, I loved him for the parental role he took with me.

David Merrick's obituary covered three-quarters of a page in the *New York Times*. He would have hated it.

Twenty-three years after I wrote my first piece about kids living in squats in Venice, I watched a cable documentary on MSNBC about homeless kids squatting in Hollywood. Most of the teenagers interviewed in 2008 said pretty much the same things I heard in 1985: "I'm disenchanted with life"; "We're tryin' to stick together"; "We're just natural-born squatters." They're still doing drugs but the ones they do now are more deadly. They're listening to different music: "Miss Murder" by AFI. The Killers' "When You Were Young." "The Long Way Around" by the Dixie Chicks. Bruce Springsteen is often heard on the street and Amy Winehouse's "Rehab" gets heavy play. The Red Hot Chili Peppers are still popular and rap flows in swirls and eddies around everything. One telling difference in current squatter culture is represented by the random girl who has a baby and is determined to keep it with her and raise it up to live on the street, just like Mom. Molly, seventeen years old and sleeping in her Olds Omega off the boardwalk in Venice in 1985, would have been shocked.

CHAPTER 13

Do or Die

"Slow Death in Venice" won an award for journalistic excellence from the Greater Los Angeles Press Club and I was seized by the kind of ambition I hadn't experienced since my first modeling jobs in New York. I did a few more cover stories for the *Weekly*, among them "Caged Kids," about teenagers placed in corporate-owned psychiatric facilities by their well-insured parents, and "Confessions from the Crossfire," an interview with a seventeen-year-old Crip. I'd asked to do a feature on gangs because of the inch or so of type I saw too often on the back pages of the *Los Angeles Times*'s Metro section, terse reports of "the shooting deaths of youths in South Central Los Angeles." Those easily missed items seemed unjust to me; these were American teenagers they were talking about. If the story had been about "youths in Beverly Hills" it would have been all over the front page.

When *Harper's Magazine* excerpted parts of the gang piece and requested that I moderate a discussion between members of the Crips and the Bloods, sworn enemies in the black-on-black gang wars, I reached out to some of the neighborhood people I'd interviewed, asked the L.A. County Probation Department for help, and was able to bring four young gangbangers to the table: an eighteen-year-old member of the Eight-Tray Gangsta Crips; his equal from the 107-Hoova Crips; the founder of the L.A. chapter of the Chicago-based Blackstone Rangers Bloods; and a twenty-three-year-old member of the Van Ness Gangsta Bloods. All of them were serious enough about the seminar to set aside their lethal differences and talk about life on streets that were unimaginable to L.A. residents securely housed in enclaves at a galactic remove from those battlegrounds. When I asked about gang killings, one of the panelists tried to explain:

"When somebody get killed who you feel close to, that make me angry enough to go kill somebody. But sometimes, after you kill somebody, you feel like 'Why did I do that? I should not even done that, that wasn't even called for.' You be thinkin' all that, then you see someone look just like the person you killed. Then you be thinkin', 'I probably didn't even kill him—he probably comin' back to get me' . . . Sometimes I start to be, like, sorry for things I done, start to think if I had stayed in school, maybe I wouldn't have been into some of those things I done. What I done in my life ain't so bad, maybe—the problem is, I done it."

When the *Harper's* seminar came out, another screenwriter acquaintance, Thomas Lee Wright, suggested I hook up with an agent. He gave me a name: Eric Ashworth of Donadio and Ashworth, literary agents based in New York. Candida Donadio, semi-retired by the mideighties, was a legend in publishing: she'd represented Thomas Pynchon when he emerged as an important voice in contemporary American literature, and bestselling authors Mario Puzo and Robert Stone were among the agency's clients.

I sent my small output of work to New York and tried to forget about it, figuring a prestigious outfit like Donadio and Ashworth would have zero interest in my local stuff. About a month later, I got a call from Eric Ashworth, and after some polite back-and-forth, he homed in:

"Time for a book."

That surprised me. It also scared me. I was hoping an agent would get me more assignments for feature pieces in national magazines; I'd never thought about writing a book. When I said so to Eric, he told me he was convinced the first book about L.A. gangs would sell, that all I'd have to do was three chapters and an outline he could show editors from different publishing houses. He promised to send me four or five successful book proposals to use as models for my own. His patience with a whining neophyte was running out—I could hear it in his voice—so I backed off, said I'd study the proposals and do my best to write a proposal for a book on the gangs.

I got the proposals a few days later, read them, and was even more frightened. I told myself I'd never be able to rise to that level of professionalism. Then I shrugged off the thought and went to work. It took about three months but after more than a few false starts, I was able to produce a proposal Eric was pleased with. He sent it out and offers began to come in. He rejected advance figures he felt were too low and then he called and said the book was going to auction. That night I heard from Craig Nelson, a rising star editor at HarperCollins. He wanted the book, he said, and made a preemptive bid for an advance payment that surpassed anything I dared to expect.

I had a book deal and no idea how to write a book. The lease on the cottage in Silver Lake ran out and I moved again, this time to Pasadena, this time with an additional member of the household: a black and white terrier mix with scruffy fur and eyes that had seen cruelty and remained loving in spite of it. Lisa found the little dog wandering the streets, starving and collarless; took him in; and called him Woofie. I babysat Woofie when she took a week's vacation with her boyfriend, fell in love, and couldn't bring myself to give him back. So Dexter, Woofie, and I were now a pack of three.

I wasted time fooling around with the precise placement of furniture and art because all those blank pages I had to fill terrified me. I bought an old conference table to use as a desk and turned the dining room, with its eighteen-foot beamed ceiling, into an office. I had yet to write word one and I'd already used up a month out of a one-year deadline. I whined to Howard Rosenberg and he told me to shut up; he'd take me to a place where I could talk to a confederation of Bloods on a regular Sunday outing in a park near the projects in Altadena. I bitched to my friend Sierra Pecheur and she put me in touch with Jim Galipeau, a deputy probation officer.

He took me on a ride-along deep into Crip territory and allowed me to observe as he sat in living rooms and at dining room tables and laid down the law to the kids on his caseload. He gave me permission to ask each family if I could come back and talk to them on my own. During the next year I went to juvenile detention camps and prisons and sat across the desk from Sherman Block, who was serving his fourth term as head of the Los Angeles Sheriff's Department. Both the sheriff and one of his adjutants told me I was asking to be raped and murdered. I persisted until Sergeant Herb Giron of the sheriff's department took me on a ride-along through the neighborhoods he patrolled. He was hard on criminal activity, but his manner of giving respect without condescension earned it back. People listened to and spoke with Herb Giron and it helped my case to be seen with him. When I went back to the streets on my own, I found that each interview led to another, like a fall of dominoes.

I was invited into a house where a sixteen-year-old gangsta placed an AK-47 with a fully loaded banana clip in my lap. I stood on street corners in Watts and Compton with active Crips and was on the scene when a stabbing occurred. I didn't witness the act but I saw the immediate aftermath of blood and a thin layer of yellowish fat over a slab of torn shoulder meat, and my only coherent thought at the moment was an urgent prayer that I not throw up on or anywhere near the injured gang member.

I was allowed into homes in an area known as the Jungle, to speak with the fierce Bloods who ruled the streets there.

I saw a thirteen-year-old Crip, a kid I met at one of the juvenile detention camps and whose story I followed up on after his release, get savagely beaten in front of his homeboys by his older sister when he called her "a dick-eatin' ho." I tried to comfort him after his humiliation, and he looked at me with the kind of contempt people reserve for well-meaning, know-nothing interlopers.

Nearly every time I went into South Central to meet with gang members I'd lose my way trying to find the 110 freeway back to Pasadena. I have no sense of direction (a gift from my mother,

along with her cheekbones), so very often, after a day spent con-
ducting interviews, I'd find myself driving along Denker or Sixtieth
or Hoover, all of them battle zones of gang warfare, hopelessly lost
and with dusk setting in. I was never scared, just frustrated and
tired and wanting to get the hell home.

Then I started taking second looks at the small huddles of
five or six young guys standing around on street corners and something clicked: they were more than likely gang members, and if
anybody knew how to get around L.A. . . . It worked: I'd pull up,
open up the passenger-side window, say I was lost, and ask for directions to the freeway. I got a few funny looks but I also got the
skinny on how to get home. Sometimes one of the homeboys would
lean in to take a closer look at me and say, "Y'all understand how
to get to the 110 now?"

I'd nod my head, but whenever I had an uncertain look on my
face, the guy would turn back to look at the others.

"She don't understand."

Then, to me again, "You got somethin' to write on?"

And I'd be given written directions spelled out in big block
letters that even I could follow easily.

Maybe I was too dumb to be scared during the time I put in
on the streets; maybe God looks out for fools. The only thing I know
with any certainty is that I was treated with courtesy and respect
by members of both the Crips and Bloods.

I knew I needed more than a notebook for gang interviews, so I
used a tape recorder, setting it up clumsily and asking anyone I
interviewed to tell me when the red light that signaled the end of a
reel came on. I did my own transcribing after each interview, hitting the rewind button again and again to make sure I got the in-
flections, the coded slang, the stop-and-go of gangspeak. What
these guys said was important. How they said it, the expression on
each face, the slash of a hand or hitch of shoulders, was vital. I had
to make each person I wrote about come alive on the page and to
do that I had to learn their language. I didn't have to speak it—that

would have been as phony as trying to pull off the elaborate hand-shakes and intricate hand-signing used by gang members—but I had to become fluent in the way they spoke. I managed by imagining gangspeak as a radio station I could tune to at will. And it worked: the instant I turned that imaginary dial, I was able to understand the language of African-American gang members. When somebody talked too fast, I'd ask them to repeat what they'd said and I'd tell them to slow down; always, slow down. I was still afraid that maybe I didn't have the goods, so I had to get it right.

At the end of 1989, I handed in the manuscript of *Do or Die*. I'd recognized those three words as the title for my book when a sixteen-year-old Crip repeated a gang saying: "Crip or cry, do or die."

Craig Nelson read the pages and called me with changes he wanted made. I sat down to work again and put the new manuscript in the mail within a couple of months. Craig approved it and told me he was ordering a first run of 45,000 copies. Howard Rosenberg shot the cover photograph of Monster Kody Scott of the Eight-Tray Gangsta Crips cradling a well-used Mac-11 equipped with a silencer. The weapon was on loan from one of the Bloods, a bull shark of a gangbanger I'd written about. He and one of his homeboys brought it to my place in a Saks Fifth Avenue shopping bag and took it apart (at my request) to prove it was unloaded. Even dismantled, it was a frightening object.

Do or Die came out in 1991 to good reviews. *Rolling Stone* excerpted a chapter and sent one of its star photographers, Matt Mahurin (now a documentary filmmaker), to shoot pictures for the illustrations. HarperCollins sent me out on a ten-city book tour and I was interviewed by newspaper columnists, radio personalities, and network morning show stars. I got my first taste of celebrity when I was leaving the NBC studios in New York and a female pedestrian stopped, touched my arm, and said, "I just saw you on the *Today* show."

The book was translated into six languages, including Japanese, and offers began to come in.

Producers from PBS called and asked if I could provide active members of the Crips and Bloods for a segment on a Bill Moyers show on the subject of hatred. I contacted guys from each side, asked if they were willing to appear on TV with their rivals, and made arrangements for the show to be videotaped in the courtyard of my apartment because it was completely neutral territory. A memorable event took place that day when I introduced two OGs (original gangstas), one Crip, one Blood, deadly rivals on the streets, both of them shot-callers with reputations built upon ruthless acts of violence. They looked at each other for a moment in serious sizing up and then they shook hands in a solemn show of truce. The younger gang members, five or six representatives of each gang, followed suit and the taping got under way. They all took their turn in front of the camera while my neighbors, all of whom had been told about the show, crowded the balconies overlooking the courtyard for a close-up inspection of the young men they had only read about in newspaper reports or seen in televised footage of arrests. I'd told them they would probably never again feel as safe as when the courtyard between us was filled with gang members on a peaceful mission. The only tense moment happened when one of the younger Crips noticed the red kerchief tied around Woofie's neck. The kid handed me his blue rag and asked for color equality on my dog.

Producer Sean Daniel, with a spread of top-floor offices at Universal Studios, took an option for a feature film version of *Do or Die*. Thomas Lee Wright was hired to write the screenplay (to date, the movie has not been made). I was interviewed by writers from the *L.A. Times*, *Time* magazine, and the *New Yorker*. There were a couple awards and Eric called to tell me Craig Nelson was ordering more copies because the book was "flying off the shelves."

Even with all that, I still couldn't believe I was a writer. I kept waiting for a tap on the shoulder and a voice behind me saying I was still a model who needed to get her ass back in the right line.

My mother and Lisa were thrilled with the success of my first book. They came to every book signing, my mom wearing her Chanel suits and good pearls, Lisa telling everyone in the stores they *had* to buy *Do or Die* because it was "a great, history-making book." It was like sliding into a warm, scented bath to see my mother and daughter so proud of me.

When Lisa decided to move to Boston in order to attend Northeastern University, my feelings were mixed. On one hand, I was proud she'd chosen to get a degree that would allow her to work as a translator within the deaf and deaf-blind communities. Still, it meant seeing her move away again. But this was what she wanted, so I wished her well and watched her take off in her Ford Explorer to begin studying for a career in a field that would allow her to exercise her natural instinct to help others. I didn't feel the same kind of wrenching ache I had when she was a kid leaving for school in London, but I knew I was going to miss my daughter all over again.

I didn't meet my agent, Eric Ashworth, until he came to L.A. on business just before the publication of *Do or Die*. He called and we made plans to meet and have dinner at his hotel. I pictured him as a soft-around-the-middle, impeccably tailored man in his mid- to late-thirties, so that's what I was looking for as I sat waiting in the lobby. I watched idly as someone who looked like a twenty-three-year-old Calvin Klein print model walked toward the area where I was seated. He stopped, looked at me, and introduced himself as my literary agent. Eric and I liked each other from the first hand-shake and spoke like old friends over a long dinner. He told me about his Sheltie, Sophie, and the African gray parrot he shared with his friend Rik. I told him about my tough-guy cat, Dexter; Woofie; and Diz, a shaggy blond puppy who wandered into my life shortly after I moved to Pasadena. We talked about his family and mine, and at some point we spoke of close friends who were desperately sick with AIDS. It was then Eric told me he had been diagnosed a few years earlier and was now in the full-blown stage of the virus. I looked across the table at him and instinct took over. I got up, moved in close, and we shared a long, hard hug. I think I fell a little bit in love with Eric Ashworth that night, and the feeling grew as I got to know him better.

He retired from the agency in 1992 and made the deal for my second book from his hospital room (Craig told me that detail and said, with admiration, that Eric was as predatory an agent as ever, even when confined to an oxygen tent). Neil Olson took over many of Eric's clients, and I can think of no other person who could have stepped into Eric's place as friend, mentor, and representative with such quiet dignity and fearsome skills. Eric still showed up at the office on good days and we had dinner together in New York when I was there for the beginning of my second book tour. He was thin and pale, there was a shunt embedded in his chest, but his sense of humor was as well honed, his interest in my work as intense. He died in 1997 at the age of thirty-nine and the picture he sent of himself and his beloved Sophie sits on my desk close to the little three-legged horse my friend Emily gave to me at school.

CHAPTER 14

Good Morning, Midnight

"She and I could have been schoolmates—we're about the same age."

"Oh, please. You look like her granddaughter."

It was always the same: we'd be in the car and my mother would nod toward an elderly woman tottering along with the aid of a cane. I'd look and respond. It was one of our small routines, like the swearing game we played when I was a kid. I enjoyed this one, too; I was proud that my mother looked so good in her eighties. She was still reed slim but she didn't try to affect a younger look by wearing skirts that were a bit too short or heels that were an inch too high. She kept to her original style of perfectly tailored suits and good jewelry. Her only concession to age and vanity was the subtly styled wig she wore as her hair began to thin. What helped give an illusion of youth was my mother's posture; she sat and stood with a straight spine and squared shoulders, but it was her walk that did the trick: she maintained her long, easy stride, head held high, arms swinging loosely. And she still had the insouciant attitude I'd admired all my life.

She liked to talk about the past: "Remember the time I came to New York when you were pregnant with Lisa and we went shopping at Bloomingdale's?"

Of course I remembered. We were on the ground floor and my mother nudged me when a woman wearing a coat made from what looked like the pelts of some tragic, long-furred species of monkey swaggered past. My mother didn't speak, didn't make a sound; that poke of elbow and slight turn of head said it all. I started to laugh and my mom nudged me again, harder this time, and hissed out my name.

"Mary Léon . . . !"

It was like trying not to laugh when someone makes a faux pas at a funeral. I caught hold of a counter edge to keep my balance. I bent over, trying to control what was about to happen. Nothing helped—I peed all over the floor in the middle of the cosmetics aisle at Bloomingdale's.

My mother took one look, turned, and walked to the next counter. The salesclerk there was staring in disbelief. People simply do not relieve themselves on the floor at Bloomingdale's.

"May I help you with something?" The clerk was addressing my mother but her gaze was spot-welded on me.

My mother picked up a bottle of cologne, sprayed some on the inside of her wrist, and sniffed it. Then she set down the bottle and looked at the woman across the counter. I was standing close enough to hear what she said.

"That poor girl. She's lost control *and* she's delusional, possibly as a result of the pregnancy." She lowered her voice slightly. "The child thinks I'm her mother . . ."

"Mom!"

She sighed and shook her head.

"You see?"

She thanked the salesclerk and sailed out of Bloomingdale's, leaving me to step out of a pool of my own piss and head for the big glass doors with as much dignity as I could muster.

The odd thing was that when I got home (my mom had grabbed a taxi and was waiting for me outside the house), all we could do was hold on to each other and laugh, as if we'd put one over on the store.

Whenever we talked about it over the years, my mother swore

it was payback for the day I stood and laughed when those monkeys grabbed her by the hair in Piedmont.

Lisa graduated with honors from Northeastern University and began work as a translator for the deaf and deaf-blind in Boston and outlying areas. She married in 1998 and Dominic LoRusso was born in February of 1999. Lisa and her husband, John, divorced the next year and she is an exemplary, if sometimes harried, single mom. Dominic is highly intelligent, curious about everything, and devoted to both parents; he spends every weekend with his dad and Lisa encourages their relationship. When he was born, she asked me what name I wanted to be called.

"Grandma."

"You don't want some kind of nickname? You know, one that doesn't sound . . ."

"Like a grandparent? How about Mrs. Bing? No, too formal. Let's stick with Grandma."

When I thought about it later, it still sounded good. I know one or two women who have grandchildren and they insist on titles that bear so little reference to being a grandparent that they could have been boarding school nicknames. That seems a little silly to me, like having your kids call you by your first name.

Lisa and Dominic came to L.A. for a short visit last year. I spent a day alone with him and it was wonderful. He went back and forth between calling me Grandma and Léon and he was very good company. He showed me some excellent card tricks and we went out for lunch and then watched a DVD about skateboarding. During our time together he pushed the envelope and tried to push my buttons. I allowed the former and delivered a loud "Hey . . . !" on the latter. We had a fine time.

My mother approved of every job I had. When I was a model she cut my photographs out of magazines and stuck them in silver frames. When she came to fashion shows in L.A. she told everyone seated nearby that I was her daughter, and wasn't I the most beautiful thing they'd ever seen? When I began to write it was her hand, warm and firm, I sensed at the small of my back, just as I'd felt it years earlier when she taught me how to dance. My mom told me I could do whatever I set my mind to and she meant it.

We still enjoyed lunches at her favorite restaurants, still took in movies and explored malls. I began to dislike the chore of shopping for clothes when I was a model, but it was one of my mother's small pleasures and her enthusiasm made it fun for me. It wasn't important to my mother that we buy anything; for her, the joy was in window-shopping and critique. We'd prowl the levels of galleries and sometimes Mom would stop short and grab my arm.

"Look at that sweater, Mary Léon. You've been saying you need a new black pullover and that's the perfect one."

And she'd pull me along into the store and stand by while I tried on whatever it was she'd spotted for me. She once urged me to buy a gold and ruby Art Deco pin when we were at Neiman Marcus but I drew a firm line with that one. Another time I caught her looking at a narrow bracelet studded with tiny diamonds and I went back and got it for her birthday. She gasped when she opened the box and then began a lecture about spending too much money.

It was the little things I noticed first: she'd order something (broiled trout or a chicken pot pie) and pick at it, lifting tiny morsels to her mouth. When I suggested we get the leftovers boxed up for her to take home for dinner, she'd shudder and say she didn't "take food out of restaurants." If I reached over to take something from her plate after she'd finished eating, my mother would mutter that I was "a table finisher" and snap out a warning about putting on weight. She'd never been much of an eater and there were very few things she liked. She had never tasted a banana, never eaten a peach. She detested vegetables and salad, hated mashed potatoes. I urged her to eat, pleaded with her not to skip meals. I bought cream of mushroom and tomato soup in cans and half-and-half to mix in with it, tuna and mayonnaise for sandwiches. We got a microwave oven and filled her freezer with chicken pot pies, macaroni and cheese, salmon. She preferred to eat cake from the supermarket.

We argued about all of it.

"Who do you think you are to tell me what to eat? I had to put up with the same thing every day at home: '*Please eat, Estelle. Please, just another few bites, Estelle.*' Same damn thing every meal. Well, you're not my mother and I'll eat what I like. I'm not going to get fat for you or anybody else."

She weighed in at ninety-nine pounds at the time. And she had cataracts. Surgery to remove them had been successful but an allergy to the post-op medicated drops left her with impaired vision. When she began to have a bad time with breathing, we went to her doctor, who sent us to a specialist. The specialist ordered the requisite tests, studied the results, and told us my mother had scarring on both lungs from an undiagnosed case of childhood tuberculosis and that the condition had been exacerbated by smoking, even though my mother quit cigarettes when she was in her forties. He was sorry, he said, nothing very much to be done about it. Oxygen canisters at home, try not to let dust accumulate around the house, get an air purifier, take short walks for daily exercise. And eat bigger portions of nourishing food, anything she wanted, because her blood pressure was, as it always had been, slightly below normal.

I convinced my mother to allow a daily caregiver to come in for cleaning and preparation of meals by playing a little hardball: I told her this was the only way she could continue to live on her own. The other end of the either-or was assisted living.

We both knew that neither of us wanted to live together. We were great at a distance with three or four daily phone calls and a few lunches a week, but our positions had reversed: I was the parental figure now. My mother resented it, I didn't like it, and things would go sour very quickly between us. I asked once (out of an overriding sense of duty) if she'd like to share a big—a *very* big—apartment with me. She didn't even need the time to think about it:

"I'd rather be dead."

I knew what she meant and the immediacy of her response was a relief. But now, a year or so later, I had to accept a grim and much more terrible truth: my mother was beginning to die. I pushed back the thought because I couldn't bear it, but I couldn't ignore the fact that she was fading away in front of me. She could no longer see well enough to drive so we sold her mint-condition Buick Regal. I still came into West Hollywood to see her two or three times a week but it was becoming increasingly difficult for her to put on her favorite suits and jewelry and walk down the stairs, shoulders squared, to my car. She persisted until even dressing for anything but a trip to the doctor's office became too exhausting. So I began to pick up sandwiches and chicken soup with matzoh balls (which she loved) from a gourmet deli near her apartment and we'd eat at the antique gaming table next to the window overlooking the patio. Her rooms still smelled faintly of Chanel No. 5 and furniture polish, and she retained shreds of her singular elegance and style, but her thighs, thin as the legs of herons, displayed the reduction she had become under the gray sweat suits she now wore to ward off chills. All that remained of my mother was an essence of the vibrant woman she had been two years, one year ago. I could almost see a rime of death frosting her skin.

I couldn't bring myself to tell her when Woofie died, couldn't tell her about finding Bobbie, my new shaggy blond shelter dog, and my sense that Woofie had waited for a replacement before he left us. I knew she wouldn't have handled his death easily, and when she asked about Woof and Diz, I told her they were both doing great.

We managed to enjoy ourselves. We talked about old times and ignored the canisters of oxygen that had become so vital a part of my mother's life. Sometimes she'd want to look through her photograph albums. We'd sit together on the long, chintz-covered sofa and she'd turn the pages slowly, talking about each snapshot as if it had been taken the day before. And sometimes I'd want to cry for what was forever gone, and sometimes I'd get the old feeling of sheet lightning in my head, the same as when we went out on drives when I was a kid and I wanted to rage at her about not being allowed to see my father. Now I wanted to scream that she had to eat, had to get better, had to return to her old vitality. I wanted to shake those matchstick shoulders and shout into her face that she could not, must not, die, because she was my mother and because I couldn't bear to lose her. I didn't say any of those things; I told her nobody could make me laugh like she could and that I loved her. And she'd offer a cheek for me to kiss.

The next appointment with my mother's doctor showed that her weight had dipped to eighty-eight pounds. The caregiver told me she'd begun to find most of the evening meal she prepared before leaving for the day hidden inside empty cartons and under old magazines in the trash container under the kitchen sink.

I confronted my mother about what I'd been told and she accused me of snooping into her life. Trying to make her eat was like forcing someone to pray. I went to a health food store and got supplemental drinks in different flavors. My mother looked at them suspiciously and ordered me to take them back; she'd give the vanilla a try but I was not to expect miracles.

I liked the caregiver, Ofelia, well enough, although I had the nagging sense she was putting on her best face when I was there. When she was out marketing one afternoon, I asked my mother about it. She bristled immediately.

"What the hell are you talking about? That woman babies me to death—she's better to me than you ever were." Her expression turned sly. "What's the matter, jealous?"

This time I just wanted to scream at her for behaving like a bitch.

A month or so later I pulled up to the curb in front of my mom's building as Ofelia was hoisting herself into what looked like a new SUV. She had a sheaf of envelopes in her hand and I saw my mother's name on one of them.

A flush of red fanned out across her pudgy cheeks.

"Oh—I was just taking your mother's mail up to her."

Bullshit, I thought. *You were just taking my mother's mail away with you.* I held out my hand.

"Don't bother. I'll take it up."

She took a step toward me and spoke in a grating whisper.

"I been meaning to tell you—your mother is going out to nightclubs every night with her neighbor, that young guy who live downstairs from her, you know?" She made a mincing gesture with one hand. "That *mariflor* is makin' her pay for everything."

I said nothing. I continued to hold out my hand for the mail and waited until Ofelia gave it to me.

"I jus' looking out for your mother . . ."

I was already halfway up the stone steps, on my way to my mom's apartment. One of the envelopes in my hand was from her bank; it contained the printout of the previous month's checks.

My mother's shaky signature was on every check; the amounts and payees were made out by Ofelia. One check was for $2,500, payable to a used car dealer as down payment on the new SUV. Other checks, some as high as $300, were written to the market where my mother had shopped for years. I knew she never spent more than $30 or, rarely, $40 whenever she went out to buy food. Ofelia had to be feeding her family at my mother's expense. This was confirmed when I found an itemized market receipt for $229 crumpled into a wad on the floor behind the trash container under the sink. Stuff my mother had no use for and never bought was listed: spareribs, six-packs of beer, hair conditioner, baby food, tampons, cartons of disposable diapers. I began a search, and to hell with my mother's complaints about snooping. There were no other market receipts in the apartment. And no bank statements other than the one I'd confiscated. When I confronted my mother with the canceled checks and marketing list, she admitted she'd been signing blank checks at Ofelia's request.

"Ofelia said you didn't want to be bothered."

Bullshit again. Ofelia may have been the initiator but my

mother signed blank checks because she didn't want me to know the amount of money she had in the bank. I'd heard it before, the one that went "I don't want you in my business."

I controlled my anger at my mother, told myself she'd been taking a final desperate stand at some kind of autonomy, and called the police. A plainclothes officer was at her door within fifteen minutes. Keeping it brief, I described Ofelia's behavior earlier in the day and showed him the bank statement and canceled check copies she'd meant to take with her, showed him the receipt from the market. My mother admitted to having signed the checks Ofelia told her were to pay the bills: telephone, gas, cable TV, and checks for trips to the market when Ofelia convinced her she was too weak to leave the house. The officer took notes, put the bank statement and the market receipt into an envelope, asked for Ofelia's telephone number, and informed us he would be going to her house to question her that afternoon.

Ofelia Suarez, who had been referred by a reputable family agency, was arrested and charged with grand theft and elder abuse.

I called the agency and reported Ofelia's actions and subsequent arrest, called Mother's bank, explained the situation, and asked for (and received) legible copies of both sides of all checks signed by my mother for the past year and a half. Then I called another agency and began interviewing caregivers again. We were lucky to find Mrs. Ida Hobbs, an intelligent and compassionate woman in her late fifties. She was a wonderful cook but she couldn't get my mom to eat—not the delicate butter-fried chicken breasts, not the fish filets blanketed in a golden crust. My mother was now down to seventy-four pounds and subsisting on tuna sandwiches on soft white bread (crusts trimmed), small glasses of cranberry juice, and, always, cake. When her doctor threatened a feeding tube, it scared her into a week or so of eating just enough to keep going without that radical procedure. But then Mrs. Hobbs said my mother was refusing to get out of bed except for bathroom breaks. She told the concerned caregiver it was because her mother—my grandmother—was holding her in her arms. When I asked my mother about it, she turned her head and refused to discuss it.

Two days later, following a hysterical outburst over the telephone when I said I'd be coming to see her that afternoon, my mother collapsed and was rushed to the hospital. When I got to her room, she waved a limp hand at me and closed her eyes. Her face was the color of unwashed linen. An intravenous line had been hooked up to one arm.

I made arrangements with Mother's neighbors, who were truly fond of her, to care for her cat. They promised to look in on Sky several times a day and said they would take turns visiting at the hospital.

"I don't think your mother is going to live out the next twenty-four hours."

Mother's doctor, who sat leafing through patients' charts at the far end of a nurses' station, was well enough acquainted with me to know I didn't want the prognosis of a death sentence buried under a frosting of euphemisms. But it was a hard thing to hear.

"No. I don't either." It was a hard thing to say, standing across the barrier of a counter, surrounded by the urgent sounds and movements of a medical center.

Estelle Lang remained the unpredictable mother I knew: she skidded into a U-turn and made a dramatic improvement. When her doctor recommended a short stay at a rehabilitation facility until she was strong enough to go home, she agreed without argument and promised to eat all the meals that would be served to her. She said she was in a hurry to get better and go back to her beautiful apartment.

The facility was clean, its staff courteous. But it wasn't a place for recuperation; this was the inexorable ice floe that carries the sick, the aged, the useless out to sea. The first time I went there to visit my mother, I passed an assembly of wheelchairs in groups of twos and threes stationed against the walls of the corridor outside each room. The people in the chairs were not talking to each other or whispering to themselves. They didn't look up or gaze curiously around at their surroundings. There were no books or magazines lying open on their laps. The occupants of these chairs rested quietly, like very old domestic animals, patient and uncomprehending inside the confines of a carrying case in the waiting room of a veterinary hospital.

My mother's body looked like a drift of feathers under the blanket that covered her. Someone had brushed her hair into a pencil-thin topknot and secured it with a pink yarn bow. Somebody's well-meaning idea of cuteness, and it made me want to slam my fist into the wall. Pink yarn tied on my mother, who detested anything that smacked of bows or ruffles, whose clothes were as crisply tailored and unadorned as men's suits. I leaned over the bed to kiss her cheek and she whispered, "Get this goddamn bow off my head."

She died two days later on October 12, 2002.

Lisa flew back from Boston (leaving Dominic with his father) and we set about the job of clearing out my mother's apartment. Leonard Salazar, Lisa's onetime fiancé, now her closest friend, offered his help. So did Glenn Brown. He and I had remained close ever since we lived in those same-floor apartments in West Hollywood when Lisa was in elementary school, he was "Uncle Glenn," and I was modeling for Rudi Gernreich.

I don't think it hit me until I walked into the apartment where she had lived for so many years: my mother—who could always make me laugh, whose stunning glamour I had tried so diligently to copy when I was a teenager, who had cheered even the least of my accomplishments—was going to be away for the rest of my life.

I managed to get through the clothes, the silk shirts and tailored suits that were her signature, without breaking down. It was the shoes, finally, that brought on the flood of tears I'd been controlling. Her low-heeled pumps, polished and stuffed with tissue paper, the blurred shape of her feet on the soles and the slight indentations of her toes inside. A dusty box at the back of a shelf in her closet held a pair of high-heeled alligator pumps. I could picture my mother reaching up for the box sometimes and taking out the shoes she loved and could wear no longer. I imagined her sitting down and sliding them on, turning a foot in different directions to admire the look and feel of the shining leather, recalling the times she strode out in them, secure in her sense of good looks and well-being.

We spent two long days folding, wrapping, boxing up. I offered Lisa her choice of her grandmother's furniture, lamps, clothes, and some of the jewelry (she was disappointed to learn that Mom had given her massive Victorian "Lincoln bed" to her favorite neighbor and that it had already been taken from her apartment). I gave the high-backed Victorian armchair that was my mother's favorite to Glenn; he'd always admired it and she would have wanted him to have it, along with the twin papier-mâché tables inlaid with mother-of-pearl on black enamel she'd placed at either end of her sofa and the pair of crystal hurricane lamps that still had all their original prisms. I kept most of her jewelry and family photographs, her silver flatware and tea service, the ebony and gilt Edwardian wall mirror, the little gaming table, her collection of antique Chinese porcelains, and the early-nineteenth-century eight-panel screen that had been the focal point of her living room.

After the movers had taken everything away and before I left my mother's apartment for the last time, I stood at the window where she once sat, looking out at the small patio that had been her view. I thought about all the times I'd seen her there, smiling and waving down at me. I thought about how she taught me to dance when I was twelve years old and how she offered me that cigarette after lunch in a Beverly Hills restaurant. Thought about the swearing game, her love of secrets, and the way she told a story. I wanted to remember everything my mother and I had ever shared: the uncontrollable laughter, the sound of her voice on my answering machine, her off-kilter sense of humor that sang along the wire of my own. I even wanted to keep the memory of our arguments. I wanted to hold on to every one of the moments that would never come again.

I stood at her window for a long moment, breathed a mist onto one of the panes, and wrote her initials. Then I picked up her cat, placed him inside his carrying case, and went back to Pasadena.

I couldn't keep Sky (because of Diz and Bobbie; Dexter had died two years earlier), so I took him to board at the veterinary facility while I looked for a new home for him. I visited every day, brought some of his toys and a couple of my mother's old towels for him to lie on. I was there, sitting next to his cage, about a week later when a woman asked if she could reach in and pet him. That was all it took. The cat and the human exchanged a long look and Sky had a home. The pictures this kind woman has sent me show him lying serenely on her bed surrounded by pillows covered in French linen. Sky and I both lucked out, and somehow I feel sure my mom arranged it.

I saw Ofelia Suarez again about six weeks after my mother's death. We were in a Beverly Hills courtroom, where Suarez pleaded guilty to all charges. She sat, eyes fixed on the floor, while a translator facilitated the dialogue between her and the judge. He looked at her with thinly veiled contempt and ordered her to make payments until the amount of money she'd stolen from my mother was repaid in full. She was to turn over a monthly money order in the amount of five hundred dollars to a probation officer and the county would take it from there. It had been determined that this so-called caregiver had stolen over fifteen thousand dollars in under a year from my half-blind, too-trusting mother.

When Suarez was asked if she understood the ruling, she whispered a reply and the interpreter said, "Yes." Then the judge spoke again, his voice glacial.

"Understand this: if you miss a single payment, I'll send you to prison immediately."

He nodded at the interpreter to translate.

Suarez whispered again and, for the first time, looked over at me. I got to my feet, took a couple of steps forward, and stared her down. If I could have slapped her face and gotten away with it, I would have. But at least, I thought, my mom was getting some kind of justice.

I miss my mother every day. Sometimes I will hear a laugh that sounds like hers or see a woman in the distance who has her walk. It might be a song by Billie Holiday; it might be that moment when I want to rush to the phone and tell her something. And there are days—and these are the most poignant—when I can almost feel her hand at the small of my back.

CHAPTER 15

The Genuine Article

Pain does not always feel like a collaborative thing. The wounding loss of a parent if you are an only child, the death of a beloved pet, or the sickening throb of a headache above one eye is yours alone at the moment it is happening. Meeting the person who is able to lift you to another level, the person who is willing to love you in spite of everything and is able to share with you whatever it is you are lacking—that's something else.

I wasn't much in the mood for anything except a walk with the dogs that afternoon. It was February of 2003, my mother was four months dead, and I was winding up a feature story on illegal car racing for *GQ*. I was thinking about Lisa and wondering idly whether or not to go to one of the newly released movies I could see using my Writers Guild card when I heard a voice coming up on my left.

"Isn't this a beautiful afternoon?"

He was a couple inches over six feet. He had posture to burn and I could see, under his jeans and T-shirt, the slim torso of someone who exercises on a fairly regular basis. He looked to be in his early twenties, with thick dark hair, features in the Matt Damon mold, round horn-rimmed glasses. I looked at him for a few seconds before I said anything; I was surprised by his sudden appearance and it's unusual for me to involve myself in conversations while dog-walking. As a rule, that's the time I spend unraveling work-related problems.

I glanced around at the quiet residential street, gold tinted in the pre-sunset light of Southern California, noticing it for the first time.

"Yeah, this is a nice time of day."

Ten minutes later we were still talking, there on the street, with Diz and Bobbie lying peacefully on the grass between us. I don't re-call anything I said; what I remember vividly is the way Gareth Seigel looked when he told me about the class of special ed students he had been the substitute teacher for that day. When he described how he'd explained a leap-year birthday to one of the boys by telling the kid how special that made him, and how the children formed a circle around him for hugs after the class ended, his voice was full of quiet emotion. I made a fast decision:

"Listen, would you like to go to the movies with me this eve-ning? It's a free screening and I can bring a guest."

He hesitated for a couple of seconds. And I wondered if I'd just done a crazy thing.

"I'd like that," he said.

I suggested an early dinner at a cafeteria I went to when I was writing against a deadline. The prices were reasonable and you could get almost any kind of no-frills dinner or sandwich to go. I liked it because it was convenient, fast, and you didn't have to think much about what you were going to order—it was all there in front of you. At some point during the meal he looked up from his plate of chicken à la king and told me the place (and its food) reminded him of the high school cafeteria back in Fort Wayne, Indiana.

"Bad?"

"Pretty bad. I'll make a real dinner for you sometime."

I liked him already. But we still had the movies ahead of us.

I went to so many movies as a kid that a few rules got devel-oped along the way: Minimum talking, particularly if the other per-son has already seen the movie and insists on saying things like "You won't believe what happens next." No crinkling of wrappers during tense scenes; if you're going to rip your way into a Butter-finger, do it during a gunfight. Get seated in time for the previews;

previews are almost as good as (and sometimes better than) the film you're there to see. Sure, it's picky; so what?

Gareth Seigel was perfect. The movie was *Gangs of New York*, and during one of the more excessive scenes, I reached for his hand. When he wrapped his warm fingers around mine and left them there, I thought about a passage in *The Catcher in the Rye* when Holden Caulfield describes holding hands in the movies with a girl named Jane Gallagher and how terrific it was. This was like that.

After the movie, when we were in front of Gareth's place (we'd taken my car and it was a pleasant surprise to find he lived two blocks away from me), I leaned over and kissed him. I didn't expect him to be the best kisser since Joe D'Alessandro, with whom I'd shared a brief session on my sofa in the eighties. But he was.

It was that easy. Everything seemed right: the smell of his skin, the texture of his hair, the way one front tooth shouldered lightly up against its neighbor.

Whatever was going on, I liked it.

He was twenty-nine years old and as we saw more of each other, I found he could bring me to the same degree of helpless laughter as my mother, that he was stunningly smart without being a smartass, that he possessed an unerring ability to recognize—and then quietly do—the right thing. I was impressed but not surprised to learn he reached the rank of Eagle Scout in his teens and had earned a degree in economics from Northwestern University. He told me about the summer after graduation when he worked as a guide at a dude ranch in Wyoming and the life-threatening incident that happened there. He wrote a short story about that summer and it was published in a national magazine. He told me about the year or so he spent working at a law firm in San Francisco and living in a basement apartment that was haunted. Told me he was divorced from a woman he'd met at Northwestern. He was the first man in my experience who didn't badmouth the ex. We talked about my mother and Lisa and writing. He read *Do or Die* and my other two books;

I read his story about Wyoming and a small book of his poetry that was about to be published.

It seemed natural for us to begin having dinner together every night. Gareth is a wonderfully creative cook and I'm not, so I was happy to be able to help with simple tasks. Often, after we finished eating, we'd pile pillows on the floor and sit close and listen to music. Glenn Gould playing Bach; a Mozart clarinet concerto; Paul Simon: *"They've got a wall in China / It's a thousand miles long / To keep out the foreigners / They made it strong . . ."*

"Something So Right" is the name of the Simon song. And that's how it felt, despite all the reasons it might have seemed wrong.

One night, after a long session of lovemaking in front of the fire at my place, I watched him walk down the long path to the street and waved when he turned back for another look. Then I whispered the thought that had been humming inside my head:

"I love this man."

We were in Gareth's kitchen one evening, a few weeks after we met, when he asked me to get a utensil out of a drawer. I groped through a jumble of cooking stuff and my fingers closed on a photograph hidden under the slotted spoons and meat pounders. I pulled it out and looked at the black and white image of five or six basketball players on the court, each player caught in that initial instant of grief when he knows it's over, that his team has just lost the game. I held up the picture and asked Gareth who had taken it.

"I did, in high school."

I studied the photograph for a moment.

"You should think about taking more photographs."

"Yeah, maybe—hey, what about that garlic press?"

A month or so later, Gareth went to Santa Fe for a visit with his younger sister, Caroline, who lives there, and their parents, who were in from Fort Wayne. He decided to drive because he'd just leased a Saab and was eager to take it on a road trip. The day he picked up the new car, he took me along to the dealership and then asked me to drive it back to his place, following along behind his old, stick-shift Mitsubishi. I was shocked: I'd never met any guy who would willingly turn over the keys to his new car—never mind the make or model—to a woman he had just begun to see. And I'm not the best driver to hit the road: I'm nervous on freeways, too easily intimidated by the maneuvers of other cars. I said all that to Gareth and he grinned.

"You'll be fine. Just drive like it's yours and let me know how it handles, okay?"

Damn right, okay.

I didn't expect to miss him that much. In every other relationship—including marriage—I valued the time when the guy, no matter who he was and how much I cared for him, wasn't around. Looking back, it seemed as if I'd always chosen to be involved with men who were often away. Whether it was a late-night rehearsal at a studio or a trip to Miami to make a drug deal, the important thing was they spent time away and left me to read or watch a movie or just sit quietly, listening to music. Now I found myself thinking about Gareth Seigel, on the road in his new Saab and in Santa Fe with his family. Every day, when I went over to his place to feed his cat, Landers (a rescue from the street of the same name in San Francisco), I'd go into the bedroom and look up at the wheat-patterned light fixture on the ceiling and think about all the times we made love beneath its dim amber glow. I ran my fingers along a row of shirts hanging in the closet and wrote a message with soap on the bathroom mirror. I did all the stuff I always thought was excruciatingly corny. And I loved it.

When he got back from Santa Fe, Gareth said I was responsible for planting the idea to take more pictures. He told me about spotting what looked like an abandoned service station, a falling-apart box of a shack on a trash-littered lot in Arizona, on the way back to L.A. Told me how he pulled over, climbed halfway up a chain-link fence, aimed the camera, and shot. What snagged his eye was a sign still in place under the sagging remains of a flattened metal roof. The letters were in comparatively good shape but one was missing, leaving the sign to read:

HELL

That black-and-white image got us started on a search for places where Gareth could shoot more photos. We'd pack a picnic lunch, load the dogs into their safety harnesses in the back seat, and drive to areas that had been pretty much abandoned by civilization. The Salton Sea, with its decaying beach bungalows tenanted only by generations of pigeons, and the expanses of empty, undeveloped blocks marked by faded street signs: Nile. Bach. Seaview. The half-submerged buildings and trailers left to rust away in contaminated water. A weathered two-story house standing alone in a plain of sand; we called it the Murder House because it looked so ominous. I loved being part of the work Gareth had become passionate about. We went into the Mojave Desert together on the hunt for the remains of an old silent movie set. On his own (because I am a coward) Gareth scaled a perilously steep hillside to get shots of what was left of one of Pasadena's historic estates after a fire burned it down to the bricks.

He began working with the master printer Michel Karman, whose work is legendary; the artists for whom he prints and whose shows he often designs will work only with him. He has printed for Irving Penn, Helmut Newton, Brad Pitt, Wim Wenders, and Sally Mann and he picks and chooses whom he will work with. When we met, Michel Karman raised the portcullis for me, just as he had done with Gareth. We see Michel often and enjoy the bouillabaisse and curries he cooks for us in his small kitchen while we nag him about the packs of Camels he smokes every day.

I'm happy Gareth's friends approve of me and I'm pretty sure Gareth feels the same way about the people who are important in my life. It makes things a whole lot easier.

* * *

Whatever distance existed between Gareth and me when we met narrowed as we spent more time together. One evening over dinner I mentioned a recurring dream I'd had for as long as I could remember. The dream takes me along a curving stone walkway that travels up the side of a medieval castle. I'm alone and it seems as if I'm searching for something. Gareth looked vaguely shocked and a few seconds slipped past before he spoke again.

"That's *my* dream, ever since I was a kid."

"What? What are you talking about?" He couldn't be serious, I thought.

"You just described my dream."

I looked across the table, searching his face for clues. He wasn't smiling.

"Is there a red flower in yours?" That would be just too spooky, I thought. In my dream there is a splash of color against all that bleak gray stone: a single red geranium on the low stone wall to my left.

"Unh-unh, no flower. But it's the same dream." He studied my face. "What do you think it means?"

I could only shake my head.

A few days later Gareth asked if he could read something he'd written to me.

I listened to a poem about splintered dreams and bastions of past solitudes. The words were beautifully placed and metered; the images evoked were stark yet entirely romantic.

Gareth told me he'd written his first poem on that horrifying morning in September of 2001 when it seemed to be the only thing he could do to keep himself sane. During our first few months together, he wrote two poems and dedicated them to me. Then he began the sonnets; they now number over two hundred and I am honored to be the one who inspired Gareth to write them.

Neither of us has dreamed about medieval castles since we met.

*   *   *

When I told Lisa about Gareth she had a big reaction:

"Mom, you have *got* to write about this! It's incredibly romantic and Gareth sounds wonderful. My God, he writes poetry about you, he cooks dinner for you, he makes you laugh. I'm jealous!" I could almost see that wide smile of hers. I heard the joy in her voice. I often wonder how my mother would have responded. She might have complained a little about the age difference but I'm confident of one thing: Gareth Seigel would have won her over.

My friends were crazy about him. He didn't try to be charming or amusing. He pulled off something much more difficult: he was completely himself. Artist Greg Colson and his wife, the glorious Dinah Kirgo (when I met her it was like a light going on); Jeff Kaufman and Julie Kirgo, Dinah's equally beautiful sister and writing partner; Paul and Ulrike Ruscha—all of them wildly talented and generous people, all of them much too smart to be easily impressed. They gathered Gareth in as one of their own, and not because I was with him. He was accepted and then loved on his own merits.

It was time for me to meet Jack and Peggy Seigel, Gareth's parents. They were in L.A. for a week or so and were staying with him. I was invited over for a glass of wine before we all went out to dinner. I rang the doorbell (Gareth had given me a key but I thought it might be pushing it to let myself in with his parents there) and his mother, Peggy, was the first to come forward, hand extended. She's an attractive woman with a beautiful smile and I was impressed with her grip; it was as strong and firm as my mom's had been. Gareth's father was soft-spoken, a little shy maybe, but welcoming. Gareth had told them about me, of course. They'd seen a couple of my photographs from the sixties and seventies in his apartment and they seemed to be dealing with it.

The cracks in the façade showed up at the restaurant. We were in a booth for four with Gareth seated next to his father, and we were still looking over the menus when I began to feel the chill. Gareth's mother was polite enough but any attempts at conversation were snipped off as neatly as thread from a spool. Gareth and his dad tried to keep it convivial but the evening was shrouded in the fog of Peggy's disapproval. I felt so sorry for Gareth. First meeting between a woman he's come to love and his parents, and he's trapped in the middle. I was tempted to turn to Peggy and speak honestly:

"Hey, lady, I understand. But it is what it is. Haven't you noticed that Gareth is happy? It's not important whether or not you like me, but it would be a hell of a lot easier on your son if you stopped behaving like this."

It would have been pointless to try. She was too locked into her antipathy toward me and my relationship with Gareth. In the oddest way, I was reminded of my own mother. Estelle Lang was the flip side of Peggy Seigel. Mom was always cool at first but she usually warmed up to the people I cared enough about to bring around to meet her. She had to work at keeping an open mind but she managed it most of the time.

I was lucky: Gareth saw things as they were. And he's a real mensch; he doesn't need parental approval in order to love me. Then something happened that proved who he is. I woke up one morning to find that Bobbie couldn't move his hindquarters because his back legs were paralyzed. I called Gareth immediately.

"Bobbie can't walk. I woke up and he can't walk or sit straight."

"I'll be right there. Don't try to lift him, just leave him where he is and we'll go straight to the vet."

Gareth picked up my dog with enormous care, laid him next to me in the back seat of his car, and drove to the veterinary hospital. The doctor examined Bobbie and took an X-ray. Ruptured disk in his back, she said. Immediate surgery, she said. Five-thousand dollars, she said.

I didn't have pet insurance at the time (I do now) or anywhere near that kind of money and said so. My words were still hanging in the air when, without hesitation, Gareth took out his credit card and told the vet to do whatever it took to give Bobbie a shot at recovery. She said she'd call the surgeon and Bobbie would be on the table within the hour. I could only look at Gareth and try to thank him with inadequate words.

We left Bobbie at the hospital and went back to Gareth's apartment to wait. The surgeon, Dr. Davison, called just before she began the operation to say if she couldn't help Bobbie, she'd "just let him go on sleeping." Gareth sat down next to me and drew me in close. We were silent for a while, then he went into the kitchen and came back with a mug of hot soup.

"Bobbie's a strong little guy, he's going to come through this. Now drink your soup and try to relax a little."

It was a very long wait and when Dr. Davison called and told me she'd removed the ruptured disk and the calcium deposits in Bobbie's spine and that he was doing well, I wept with gratitude for her surgical skills and for Gareth's heroic generosity and tenderness. And I thanked God for keeping watch over our Bobbie.

He had to learn to walk all over again, a few steps a day. Gareth and I took turns massaging his back legs and he made steady progress. Within two months you could barely see the little kick-out in one hind leg when he ran, the only reminder of his ordeal. The first time he moved at all was the day he came home from the hospital. He was sleepy from the medication but when he saw Gareth, he lifted his head and thumped his tail. That's how we knew Bobbie was going to be okay.

"Mom. *Mom*! Leonard died . . . he died and he was too young!"

Lisa's voice pushed its way through chest-heaving sobs. I tried to calm her, asked her to tell me what had happened. Sudden heart attack during the night, gone before the paramedics arrived. Lisa would be flying in from Boston in two days and she would stay with Leonard's aunt, with whom she'd remained close. She wasn't bringing Dominic with her. No, I didn't have to pick her up at the airport. Yes, she'd call when she got in; yes, she'd make arrangements to see me at some point.

Gareth kept me from taking her coolness personally by reminding me that none of this was about me; I had to keep myself out of the equation and be there for Lisa when, and if, she needed me. I didn't plan on going to Leonard's funeral. I'd been very fond of him and we'd had dinner from time to time after Lisa moved to Boston. But I didn't know his aunt and I didn't feel slighted when I wasn't asked to the service. I don't like funerals and my family stopped having them after my grandfather's death.

When Lisa called, Gareth suggested we pick her up and take her back to Pasadena for dinner at his place. She was waiting outside the aunt's house when we pulled up, and she looked like someone who has just come out the other side of a terrible illness. She was quiet during the drive back from Hollywood. She sighed often and said Leonard's name softly a few times. She cried a little. My mother and Hotten had been old when they died, Cass went when Lisa was still a child, and Harry Cohn wasn't an integral part of her life. Leonard's death was her first collision with the sudden loss of a closely held friend.

Lisa managed to eat some of the special meal Gareth prepared and she made a valiant effort at conversation, but she was constantly pulled back into grief. After we left the table, Gareth put on a Paul Simon CD and suddenly Lisa was up and moving, swept into the rhythms of "You Can Call Me Al" and "Under African Skies." Gareth and I sat quietly and watched, and when the tempo slowed, I got up, put my arms around my daughter, and began to dance with her. Her body felt so slight and her hair smelled, as always, like eucalyptus. We moved together like that for a few minutes. It was the closest we'd been in a long time and I was sorry when she pulled away and sat down, but grateful for having been able to reach out and touch her. When I sat next to Gareth again, he clasped my hand, and the feeling of being understood and loved without the need to talk about it was everything I needed.

When Lisa left for Boston I knew the distance between us was still there. It hadn't grown but I was saddened to think it might never go away. The only thing I could do was continue to be there for my daughter in any way she could accept.

* * *

I knew I wanted to write about DeShion "Red" McIntyre five minutes after I met him at a televised gang seminar in 2005. The taping was still an hour or so away, and while every other guy there
was engaged in the kind of informal chest-thumping that goes
on when gangbangers get together in a neutral setting, I noticed
a man standing quietly next to a young woman holding a baby. I
watched them for a while before I walked over and introduced
myself.

Red McIntyre is in his late thirties, a tough little workhorse
of a man with an easy smile, close-cropped red hair, and a spray of
freckles across the bridge of his nose. The smile cannot quite mask
an unmistakable quality of cool assessment behind his light brown
eyes; it lets you know he's wary of your game. That was how he
looked at me during the first few minutes of our conversation that
night. When I said I was the author of *Do or Die*, it was like an
alarm had been switched off. He relaxed and we began to talk.
When I asked if he was still involved with the old neighborhood,
he grinned and shook his head.

"Naw. I'm done puttin' in that kinda work. I'm with the Forest Service now."

"Doing what?"

"I'm a firefighter."

It was like pulling that final high card in a straight flush. This
would be the first time I could tell a gang-related story with a vic-
torious finish. If Red McIntyre was the real deal, he would prove
there are people who can will themselves to change no matter what
they come from.

I told Red his story might be something worth telling and
asked if he'd allow me to interview him. I asked if he'd be willing
to come to my place for the interview.

"No problem."

I pitched the idea to Laurie Ochoa, editor in chief of the *L.A.
Weekly*, as a cover story. She liked what she heard and we talked
terms. My only demand was that I needed enough space to write

as many words as the piece required. She agreed and I went home and made arrangements to meet with Red on his first day off.

Red McIntyre leaned back against the cushions on the big reading chair in my living room and gulped down more than half a bottle of water, as if just speaking about forest fires got him thirsty. Then he settled in and began to talk about his past as a hard-core Crip. His weapon of choice was a .40 Glock. "We was programmed to kill dudes from enemy sets before first period." He ducked his head a little when he said this. He was talking about elementary school.

It was difficult, during that initial interview, to equate the man, whose hands were so gentle on the two dogs that crowded up against his chair, with the remorseless gang member he described in such chilling detail.

When Gareth called to ask if I'd be done with the interview in time for dinner, I asked if I could bring Red along.

"Sure, Boo. There's plenty of food, and I'd like to meet him."

I don't remember when the nicknames started but the endearment is the same for each of us; we're both "Boo."

Gareth and Red shook hands at the door of Gareth's apartment and Red walked inside slowly. He was a little shy, a little tentative, but Gareth's easy warmth was contagious and within minutes they were sharing a beer, deeply involved in a conversation about the lung-bursting work of putting out forest fires. I watched the two men, one an Indiana Eagle Scout with a sash full of merit badges, the other an escapee from the nightmare alley of gang life. Red walked slowly around the living room, studying each of Gareth's framed photographic images, asking questions, making comments. The shot of an empty swimming pool covered with graffiti brought out a rueful grin. When Gareth began to cook, Red leaned over the kitchen counter to watch, comfortable enough now to make conversation. When I went in to set the table, he insisted on helping.

It was a good evening, filled with talk about teaching, fire-fighting, writing, and the current crop of young gang members still in school. Red and I made plans to meet the next week for our final interview and an idea began to take hold at the back of my mind.

"This is a guy who looks for the exits in every room he walks into. Red's met Gareth; he's comfortable with him. He'll relax more if someone he knows is taking the pictures."

Gareth and I were seated in Laurie Ochoa's office. She had leafed through his portfolio and now she nodded her head.

"I'll run it past our photo editor but I think it makes sense, too."

Gareth and I didn't talk much during the drive from Pasadena to meet Stanton Florea, the fire information officer for the U.S. Forest Service who would take us into the Sequoia National Forest, where Red was part of a crew fighting a sleeper fire (a fire that gets started in a single tree after a lightning strike, smolders, and then flares) that had been burning for three and a half days. I was thinking about whether or not I'd be allowed to get close to the fire line and, if I could, whether there would be any opportunity to speak with the men. I knew if I thought about the heat of the fire and the smoke, I'd start to get nervous. I knew also that Gareth would move right in next to the firefighters (careful not to get in their way) if nobody stopped him. Nothing got on his nerves.

"You okay?" Gareth shot a fast glance at me.

"Sure. Just the usual preinterview stuff."

I was also thinking about the dogs. They couldn't come along on this trip so I'd boarded them with a woman who worked at the veterinary hospital. She'd taken care of them before and they did well with her, but when she and her husband came to pick them up this time, Diz kept looking back over his shoulder at me as he was led away. I knew I was being neurotic but he'd seemed so wistful, and now I couldn't get rid of that image. I reached for a bottle of water and went back to making a mental list of things to ask in the interviews.

We met Stan Florea at a 7-Eleven on a corner of a barren stretch of land with a disturbing history: it was the place where Rodney King had been beaten into submission by six LAPD patrolmen. There used to be a service station next to the 7-Eleven but it was torn down after too many tourists with a taste for the sensational stopped to gawk.

Florea told us the plans had been changed. Red was back at his post at the Valyermo station and we were to go there. We followed the mint-green U.S. Forest Service station wagon through what looked like fields under cultivation and canals from which Sikorsky Type 1 helicopters suck up as much as 2,500 pounds of water (through the long mosquito-like extensions dangling from their bellies) to be dropped on fires.

The Valyermo station might look like a collection of large, well-kept tourist cabins if it were not for the Forest Service flag and the mint-green fire engines parked around the property.

We met the crew, an elite squad known unofficially as the Hot Shots, and Gareth set up and began taking pictures of Red while I introduced myself to the young guys I would interview. We spent the day with the Valyermo Hot Shots. Gareth went out with some of them on one of their regular two-hour training hikes and photographed them in silhouette, walking single-file along a ridge, each man carrying the regulation sixty-five pounds of gear needed on a fire line. When they got back, Gareth came into the rec room, where I was interviewing some of the other guys, a couple of them ex–gang members, one with the bullet scars to show for it. Somebody asked if we'd each like to try an MRE (meals ready to eat), the foil-encased meals (main course and cookie-like dessert) they took out with them to fires. You open the wrapping and the food heats automatically. Gareth had a kind of stew with vegetables; I had spaghetti with tomato sauce. Not great eating, but good enough if you've got only a brief rest from battling a fire in Southern California or a time-out during war in Iraq. After we ate, Gareth and I stayed in the rec room, questioning the guys like a tag team, each of us bouncing off the other with perfect timing. And as we interviewed the young firefighters, we exchanged glances more than once in silent acknow-ledgment of a partnership that worked on so many levels.

It had been a long day and we stopped at a restaurant in Sierra Madre on the way home. I called to see how the dogs were doing.

"Not so good—Diz has been throwing up blood. I'm taking him over to the hospital now for an X-ray."

I told the woman we were on the way. Gareth ate his meal quickly; I couldn't eat at all. I kept trying to push back the feeling this was not going to turn out well.

The woman, Marisa; her husband; and their seven-year-old son were already at the veterinary hospital when we got there. Marisa had taken the X-ray; she said it showed that Diz had swal-lowed a needle. I didn't ask to see it; my only thoughts were for my dog. He had been lightly sedated and was in a large cage in the big examining room trying to sit upright but listing to one side be-cause the medication had kicked in.

"Listen, Marisa—can I stay here? I can sleep in the cage with him or lie on some blankets next to it so if he wakes up during the night, he won't be scared."

"It's not allowed, but he'll be fine. Really."

Marisa reached for my hand, pressed it, and went out to the lobby, where Gareth was waiting with Bobbie. Her husband and son stayed in the room with me and Diz and the kid stepped up close to the cage. He watched the drowsy little dog for a few sec-onds, then he turned to look at me.

"Your dog's going to die."

I wanted to shake him. I couldn't do that, so I yelled.

"Don't you *dare* say that! He's going to be fine."

I looked over at the father, trying to catch his eye because I wanted him to yell at his son, too; what the kid had just said was terrible. The man jingled the change in his pockets and gazed in the other direction. Then Marisa bustled back and said it was time for us to leave. Her kid ran to her side and leaned against her. I took off my sweater and spread it out on the bottom of the cage so Diz could lie on it and be comforted. I whispered to him for a few seconds and kissed his face. Then I went out to Gareth and Bobbie.

Diz was kept in the hospital while the vet waited for the needle to pass; he was twelve years old, he had a heart murmur for which he took medication, and they wanted to wait before putting him through a surgical ordeal. I brought in a couple of my T-shirts for him to lie on, stroked his cashmere fur, and told him we missed him, that home wasn't the same without him. He was at the hospital for three or four days, then they called me: Diz could come home tomorrow. Bobbie and I took him out for a walk the day before I was to pick him up and he addressed every tree and bush along the way. Then we sat with him in one of the examination rooms and I petted and kissed him, told him how much I loved him and how happy I was he'd be home with us tomorrow.

The next morning I called the hospital to ask when I could pick up my little Diz. The receptionist told me to hold on. Then one of the technicians came on the line.

"Diz died in his sleep last night; one of the techs found him this morning. I'm so sorry."

I hung up the phone, reached for Bobbie, and cried into the soft fur at the back of his neck. I knew I couldn't allow myself to wallow in "If only . . ." thoughts of self-recrimination, but it was hard not to think about how Diz had looked back at me as he and Bobbie were being led away the night before Gareth and I were to go to the fire station, how dopey and sweet he'd been when we saw him that night at the hospital. Gareth didn't tell me not to feel bad. He didn't say "You're being too emotional" or "You've still got Bobbie." He said, "We're going to get through this together." It was the "we" that provided the support I could lean against.

Diz did come home a few weeks later: his ashes rest with Woofie's and Dexter's inside a sweet-smelling cedar box on my desk.

My story about DeShion "Red" McIntyre came out a couple of months after I handed it in to the *L.A. Weekly.* Nothing had been edited out and Gareth's photographs of Red and his fellow fire-fighters popped on the page, even with the loss of detail you get in newsprint.

During the first interview, I asked Red what forced evacuations were like. He looked around my living room at the art on the walls, the piano with the silver-framed pictures of family, friends, and pets marching across its gleaming top, the shelves of books, a few of them left over from my mother's childhood.

"Sometimes it's more than fire you got to fight."

I understood but I was thinking about other kinds of battles, the ones you have to win in order to keep what you hold dear, the ones that don't include the crackle and lick of an oncoming fire.

What holds Gareth and me together is stronger than tungsten carbide and it is a fusion of love, passion, respect, and the ability to keep making each other think as well as laugh. He is different from any other man I've been involved with: we don't just get along; he's inside my head. I don't have to explain myself to Gareth; he gets it every time and says it's like that for him, too. We get each other.

We have dinner together every night, sometimes we watch movies on TV, sometimes we catch a new release at a theater. We like reading for two or three hours at a clip in comfortable silence. We meet with close friends as often as we can all get together and when the conversation gets around to politics everybody has to yell to make sure his or her opinion is heard. I cut his hair every six weeks or so. When he has time, he drives around L.A. looking for subjects to photograph. When I'm not trying to make up for a blown deadline, I go along and ride shotgun. Weekends, we might visit one of the museums around town: the Getty, LACMA, or Norton Simon, which is within walking distance. Gareth is crazy about one of the paintings there: Van Gogh's portrait of his mother. I like it too, although I've never had an urge to touch it.

There are many reasons for me to love Gareth Seigel. Some are intangible, others more easily explained: He gives me vitamins and then follows up to make sure I take them. He reminds me to do my exercises. He cooks healthy food that looks good and tastes delicious. He laughs and tells me to shut up when I complain about the dearth of cheeseburgers and barbecue in our diet. He buys salads and fresh fruit and puts them in my refrigerator for lunch when I'm working. He is gentle and loving with his cat, who has many divalike ways, and he's like that with me and many of my divalike ways. He points out my blind spots even when I don't want to see, and I return the favor. He compares some of our rougher rides to the dangerous passage of that odd couple in *The African Queen*. He speaks fluent, unabashed dog-talk and lets Bobbie wash his face with his big pink tongue. He is a true friend to my daughter, both in L.A. and on the phone to Boston. He continues to write exquisite sonnets to me. He says being with me is like having breakfast, lunch, and dinner at Tiffany's. Being with Gareth is even better: he's that long drink of cold water when you're dying of thirst and the thermometer on the wall reads 105 degrees and climbing.

One more thing: It's Gareth Seigel who has taken my mother's place in telling me I can do what I set my mind to. Or, in a few instances, what he sets his mind to. It is now Gareth's voice I hear when I feel I'm out of whatever it takes to make whatever is necessary work. He may have taken his sweet time getting here, but the way I look at it, it was worth the wait.

Epilogue

I learned things writing this book. The memories have always been there, floating lazily on currents, like hawks circling down until they reach a level where they can be tracked. But before I began, I had to understand I couldn't control them; I just had to relax and go along with them to wherever I was being taken. When I had to put down some hard things about my mother, I found her spirit, still alive in me and impatient at those moments when my eyes welled with tears. It was then I could almost hear her voice telling me to just get the hell on with it. In writing about her, I realized it was all the ways she lived her life that informed mine to the degree where I would make it—or not—on my own terms.

I found that to write about loss, whether it is a parent, other family members, or a beloved pet, is to relive that moment of agony as you struggle to make sense of your feelings through the tears trailing down your face. There is no "I'll think about it tomorrow" at those long moments; there is only the past coming at you like a runaway train.

I learned I didn't have a clue about who I am or what I have or might become until I got a good look at myself in the eyes of those people who have gone for more than just a limited ticket to my life.

I found a few things I have going for me and against me: I'm either a dumb person at the core of a smart one or an intelligent woman who can make some really stupid choices. Both cases are difficult to deal with, particularly for those close to me. I am ambitious, lazy, and impatient, intensely loyal and maddeningly stubborn. I am always ready to fight for someone not equipped to do battle for themselves. I've learned to be grateful for what I have but I will never stop going after what I believe is necessary. I will not swap fierceness for a lower stress factor in my life.

Raising my daughter to young womanhood and seeing her become a fine and loving mother to her son has earned her my admiration and respect. Writing about the people who came into my life and moved the pieces around, shaping and reshaping me in ways both small and profound, has given me a much clearer picture of myself. I haven't always liked the view but one thing is certain: it keeps on changing.

Acknowledgments

I am deeply indebted to those people who have been so tirelessly supportive of me: Gareth Seigel, for willing me to write this book and for all the other reasons he knows so very well. Mark Pickell, great friend and neighbor, computer whiz without peer. Larry DuBois, for pushing so hard and believing so long. My love and eternal thanks to Hal Dresner. And loud shout-outs to Jerry Korda, Paul Ruscha, Glenn Brown, Eric Mankin, Jeff Kaufman, Greg Colson, Keshon Cooper, Keith Allison, and David Pearl.

I can only deliver a deep bow to Dennis Hopper for making the image so much better than the real thing. Also, another bow to Tom Waits for writing such great, quotable lyrics.

Love and thanks to the women in my life: Victory, Regina Hyde-Scott, Dinah Kirgo, Julie Kirgo, Sandra Schneider, and Sierra Pecheur. Great dames, every one of them.

Endless appreciation to Neil Olson, my friend, mentor, and great white of a literary representative, and to Kathy Belden, the editor every writer dreams about. Her unerring eye and extraordinary guidance made this damn book better than it has any right to be. My great thanks to Jenny Miyasaki for her eagle eye and intractable good taste. And my gratitude to Aja Pollock, as well, for many of the same reasons.

My biggest love to Lisa Bing, Dominic LoRusso, the memory of my mother, Estelle Lang, and all those members of my family who are gone but remain alive in memory and loved forever.

Finally, thanks and nose-kissing love to Bobbie Bing, the best dog in the world, and to the spirits of the three bums who came before him.

A Note on the Author

A former model, Léon Bing is the author of *Do or Die*, a profile of the archrival gangs the Bloods and the Crips, which she wrote after spending extensive periods of time among the two factions.